Creative Accounting and the Cross-Eyed Javelin Thrower

Creative Accounting and the Cross-Eyed Javelin Thrower

DOREEN McBARNET
and
CHRISTOPHER WHELAN

JOHN WILEY & SONS, LTD
Chichester · New York · Weinheim · Brisbane · Singapore · Toronto

Published 1999 by John Wiley & Sons Ltd,
Baffins Lane, Chichester,
West Sussex PO19 1UD, England

National 01243 779777
International (+44) 1243 779777
e-mail (for orders and customer service enquiries):
cs-books@wiley.co.uk
Visit our Home Page on http://www.wiley.co.uk
or http://www.wiley.com

Other Wiley Editorial Offices

John Wiley & Sons, Inc., 605 Third Avenue, New York, NY 10158-0012, USA

WILEY-VCH Verlag GmbH, Pappelallee 3, D-69469 Weinheim, Germany

Jacaranda Wiley Ltd, 33 Park Road, Milton, Queensland 4064, Australia

John Wiley & Sons (Asia) Pte Ltd, Clementi Loop #02-01, Jin Xing Distripark, Singapore 129809

John Wiley & Sons (Canada) Ltd, 22 Worcester Road, Rexdale, Ontario M9W 1L1, Canada

Library of Congress Cataloging-in-Publication Data

McBarnet, Doreen J.
Creative accounting and the cross-eyed javelin thrower / Doreen McBarnet, Christopher Whelan.
p. cm.
Includes bibliographical references and index.
ISBN 0-471-98835-9
1. Financial statements–Great Britain. 2. Corporations–Great Britain–Accounting. 3. Corporations–Great Britain–Accounting–Corrupt practices. I. Whelan, Christopher. II. Title.
HF5681.B2M353 1999
657'.3–dc27 99-12643
CIP

British Library Cataloguing in Publication Data
A catalogue record for this book is available from the British Library

ISBN 0-471-98835-9

Typeset in 11/13pt Palatino by Mackreth Media Services, Hemel Hempstead, Herts.
Printed and bound by Antony Rowe Ltd, Eastbourne
This book is printed on acid-free paper responsibly manufacured from sustainable forestry, in which at least two trees are planted for each one used for paper production.

Contents

PART VI CONTROL?

Appendices

Foreword

Financial reporting matters. Financial reports demonstrate companies' accountability to their shareholders and provide a basis for decision-making. Unreliable financial reports create distrust and distort decisions.

In 1990, new arrangements were introduced for the setting of United Kingdom accounting standards. Concern had developed that existing arrangements had come under strain and were not able to provide standards on a timely basis to deal with the needs of rapidly moving markets. A review committee under the chairmanship of Sir Ron Dearing (now Lord Dearing) recommended a new framework for standard-setting. The 1990 initiatives largely adopted the Dearing committee's recommendations.

At the root of the difficulties experienced during the 1980s lay the relationship between accounting standards and the law. Unsurprisingly, therefore, this relationship lay at the heart of the Dearing committee's proposals and of the success they have achieved in maintaining confidence in financial reports.

Any system is likely to have weaknesses as well as strengths. However strong the Dearing arrangements are thought to have been, it is wise to analyse their practical effect. This welcome book offers an analysis of the practical experience of the Dearing arrangements, and, as such, should prove valuable to finance directors and practitioners as well as standard-setters and policy-makers.

Chris Swinson, President of the Institute of Chartered Accountants in England and Wales

Acknowledgements

We have been monitoring the development of the new regime in financial reporting, and the factors that shaped it, for over a decade. To begin with, the interest was incidental, arising naturally in the course of research projects on tax avoidance and European company law harmonisation. Later, our attention firmly caught by what the new regime was trying to accomplish, we focused on the new regime itself.

This book is concerned only with the enforcement of the new regime – other work addresses the wider issues raised – but it tries to offer a broad analysis of enforcement. To inform that analysis, it draws at various points on the range of research projects we have worked on over several years.

These projects have involved in-depth interviews with a wide range of people: regulators in the UK, France and Germany; officials at the European Commission; UK government department officials; leading members of the accountancy profession and especially the big firms; barristers and solicitors, corporate counsel, bankers and consultants. We have talked at length to the key players in the new regime, at the FRC, ASB and FRRP. We'd like to thank all those who have given their time to share their experiences and reflections with us.

Some of the interviews – especially with companies involved in Panel investigations – were undertaken on the basis of strict confidentiality, and we have been careful to abide by that. We have also chosen to cite published records wherever possible, and to opt for public statements in preference to interview material where there was an overlap. With confidentiality in mind, some of the research has been used indirectly or to raise questions rather than being cited per se. Likewise we have chosen to present most of our examples of legal arguments as 'potential' or 'hypothetical' whether they are based on our own or others' readings of the regulations, or on practices described to us as ongoing.

Our research has involved extensive documentary analysis, some in the public domain, some private, and thanks are due to those who provided access. Appendix 1, Foreword to Accounting Standards is reproduced by kind permission of the ASB. Copyright is retained by the ASB Ltd. Appendix 2, The Companies (Revision of Defective Accounts and Report) Regulations 1990 (SI1990/2570) is reproduced with the permission of the Controller of Her Majesty's Stationery Office.

The research projects which provide the background to this book, and to a greater or lesser degree informed the analysis, have been funded from a range of sources. We should like to thank the Jacob Burns Fund for Socio-Legal Studies, the British Academy Humanities Research Board, the Economic and Social Research Council (award numbers: E06250033 and R000231235) and the European Commission. We should also like to thank our departments, the University of Oxford Centre for Socio-Legal Studies and the University of Warwick School of Law, for their support.

Thanks to Chris Swinson for writing a Foreword to the book. Thanks too to those who commented on the ideas presented here, including anonymous reviewers whose constructive criticism we have taken on board.

Valuable research assistance was provided by Julia Maibach and Rachpal Kaur. Last, but very far from least, we owe an extremely large debt of gratitude to Lesley Morris who, in patiently typing the 'final' draft of the book over and over again, came face to face with the downside of creative accounting!

Who's Who

The Honourable Mrs Justice Arden, formerly Mary Arden QC – author of the opinion 'The true and fair requirement'. See Appendix 1

Robert Bruce – *The Times*

Allan Cook – Technical Director, Accounting Standards Board

Lord Dearing, formerly Sir Ron Dearing – Chairman of the Dearing Committee and first FRC Chairman

Edwin Glasgow QC – Second FRRP Chairman

Peter Goldsmith QC – Third (current) FRRP Chairman

Sir Sydney Lipworth – Second (current) FRC Chairman

Brian Singleton-Green – Editor, *Accountancy*

Chris Swinson – President, Institute of Chartered Accountants in England and Wales

Sydney Treadgold – ASB, FRRP Secretary until 1998

Simon Tuckey QC – First FRRP Chairman

Sir David Tweedie – ASB Chairman

Karel Van Hulle – European Commission DGXV, Head of Financial information and company law unit

List of Abbreviations

ACCA	Certified Association of Chartered Accountants
ACT	Advance Corporation Tax
APB	Auditing Practices Board
ASB	Accounting Standards Board
ASC	Accounting Standards Committee
CA	Companies Act
CBI	Confederation of British Industry
CCAB	Consultative Committee of Accounting Bodies
DGXV	European Commission Directorate – General XV
DTI	Department of Trade and Industry
EC	European Community
ED	Exposure Draft
EITF	Emerging Issues Task Force (USA)
EPS	Earnings Per Share
ESOP	Employee Share Ownership Plan
EU	European Union
FASB	Financial Accounting Standards Board (USA)
FRC	Financial Reporting Council
FRED	Financial Reporting Exposure Draft
FRRP	Financial Reporting Review Panel
FRS	Financial Reporting Standard
FT	Financial Times
GAAP	Generally Accepted Accounting Practice
IASC	International Accounting Standards Committee
ICAEW	Institute of Chartered Accountants in England and Wales
JV	Joint Venture

PN	Press Notice (FRRP)
SFAS	Statement of Financial Accounting Standards (USA)
SORP	Statement of Recommended Practice
SSAP	Statement of Standard Accounting Practice
TR	Technical Release
UITF	Urgent Issues Task Force

PART I

SETTING THE SCENE

1
The Challenge

Creative accounting was one of the key themes in corporate finance and corporate governance in the 1980s. Controlling it became one of the key issues of the 1990s. In this book, we ask whether creative accounting can be controlled? If it can, how can it be done? If it can't, why not?

Creative accounting is one of the primary targets of the new regime of financial reporting in the UK. The campaign to clean up accounts has been spearheaded by Sir David Tweedie, Chairman of the Accounting Standards Board. Armed with new weapons, the Financial Reporting Review Panel has been created to police company accounts. If the Panel believes accounts have not complied with accounting standards or with company law it has the power to go to court and the court can order the company to revise them and make directors personally liable for all the costs involved.

The Cross-Eyed Javelin Thrower

When Sir David Tweedie is asked whether the new regime will win the battle against creative accounting he responds, characteristically, with a joke:

> We're like a cross-eyed javelin thrower competing at the Olympic Games: we may not win but we'll keep the crowd on the edge of its seats!

The comment highlights the uncertainty still surrounding the prospects of the new regime. The outcomes will have implications for business and regulation beyond the realms of accounting, and beyond the UK. Financial reporting is a key aspect of corporate governance, and the challenge of creative accounting goes to the heart of business regulation and business ethics.

CREATIVE ACCOUNTING

By the early 1990s, creative accounting was well and truly recognised by national and international regulators as one of their major headaches. The excesses of creative accounting – and creative accountants – had been widely reported.

In the UK in 1986, the financial journalist Ian Griffiths published his best-seller *Creative Accounting: How to make your profits what you want them to be*. The book claimed (on page 1) that:

> Every company in the country is fiddling its profits. Every set of published accounts is based on books which have been gently cooked or completed roasted . . . It is the biggest con trick since the Trojan horse.

His claim was soon to be borne out by other surveys of corporate practice (Pimm, 1991; Pijper, 1993).

Off Balance Sheet Financing

A particular concern was being expressed about off balance sheet financing, which Robert Bruce of *The Times* has described as "the greatest creative accounting sin of the late 1980s" (20 February 1997). Many complex arrangements were developed. If accounted for in accordance with their legal form, they resulted in accounts that did not reflect their commercial reality. The effects of off balance sheet financing make it harder for the reader of the accounts to assess the true economic position of the reporting entity because they obscure the true extent and nature of its borrowings, its assets and the results of its activities (FRS 5, Appendix III, para 4).

Terry Smith, formerly of UBS Phillips & Drew, kept the spotlight on creative accounting with his book, *Accounting for Growth: Stripping the camouflage from Company Accounts*, in 1992. Smith, with his colleague Richard Hannah, had looked at 200 companies listed on the International Stock Exchange and indicated those which were using one or more creative accounting techniques (Smith and Hannah, 1991). This, he said, "became affectionately known as the 'blob guide'" (Smith, 1992:4).

Advantages of Creative Accounting

Creative accounting can be an attractive option for company directors. There are many potential advantages. Creative accounting can:

- boost reported profits/minimise reported losses;
- manipulate key ratios used in market analysis;
- conceal financial risk;
- circumvent borrowing restrictions;
- escape shareholder control;
- enhance management performance (and performance-related management pay);
- gain access to finance, that would otherwise be impossible to raise.

While a company is riding high on the market, shareholders can benefit from the effects of creative accounting too.

Disadvantages of Creative Accounting

But there is a downside: the potentially adverse impact of creative accounting on investors, creditors, employees and others. The role of creative accounting both in concealing shortcomings in corporate performance and in contributing to the downfall of particular companies has been amply demonstrated. The demise of companies such as Polly Peck, Maxwell Communications Corporation and Saatchi & Saatchi is well known: all were enmeshed in various forms of creative accounting. Terry Smith claimed that his 'blob guide' of creative accounting "proved to be an amazingly accurate guide to the companies to avoid" (1992:4).

Perfectly Legal

The attraction of creative accounting as a means of enhancing accounts – and the headache for those policing it – has been that it can always claim to be 'perfectly legal'. The phrase has cropped up time and again in press commentaries on the latest smart devices. The Dearing Committee, reviewing accounting regulation in 1988, observed:

> There is little evidence that companies are engaging in flagrant breaches of accounting standards . . . However . . . there is strong pressure on auditors from time to time to accept interpretations of accounting standards which conform to the interests of preparers rather than with the spirit of the standard. (1988:12)

Creative Compliance

The problem for enforcement was that what was going on was not so much *non*-compliance – 'flagrant breach' of regulations – as what we call '*creative* compliance'. Advantageous interpretations of grey areas, seeking out loopholes in specific rules, or dreaming up devices which regulators had not even thought of, let alone regulated, are the essence of creative accounting.

Faced with regulations which would reduce reported profits, earnings per share or the balance sheet, companies were finding imaginative ways to package deals or interpret rules such that their accounts could claim to *comply* with regulations at the same time as avoiding any disadvantageous impact they would otherwise have had. This was not 'flagrant breach' of rules, but it was not the result the regulators intended. To the regulators it was not in the spirit of law and standards.

The Dearing Committee's observation pointed to two problems: the need for a stronger agency of enforcement, and the need for new regulatory weapons to capture creative accounting, pre-empting the 'perfectly legal' claim. And this, in a nutshell, is the strategy of the new regime. There is the new statutory agency to enforce regulations – the Financial Reporting Review Panel – and new, stronger, regulations for it to enforce. Financial Reporting Standard (FRS) 5, for example, confronts head-on the issue of off balance sheet financing.

How has the new regime fared in controlling creative accounting, and how will it fare in the years to come?

WILL THE NEW REGIME WIN?

Some commentators declared the new regime a success from the start. Robert Bruce wrote about the Panel in *The Times* in early 1992: "Enforcement . . . is proving heady, invigorating and effective stuff" (6 February 1992). Later in the year, after the much-publicised 'climbdown' by Trafalgar House, when the Panel had threatened to take the directors to court, he commented that it had the "look of a big game hunter in the financial jungle" and Trafalgar House was its "biggest trophy so far" (16 October 1992). Pijper's view, in his book on creative accounting, was that the Panel has been "a powerful influence in improving the clarity of disclosure" (1993:25).

More recently, in UK GAAP, Ernst & Young said of FRS 5, the "centrepiece of the ASB's assault on creative accounting" (*FT*, 18 February 1997):

> FRS 5 has so far been fairly successful in curbing the wilder excesses of creative accountants. [It has] provided useful ammunition against contrived schemes that rely on artificial structures or improbable interpretations of events. (1997:976)

Directors of companies investigated by the Panel have said the same thing. Keith Hamill, then group finance director of Forte and chairman of the CBI's Financial Reporting Panel, told a conference in 1995 on 'The Future of Accounting – Principles or Rules?' that "the ASB has largely achieved the important objective of seriously restricting 'creative accounting'" (KPMG, Financial Reporting Update, February 1995). Graham Pomroy, group financial controller when BET's 1993 accounts were investigated by the Panel, has advised companies not to take the Panel to court: "I don't think you would stand a dog's chance" (quoted in *Accountancy*, December 1996:42).

Or Not?

Griffiths published a second edition of his book in 1995. In this he too acknowledged the achievement of the ASB in bringing:

> some order to the chaos which [in 1990] passed for a regulatory framework. Indeed under Sir David Tweedie's leadership the ASB has made tremendous progress in restoring the credibility and integrity of accounting standards.

But, Griffiths also argued that his "basic premise" in 1986 that every company in the country is fiddling its profits "still holds true" in 1995:

> While many of the more flagrant abuses . . . have been outlawed those who are charged with the responsibility of preparing a set of accounts still have an extensive range of techniques available to them which can be used to massage the figures which are presented to the watching world. (1995:vii)

He concluded that while the Review Panel's teeth are "sharp" (xi) and there have been other improvements, "creative accounting still flourishes . . . there is still tremendous scope for manipulation" (xi, xviii). No wonder that he called this edition *New Creative Accounting*.

Ernst & Young's apparent praise for the new regime in 1997 was similarly equivocal. Regarding the pattern of Panel decisions:

> many of them have involved relatively minor misdemeanours by companies who are not household names, and this has led some commentators to express the concern that the Panel has still to establish its credibility in policing the more difficult areas of UK GAAP.

But they concede: "there have been exceptions, where the Panel has successfully challenged major companies on important matters" (1997:23).

New Weapons in Action

1997 saw the new weapon of FRS 5 brought successfully into action in the *Associated Nursing Services* case. Here, the Panel, in a landmark ruling, forced the company to revise *two* years' sets of accounts in order to bring on balance sheet its sale and leaseback transactions and to consolidate two deadlocked joint venture companies. Making a company unravel such transactions in order to report the *substance* of transactions can be seen as a very significant development indeed. And according to the chairman of the company, Sir Neil Macfarlane, the investigation and action by the Panel would have "far reaching implications . . . for hundreds of companies in the UK which have entered into sale and leaseback transactions" (quoted in *FT*, 18 February 1997). This was not ANS' only brush with the new regime and its experience so far is instructive.

ANS had been the subject of an earlier Panel investigation in 1992, as a result of which the company had changed its accounting policy. Subsequently, the company "introduced" FRS 5 which led to the assets and liabilities of two nursing homes developed with Business Expansion Scheme money being brought on to its balance sheet (*FT*, 3 June 1994). The company had a commitment to buy the homes after five years. The effect of complying with FRS 5 was to increase gearing from 84% to 92%, and to reduce pre-tax profits from £2.8 million to £2.3 million; the previous year's profits were restated too, down from £1.82 million to £1.58 million. At this time the company also announced a £10 million rights issue to cut gearing to about 20% and to fund new homes via joint ventures (*FT*, 3 June 1994). It was these off balance sheet joint ventures that the company was forced to consolidate following Panel intervention in 1996/97.

Regulatory Will

The regulators have emphasised their strong determination to tackle creative accounting. The effect of Review Panel action on shareholders' funds and earnings per share figures has been significant: "the majority of the primary statement changes required by the Financial Reporting Review Panel *reduce* earnings or shareholders' funds" (Brandt *et al.*, 1997:36, emphasis added). The first ANS case resulted in a decline in shareholders' funds of 18.95%, while the case involving Trafalgar House resulted in a fall in EPS of 279.66% (*ibid*).

Tweedie has warned the auditing profession and preparers that he will not allow the abuses of the 1980s to spring up again without challenge. Of FRS 5, he has said:

> If new schemes should nevertheless be developed to circumvent its provisions, we will refer them to the UITF or, if necessary, will revise the FRS itself. (ASB Press Notice 44, 14 April 1994)

The UITF, the Urgent Issues Task Force, is the ASB's 'rapid reaction' force. It facilitates a rapid regulatory response to new issues as they emerge: "a safeguard against opportunism and minimalism" (FRC, 1991: para 2.20).

The Panel has dealt with 317 cases (to the end of 1998). There has as yet been no resort to the court but former chairman Edwin Glasgow QC emphasised that this

> has not been due to any lack of determination on the Panel's side – rather the opposite. We never threaten what we are not prepared to carry out. (FRC, 1996:31)

Sir Sydney Lipworth, chairman of the Financial Reporting Council, which oversees the new regulatory regime, referred to the "significant expenditure preparatory to litigation" – £259,000 – spent in 1997:

> The fact that this expenditure was incurred signals the Panel's determination not to be deflected or delayed from pursuing an action in court if it believes that to be necessary. (FRC, 1998:15)

In the face of such a display of regulatory determination and will to enforce the new regulations, many companies may have taken the opportunity to 'clean up' their accounts.

A Below the Waterline Effect?

And it does appear that under the new regime financial reporting has improved and some creative accounting has been eliminated. One example is the decision of British Airways, citing FRS 5, to bring on balance sheet the leasing arrangements of 24 aircraft. Previously, the company had treated them as 'extendible operating leases' (see Chapter 13).

Another example is given in Ernst & Young's UK GAAP. It

analysed the 1994 pre-FRS 5 accounts of Forte, focusing on its sale, leaseback and repurchase agreements. The analysis (at p. 1024) suggests that

> the leases had been structured in such a way that the lessors received no more than a lender's return, indicating that the substance of the transactions may have been that of a financing. [T]his, in fact, did prove to be the case as, following the implementation of FRS 5, a substantial proportion of these assets were brought back on balance sheet – as explained in Forte's 1995 accounts.

£415 million worth of assets and £475 million of associated future obligations were included in the 1995 balance sheet, and the 1994 figures were restated on the new basis. This can be seen as a 'success' for the new regime. As Ernst & Young point out, since the original proceeds Forte received were £407 million while future lease obligations were £475 million,

> This must raise at least some doubt whether Forte had disposed of all the risks associated with the assets at the time the original transactions were entered into. (1997:1026)

This too was achieved without the need for Panel enforcement (although Forte's 1991 accounts had been the subject of an earlier Panel investigation). The same is true of other companies – First Choice Holidays (formerly Owners Abroad) included two additional aircraft and one engine on its October 1994 balance sheet citing FRS 5. The assets were held under leases with options to repurchase at set dates and prices. They had been treated as operating leases but were re-classified as finance leases (*Accountancy*, March 1995:104). Vaux Group applied FRS 5 "just in case" in its 1994 accounts in relation to rents on sale and leaseback agreements for two hotels where the group had an option to repurchase the assets. As a result, profits were reduced and debt of £26.1 million and fixed assets of £24 million were included on the balance sheet (*Accountancy*, March 1995:104).

Such voluntary compliance has been described by Sir Sydney Lipworth as reflecting a

> below the waterline influence that cannot be measured but is nevertheless . . . very real. The mere presence of the Panel

> undoubtedly serves as a deterrent to those who might otherwise contemplate adopting an accounting treatment that is on the wrong side of the divide. This deterrent effect can only be for the good. (FRC, 1997:13)

Edwin Glasgow has claimed that "the overwhelming majority of the worst practices that undeniably took place ceased overnight when the Panel went into business" (*Accountancy*, April 1993:35). It is not surprising that the Panel has been described as the "military wing" of the ASB that "supplies the muscles to back up Sir David's principles" (*FT*, 8 February 1996). So, the 'mere presence' of the Panel may be operating in itself as a powerful deterrent.

RESISTANCE

But what of those who are not deterred? Business is not in the habit of capitulating long term in the face of new regulations. Much more likely is a renewed search for 'perfectly legal' routes for enhancing accounts.

The Panel can, of course, step in to review practices it sees as unacceptable, armed with new standards and powers to seek revision of accounts. But what if directors remain undeterred by the Panel's view that the accounts are defective? What if directors do not capitulate, but challenge the Panel's view instead. What if they mobilise the *law* to do so?

Sir David Tweedie has described the enhanced role of law in the status and enforcement of financial reporting regulation as a "great leap forward" (*FT*, 3 June 1993). But can the law be used by directors too? What of those who are prepared to take on the 'military wing'? How would enforcement work in the face of persistent resistance?

Enforcement and Enforceability

This book looks at the potential for successful enforcement and at the potential for successful resistance. But the book is not a manual. There is no 'magic formula' on how to exercise control or escape it. There is no guarantee that this carefully constructed creative device will work; no guarantee that this carefully constructed regulation to control it will work either. Because that is not how law enforcement operates in the real world.

Law enforcement is a *process* in which many factors come into play to influence outcomes in individual cases. It is in the nature of law enforcement that there are choices to make, strategies to follow, discretion, bargaining. It is in the nature of the legal process that there can be two sides to every case, competing interpretations of what the law means or how it should be applied, that even regulations claimed as panaceas can be open to challenge. It is in the nature of contests in court that outcomes are uncertain.

That is why Sir David Tweedie cannot know whether his javelin thrower will win or not. The process of legal enforcement may be the key issue for the success or otherwise of the new regime, but it is characterised by unpredictability.

Throughout this process, however, *both* sides have an input to make. This book looks at enforcement from both sides. It looks at strategies of control and strategies of resistance. It looks at the weapons available to the Panel, and at the weapons companies might – and do – use in response. It looks at *enforcement* and it looks at *enforceability*. It looks at the factors and strategies that will ultimately determine whether the new regime succeeds in controlling creative accounting or not.

THE STRUCTURE OF THE BOOK

Framework

In the next chapter we set out the new framework of enforcement. The assault on creative accounting has been developing throughout the 1990s and is still developing. Some of the more powerful weapons have been available to the Panel in practice only recently.

Enforcement

In Part II we look at the Panel and the process of review.

- How are the new weapons brought into play?

- How does the Panel discover and detect defective accounting?
- What strategies does the Panel adopt in investigation and enforcement; what are their strengths and weaknesses?
- What has the Panel achieved so far?
- What message is conveyed by its record?

Enforceability

In Parts III and IV we look at strategies of legal confrontation. We shift the focus from *enforcement* to *legal enforceability*.

- How powerful *are* the new weapons?
- What *legally* is creative accounting?
- Is there still scope for companies to look for loopholes in the new regulations?
- What legal arguments can a company employ to resist the Panel's 'recommendations' and argue its practices, even under the new regime, are 'perfectly legal'?
- How can the Panel respond?

The Law in Action

Part V looks at the law in action. It looks at the impact of legal arguments in practice. And it sets enforcement and enforceability in a wider political and regulatory context.

- What would happen if a case went to court?
- Why are courts unpredictable?
- How do legal arguments affect enforcement?
- Can technical arguments be used *tactically*?
- Can creative accounting be controlled by means other than the Panel and the courts?
- What impact might other current regulatory developments in the UK and internationally have on the control of creative accounting, now and in the future?

Control

Finally in Part VI we stand back and ask:

- Who is winning?

- Is the new regime achieving a change of climate?
- What is the basis of control to date?
- What factors will affect the new regime's potential to succeed in the long run?
- Will the spirit of the law prove to be the spirit of the age?
- Will creative accounting result in creative control?
- Will the cross-eyed javelin thrower reach its target?
- And what are the implications for regulation and business beyond the arena of financial reporting?

2
The Response

THE DEARING REPORT

The new financial reporting regime was created following the report of a Committee under the chairmanship of Sir Ron Dearing (now Lord Dearing). The Committee was set up by the Consultative Committee of Accounting Bodies (CCAB) to review the structure and process of standard setting, the relationship between accounting regulation and the law, and enforcement of financial reporting regulation. In its report in 1988, the Committee found the standard setting process then operating under the Accounting Standards Committee (ASC):

- to be too cumbersome to keep abreast of rapidly changing circumstances;
- as encouraging compromise because of the need to achieve consensus among the bodies involved; and
- as inadequately resourced (the ASC being largely voluntary, part time and unpaid).

Accounting standards, weakened by compromise, were seen as frequently allowing too much choice and as being ad hoc, lacking a consistent conceptual framework.

Enforcement

There was also concern over enforcement. The Committee

noted a gap in enforcement and sanctions:

- The strength of auditors vis-à-vis directors, and their independence were questioned:

  companies are increasingly prepared to challenge auditors, to shop for opinions, to seek counsel's opinion on the auditor's views and to change auditors. It would be idealistic to assume that all auditors at all times are unmindful of the risk of losing business. (Dearing, 1988:11, 5.14)

- Professional bodies could only discipline their members, but

  The primary responsibility for accounts lies with the directors who approve them and they (apart from any directors who are professionally qualified accountants) are not answerable to the six professional accountancy bodies. (Dearing, 1988:32, 15.5)

- The Department of Trade and Industry could confront directors it saw as contravening the Companies Act, but only through the criminal law, seen by the Dearing Committee as too heavy handed, and rarely used.

In short, the law was not being adequately enforced. The Committee therefore recommended a new institutional structure.

NEW STRUCTURES

Following the Dearing Report, a new structure for the making and enforcement of accounting regulation was created in the Companies Act 1989 and related legislation. The role of law in accounting was enhanced. The intent, however, was not to replace 'expert' regulation, but to strengthen it by adding to the duties of directors with regard to standards, and providing new powers and sanctions to the regulators. It was recognised that the ASC had lacked authority and teeth. In its place a multi-tiered regulatory structure was set up.

Financial Reporting Council

The Financial Reporting Council, comprising representatives of the accounting profession, industry, finance and government, was established. Its function is to promote sound financial reporting and to review the development, application and observance of accounting standards. It oversees the multi-pronged structure of the ASB, the Financial Reporting Review Panel and the ASB Committees, the most important of which is the Urgent Issues Task Force. The Council does not become involved in the detail of the activities of these bodies but provides them:

> with a high level and widely experienced resource on which to draw for guidance on key issues. This 'behind the scenes' function of the Council is an essential and much-valued part of the overall framework. (FRC, 1998:9)

Accounting Standards Board

The ASB, which was set up in 1990, draws its membership from the same pool as the FRC, unlike the old ASC which was appointed by and from the profession. The ASB sets standards on its own independent authority, "needing no external approval for its actions" (FRC, 1991:46). The ASC, by contrast, required the approval of the six accountancy bodies which make up the Consultative Committee of Accountancy Bodies.

Urgent Issues Task Force

The ASB established in 1991 an Urgent Issues Task Force as its trouble-shooter, its main role being to:

> assist the ASB in areas where an accounting standard or Companies Act provision exists, but where unsatisfactory or conflicting interpretations have developed or seem likely to develop. (FRC, 1991:47)

It can publish a consensus opinion or 'Abstract' on the desirable treatment to be used and expect companies to follow it as "authoritative guidance" (FRC, 1991:8).

Financial Reporting Review Panel

A Financial Reporting Review Panel has been established with the power to examine departures from accounting standards and the accounting requirements of the Companies Act.

Membership is drawn from representatives of the business and financial community and members of the accountancy and legal professions. The Panel, again following the Dearing Report, spells out what revision or additional information is needed in order that financial statements give a true and fair view.

Funding

Funding for these bodies comes from three 'broadly equal' sources:

- the accountancy profession, via the CCAB;
- the government – mainly from the Department of Trade and Industry, but also with contributions from the Northern Ireland Department for Economic Development and the National Audit Office; and
- the City – three-quarters of which comes from the London Stock Exchange which raises funds through a levy of listed companies; half of the remainder comes from the Bank of England on behalf of the banking sector, and the other half from the Association of British Insurers, the National Association of Pension Funds, the Association of Investment Trust Companies and the Association of Unit Trusts and Investment Funds.

According to Sir Sydney Lipworth, its pattern of funding is "one of the FRC's great strengths, and a practical manifestation of the broad base of its support" (FRC, 1997:14; repeating FRC, 1996:8).

THE MIGHT OF LAW

Dearing did not recommend that standards should be incorporated into law

> because this inescapably requires a legalistic approach and a reduction in the ability of the financial community to respond quickly to new developments. (1988:23,10.2)

Rather, standard setting should be in the hands of "auditors, preparers and users of accounts" (10.2), an "expert" body (1988:44, R9). However, in several significant ways, accounting standards and the new regulatory regime were incorporated into the *legal* framework of accounting regulation.

In one sense this has always been the case. In tax cases, for example, 'ordinary principles of commercial accountancy' has become a time-honoured expression. When they are followed, according to the courts, tax legislation will have been complied with (unless there is specific legal provision to the contrary). Accounting standards will be referred to by the court to determine what they are at any given time. The link between these principles and the financial reporting requirement to give a true and fair view has also been made, for example by the Court of Appeal (*Johnston*, 1994).

Accounting standards have been recognised in other cases too. According to Mr Justice Woolf in *Lloyd Cheyham* (1987), in determining whether an accountant had been negligent, accounting standards "are very strong evidence as to what is the proper standard which should be adopted." In financial reporting in the 1990s, however, accounting standards can be seen as having an even firmer legal basis.

Standards

Following Dearing, ASB standards have statutory recognition. The Companies Act 1989, which amended the Companies Act 1985, acknowledges the role of accounting standards. Accounting standards are defined as "statements of standard accounting practice issued by such body or bodies as may be prescribed by regulations" (Companies Act 1985 s. 256).

The ASB has been designated as the body responsible for issuing SSAPs under this section (Accounting Standards (Prescribed Body) Regulations 1990 (SI 1990/1667)). Companies are required by law to state in their accounts

> whether they have followed applicable accounting standards and to give the particulars and reasons for any material departure from them. (Companies Act 1985, Sched. 4, para. 36A)

The ASB has carefully set out in its Foreword to Accounting Standards (1993) what it sees as the legal basis of the new regulatory authorities and of its standards.

The 'True and Fair View' Requirement

The statutory requirement in financial reporting is the requirement to give 'a true and fair view' . This is the long established 'overriding' requirement of the Companies Acts. The ASB's claim in the Foreword to Accounting Standards is that, to meet this true and fair view, companies must comply with accounting standards. Counsel's opinion (by Mary Arden QC, now Mrs Justice Arden) is appended to the Foreword in support. Both the Foreword and the Opinion are set out in full in Appendix 1.

Arden's opinion, in a nutshell, notes that:

- "the Companies Act 1989 now gives statutory recognition to the existence of ASB accounting standards and by implication to their beneficial role in financial reporting" (para. 5);
- statutory policy favours both the issue of accounting standards and compliance with them (para. 7);
- Schedule 4 (para. 36A) of the Act requires directors (a) to state expressly whether accounts have been prepared in compliance with standards and (b) to declare any departures from them (para. 5);
- s.256(3) (c) contemplates the investigation of departures from accounting standards (para. 7);
- these changes she expects to "increase the likelihood" that "the courts will hold in general compliance with accounting standards is necessary to meet the true and fair requirement" (para. 7);
- the status of standards is also enhanced by the fact that they are set by a body which now includes more than the profession in its membership (para. 8);
- whether accounts satisfy the true and fair requirement is a question for the court but "the task of interpreting the true and fair requirement cannot be performed by the courts without evidence as to the practices and views of accountants" (para. 14).

Arden concluded that

> an accounting standard which the court holds must be complied with to meet the true and fair requirement become[s], in cases where it is applicable, a *source of law* in itself in the widest sense of that term. (para. 15 emphasis added)

In consequence, the ASB states:

> Accounting standards are authoritative statements of how particular types of transaction and other events should be reflected in financial statements and accordingly compliance with accounting standards will normally be necessary for financial statements to give a true and fair view. (para. 16)

The ASB has adopted the ASC's standards (SSAPs) to give them the same status in law as its own Financial Reporting Standards (FRSs).

UITF Abstracts

UITF Abstracts do not constitute 'applicable accounting standards' under the Companies Act. But, in the opinion of Mary Arden:

> the Court is likely to treat UITF Abstracts as of considerable standing even though they are not envisaged by the Companies Acts. This will lead to a readiness on the part of the Court to accept that compliance with abstracts of the UITF is also necessary to meet the true and fair requirement. (para. 12)

In addition, the Councils of the CCAB bodies expect their members to observe Abstracts in the same way as standards. Thus, UITF statements are also stipulated to be part of the "corpus of practices" on what constitutes a true and fair view (ASB, Foreword to UITF Abstracts, 1993, para. 13) and should be read in conjunction with accounting standards. The Foreword to UITF Abstracts explains the authority, scope and application of UITF Abstracts (see *Accountancy*, March 1994: 127–8).

The Role of the Panel

The Financial Reporting Review Panel has been designated as the body which polices defective accounts (Companies (Defective Accounts) (Authorised Person) Order 1991 (SI 1991/13)).

The Panel has set out its role as follows:

> the main focus is on material departures from accounting

standards where such a departure results in the accounts in question not giving a true and fair view as required by the Act. (FRRP Press Notices)

It has the power to apply to the court for a declaration that accounts do not comply with the requirements of the Companies Act and an order requiring directors to prepare revised accounts (CA 1985, s.245B).

NEW POWERS OF ENFORCEMENT

Compulsory Revision of Defective Accounts

The compulsory revision of accounts is regulated generally by The Companies (Revision of Defective Accounts and Report) Regulations 1990 (set out in Appendix 2). Accounts can be revised either in *full*, via a *replacement* of the original defective accounts, or *partially*, via a Supplementary Note setting out the corrections to be made (Reg. 2). Revised accounts are subject to exactly the same requirement to give a true and fair view as the original accounts (Reg. 3(2)) and non-compliance with the requirements of the Regulations exposes directors to the same liabilities to prosecution and fines as in the original accounts (Reg. 4(2) (b)).

Revised accounts should be prepared as if they were being prepared at the date of the original accounts. So, assets and liabilities, income or expenditure arising *after* that date are *not* to be taken into account. Where auditors have already reported, they must do so again. The report states whether the revised accounts have been properly prepared under the Act, and in particular, whether a true and fair view has been given by them.

Circulation of Revised Accounts

The Regulations explain how revised accounts should be circulated. If the original accounts have already been sent out (to members and debenture holders for example), directors must send them a copy of the revised accounts or of the Supplementary Note together with a copy of the auditor's report not more than 28 days after revision (Reg. 10(2)). The directors must also send them to anyone else entitled to receive accounts at the date of revision (Reg. 10(3)).

Before approving the revised accounts, the directors are obliged to state, in a "prominent" position, how the original accounts failed to comply with the Act and how this has been put right (Reg. 4(2)). This is reinforced by the requirement that *auditors* not only give an opinion that the revised accounts have been properly prepared and give a true and fair view, but also state in their report whether in their opinion the original accounts "failed to comply with the requirements of the Act in the respects identified by the directors" (Reg. 6(3)).

If the original accounts have been laid before a general meeting, then the revised accounts must be laid at the next general meeting (Reg. 11(1), (2)). If the original accounts have been filed with the registrar, then a copy of the revised accounts or Supplementary Note, together with the auditor's report, must be filed with the registrar within 28 days of approval of the revision (Reg. 12(1), (2)).

Cost of Compulsory Revision

The Companies Act provides that if the court finds the accounts did not comply with the Act it can make an order regarding the costs of the court case *and* any reasonable expenses incurred by the company in preparing revised accounts. These costs must be borne by such of the *directors* who approved the defective accounts (Companies Act, s.245B(4)). Unless directors can show that they were not directors at the time or took "all reasonable steps to prevent" the accounts being approved they shall be "taken to have been a party to their approval."

Directors only hope then is to plead mitigation or 'pass the buck' – the court shall have regard to whether the approving director knew or ought to have known that the accounts were defective. It may exclude a director from the costs order or it may order the payment of different amounts by different directors (s.245B(5)).

Voluntary Revision of Defective Accounts

The Companies Act also provides that directors may 'voluntarily' prepare revised accounts if they did not comply with the Act (s.245(1)). If the accounts have already been laid before a general meeting of the company or filed with the registrar, the revision must be confined to those respects not complying and any necessary alterations (s.245(2)).

NEW CONTROLS ON CREATIVE ACCOUNTING

These remedies and sanctions can, of course, only come into play for 'defective' accounts. The Panel also has at its disposal an arsenal of statutory provisions and accounting standards (many new) which aim to bring creative accounting into the net of 'defective' accounting. These have been provided by:

- the European Community's Seventh Directive; implemented in
- the Companies Act 1989 (which amended the 1985 Act); and
- the ASB in various accounting standards.

The ASB's assault on creative accounting has been developing throughout the 1990s, with its 'centrepiece' , FRS 5, in gestation since 1985 but not in place until 1994. With the inevitable lag for publication of accounts, scrutiny for defects, and the process of review, the Panel's first case using FRS 5 emerged only in 1997. In short, it is only very recently that the Panel has been able to tackle creative accounting with its full arsenal of new weapons. What are they?

Statutory definition of a subsidiary

The Companies Act, implementing the Seventh Directive, has set out new statutory definitions of a 'subsidiary undertaking'. This change was designed to tackle one of the recurrent techniques used in a whole range of off balance sheet financing devices in the 1980s, the *controlled non-subsidiary* or what we call the 'orphan' subsidiary – a subsidiary without a parent. This corporate structure functioned like a subsidiary but was constructed to fall *outside* the then Companies Act definitions, and so outside group accounts. The new broader definition would capture any relationships where there was 'actual exercise of dominant influence' and a 'participating interest' .

Guidance on its application was given by the ASB in FRS 2.

FRS 5 and 'quasi-subsidiaries'

The new statutory definition, however, could still be exploited. The ASB therefore provided a weapon against 'quasi-subsidiaries' designed to fall beyond the reach of the statute. FRS 5 required consolidation of a 'vehicle' which

> though not fulfilling the statutory definition of a subsidiary, is . . . controlled by the reporting entity and gives rise to benefits for that entity that are in substance no different from those that would arise were the vehicle a subsidiary. (FRS 5, para. 7)

Standards against specific forms of creative accounting

The ASB has tackled specific forms of creative accounting in specific new standards. In FRS 3, for example, on 'Reporting Financial Performance' , it tackled the scope for using 'exceptional' and 'extraordinary' categories to enhance accounts. Introducing FRS 6 ('Acquisitions and Mergers') and FRS 7 ('Fair Values in Acquisition Accounting'), Sir David Tweedie stated that "Accounting for acquisitions has long been seen as a fertile ground for manipulating figures" (quoted in *Management Accounting*, November 1994:3).

FRS 6 sets out to put right inappropriate use of merger accounting. The acquiring group's earnings could be enhanced by including the results of the acquired company for the whole of the year rather than just from the date of acquisition. The basic principle of FRS 7 is that in attributing fair values to assets and liabilities acquired they should reflect the circumstances at the time of acquisition, and should not reflect either the acquirer's intentions or events subsequent to the acquisition. As a result, provisions for reorganisation costs and future losses should now be excluded. According to Kirk,

> Some of these provisions were undoubtedly genuine but it was impossible for the ASB to determine these from pure creative accounting. (Kirk, 1995:52)

Anti-avoidance rulings

The UITF has issued specific Abstracts to give guidance on grey areas, preventing the spread of practices it considers inappropriate. For example, UITF 3 addresses the treatment of goodwill on disposal of a business. It requires that the profit or loss on such disposals be calculated by including, as part of the cost, the attributable amount of purchased goodwill, even where it had been eliminated previously against reserves. This tries to stop companies reporting a profit on disposal when in fact the business had been sold for an amount substantially less than its purchase price (the purchased goodwill had been written off directly against reserves).

The UITF aims to provide rapid response anti-avoidance rulings. UITF Abstract 12 on Reverse Premiums, for example, was produced within six months of the referral by the Review Panel following the *Pentos* case (PN28). UITF 5 and 17 were also anti-avoidance measures.

FRS 5: reporting substance

FRS 5 goes far beyond quasi-subsidiaries. It sets out a basic requirement that 'reporting entities' report the *substance* of transactions, if necessary overriding the legal form of the deal. In other words, FRS 5 creates an "overriding principle" (PN47). This is seen as a key weapon in the armoury against creative accounting because it attacks the whole idea, underlying many techniques of creative accounting, of reporting according to some artificial packaging rather than commercial reality. FRS 5 requires that

> the commercial effect of the entity's transactions, and any resulting assets, liabilities, gains or losses, should be faithfully represented in its financial statements. (FRS 5, para 1)

Other standards also reflect this basic principle. FRS 4, for example, concentrates on recording the commercial reality rather than the legal form of capital instruments issued by a company.

Principles and rules

This emphasis on principles is itself a conscious strategy to counter creative accounting. Though the new standards and abstracts often tackle quite specific issues and set out very precise rules, the ASB sees its basic approach as one that prefers principles to detailed rules.

- Principles are seen as the only way to capture "a complex area that cannot be reduced to a few simple rules without the danger of oversimplification" (FRS 5, Appendix III, para 18).
- Principles can be used to fill regulatory gaps, guiding preparers of accounts on "topics that do not form the subject of an accounting standard" (ASB, Draft Statement of Principles, 1991, para 1).
- Specific rules with very precise definitions and criteria invite creative compliance – complying with the specific letter of the law but not its spirit.
- Specific rules also foster cat and mouse games, with regulators catching one creative device with a specific rule, only to find a new technique taking its place.
- The goal of the ASB was to pre-empt these problems by setting out general principles both in a broad statement of principles and in FRSs themselves. As Tweedie stated in the first FRC report:

  > We believe this is the surest means of forming standards that will remain relevant to innovations in business and finance and which are most likely to discourage ingenious standards avoidance practices. (FRC, 1991, para. 5.5)

The true and fair override

The Companies Act also expresses a principle in the 'overriding requirement' that companies give a true and fair view in their accounts. Indeed, the true and fair 'override' in special or exceptional circumstances allows departure from specific provisions in statute or standards to the extent necessary to give a true and fair view. It has therefore been seen, not least by Sir David Tweedie, as a useful weapon against accounting treatments which comply with the letter of specific provisions but not their spirit.

In the 1980s there was some dispute over the reach of the override and in the 1989 Companies Act the DTI changed the statutory provisions to make it more readily accessible.

THE SPIRIT OF THE LAW

The first chairman of the FRC, Sir Ron Dearing, talked of the new regime's goal as accounts that were genuinely informative, "applying the spirit as well as the letter of law and accounting standards" *The Times*, 24 January 1991). The emphasis on substance, principles, and the overriding requirement to give a true and fair view, can all be seen as routes to achieving this goal. But the reference to *application* of law and standards is significant too.

The ASB has expressly stated:

> In applying accounting standards it is important to be guided by the spirit and the reasoning behind them. (ASB, Foreword to Accounting Standards, 1993, para 17)

The new regime wants more than just technical compliance with the letter of regulations – so often at the root of creative accounting. It wants compliance with the spirit of the law.

A successful formula?

The new regime has established a statutory enforcement body and equipped it with a range of weapons intended to counter creative accounting. In the end its success will depend on the enforcement and enforceability of those weapons. In Part II we turn to the Panel's enforcement strategies, its record so far, its strengths, and its potential vulnerabilities.

PART II
ENFORCEMENT

3
Discovery and Detection

For the Panel to control creative accounting, it must first detect it. While auditors review each and every set of accounts, the Review Panel does not. So how *do* cases enter the system? How *is* the law brought into play and Panel investigation set in motion? Is the process of detecting cases likely to expose creative accounting; or will it go undiscovered?

ACTIVATING ENFORCEMENT

The enforcement process can be triggered in one of two ways. The initiative can be taken by a third party – and the agency reacts – or the agency itself can seek out its own cases to investigate. Agencies may choose to be 'reactive' or 'proactive' .

Dual Vigilance

In practice, they usually adopt both strategies to a greater or lesser extent. Police react to citizen complaints; they also target particular activities and areas. Customs and Excise and the Inland Revenue are typically proactive in instigating investigations, but they also respond to particular complaints brought to their attention. In other words, systems of dual vigilance – to one degree or another – operate with both 'top-down' and 'bottom-up' monitoring. With the Review Panel, however, this is *not* the case. The Panel has made clear it has little or no inclination to be proactive. What is its strategy?

The Review Panel Strategy

The Review Panel's approach, according to its current chairman Peter Goldsmith QC, is "deliberately reactive rather than proactive" (FRC, 1998:62): "it will not itself monitor or actively initiate scrutinies of company accounts for possible defects" (FRRP Procedures for Handling Individual Cases, September 1993, para. 6; see Appendix 3). The only exception is to monitor the accounts of companies required to take remedial action to ensure they have done so *and* to check them more widely.

This has always been the Panel's approach, and it was reaffirmed by Sir Sydney Lipworth in 1996:

> The Panel, supported by the [Financial Reporting] Council, has rightly rejected the idea that it should become proactive instead of reacting only to cases drawn to its attention. (FRC, 1996:8)

One reason for this is resources.

Resources

The resources available to the Panel it says necessarily make it reactive. With nearly 2,500 companies to police, multiplied many times if subsidiaries are taken into account (and they too can be investigated by the Panel), a proactive policy would require the commitment of resources that the Panel and the new accounting regime simply do not have at their disposal: "it would be prohibitively resource-intensive and wasteful for it to search for accounting failures proactively" (Sir Sydney Lipworth, FRC, 1998:14). (We look at Panel resources further below.)

Whistleblowing

Instead, cases are currently identified through what Glasgow terms "whistleblowing" . There are several recognised routes for matters to be drawn to the Panel's attention:

- cases referred to the Panel by individuals or corporate bodies;
- qualified audit report in respect of listed companies (routinely drawn to the Panel's attention by the Stock Exchange).

Dearing thought this would be the main source of Panel cases. In fact, in the Panel's view, very few qualifications "go to the heart of accounting." Many are "going concern" qualifications, which the Panel does not investigate;
- departures from accounting standards or other requirements flagged in the accounts;
- press comment. The Trafalgar case, for example, was prompted by comment in the 'Lex' column of the *Financial Times*.

Getting cases in this way means that the Panel has relinquished control over the source of its case load and is totally dependent on others for its cases. Does this matter?

Motivation

One of the potential problems with whistleblowing via individual or corporate referrals is that it requires motivation on somebody's part to blow the whistle. That motivation may be something other than a simple wish for good accounting. Edwin Glasgow has conceded that sometimes complaints have been

> motivated by personal disagreement; they are one way of reflecting an ongoing row . . . We have had companies that are in litigation with one another referring each other's accounts to us. (quoted in *Accountancy*, December, 1996:42)

One example of this was the second Butte Mining case (PN43. Press Notices – PNs – on cases are noted in detail in Appendix 5). The complaint – which turned out, in the view of the Panel, to be well founded – was made by the Robertson Group, a subsidiary of Simon Engineering, which held a 4% stake in Butte. However, at the time, Butte was pursuing this company over a claim for £100 million (*FT*, 2 October 1996).

Another situation that produces referrals is, according to Glasgow, a hostile takeover:

> with potential take-overs people tend to look more critically at the accounts . . . and have an agenda which has nothing to do with accounting standards but to do with strengthening their position. (*Accountancy*, December 1996:42)

An example of this involved Etam, the fashion retailer. Having survived a hostile takeover by Oceana, Etam complained to the Review Panel about Oceana's accounts. Oceana had equity accounted its 34.4% share in Etam (and claimed 34.4% of Etam's £7.1 million profits as its own). To equity account in this way Oceana had to have a 'significant influence' over Etam. In fact, Oceana's only power was to block, via its 34.4% holding, special resolutions at an annual general meeting (which required a 75% majority). The Panel cleared Oceana (*FT*, 12 November 1992).

It is anybody's guess whether or not this kind of whistle-blowing produces appropriate cases. The same goes for cases picked up from press comment. Where does the press get its information from; how reliable are its sources?

The Panel is aware there are drawbacks in some of its sources. It has been "slightly more sceptical" about press comment than Stock Exchange referral, and "very wary of being sucked into contested bids – you can always find something to sneer about if you look".

But there is a much greater problem with a whistleblowing strategy than the danger of inappropriate cases being chosen by whistleblowers. What if the whistle is not blown at all? In an exclusively reactive strategy, if the whistle is not blown – whether by referral, directors' disclosure, auditor's qualification or press comment – there will be *no* cases; so there will be no enforcement. The Panel has actually dealt with remarkably few cases over its eight years. Why might the whistle not be blown?

First the Good News

One answer may be that the standards of financial reporting have improved and that instances of creative accounting have dropped away. The Panel's confidence in its whistleblowing strategy is based partly on its assumption or hope that if there are few or no complaints 'out there' then there must be general satisfaction and contentment with corporate accounts.

And in recent years, the number of cases the Panel has "substantively considered" has declined (see Appendix 4).

There were 43 cases between November 1993 and December 1994 period but only 34 cases in 1995: a "significant fall" according to Glasgow (FRC, 1996:32). In 1996 the number rose to 40, but in 1997 it fell again this time to only 26. As Peter Goldsmith put it in 1997 "the Panel's current workload is low" (FRC, 1998:64).

He hoped this was 'good news':

> It is certainly good news for financial reporting if standards of compliance have improved, whether because of the deterrent effect of the Panel's existence or for more worthy reasons. (FRC, 1998:64–5)

But both Goldsmith and Glasgow are aware that there is another possibility.

Now the Bad

According to Glasgow, "It is not easy to determine the reason for this reduction. If it means that serious cases are slipping through the net it is obviously worrying. . ." (FRC, 1996:32). Goldsmith hopes

> that the fall-off in Review Panel business reflects a general improvement in the standard of compliance . . . rather than that serious failures of compliance have escaped the Panel's attention. (FRC, 1998:64)

Any enforcement strategy will suffer from the problem of the ones that get away. This may, however, be exacerbated by a purely reactive strategy – especially where creative accounting is concerned.

Hidden Creative Accounting

For a start, one of the inherent characteristics of creative accounting is that it is difficult to spot. Devices and the transactions in which creative accounting techniques are employed are often complex. Even 'sophisticated' readers of accounts might miss them. And then there's the question of what we might call 'off-the-peg' versus 'tailor-made' techniques. It may be relatively easy to spot 'off-the-peg' schemes such as ANS' sale and leaseback deal arranged and marketed by Nursing Home Properties (*The Times*, 20 February 1997). The press is relatively likely to pick up on a marketed technique, repeated throughout a sector. Tailor-made, one-off, constructions may, however, be hard to spot.

But that is not the only problem. Even if whistleblowers suspect creative accounting is going on they may still not draw the accounts to the attention of the Panel. Why not?

CONFLICT OF INTEREST

If there are motivations at times for the whistle to be blown *in*appropriately, there can also be motivations for it *not* to be blown when, in the regulators' eyes, it should be. For many potential whistleblowers there may be a potential conflict of interest which deters them from whistleblowing.

Shareholders

One possible outcome of a Panel investigation, if the accounts are found to be defective, is adverse publicity which may affect the share price. For the current investor affected by the share price, whistleblowing may represent a degree of altruism which it is unrealistic to expect. Even though the Panel emphasises the confidentiality of its investigations, it will not and cannot guarantee that information about companies will never be released.

Indeed, since creative accounting may have a *positive* impact on the accounts and, by implication, the share price, at least temporarily, the attitude of the rational investor may well be: long may it continue (and continue to escape detection). Which shareholder would have put at risk, by bringing in the Panel, the spectacular share price performance of Polly Peck International as shares grew from 7p to 418p and market capitalisation rose to £1.5 billion, to make the company, as Chairman Asil Nadir described it, "the best performer of the decade, around the world"? (*Fortune*, 16 March 1992).

Auditors

Auditors are another set of potential whistleblowers specified by the Panel, though auditors would be quick to remind the Panel of the limit of their investigatory role. They "are watch-dogs but they are not expected to play detective" (Maw *et al.*, 1994:59). In any case, as we saw in Chapter 2, one of the reasons for introducing the Panel was a concern, expressed for example by the Dearing Committee, that auditors were not blowing the whistle enough in the 1980s.

This view was still being aired in the 1990s. Andrew Jack, the *FT* journalist, set it out in graphic language:

> all too frequently auditors treat the directors of the company as the client. It is the board which sacks, appoints and pays the auditors, meets the audit partner, negotiates the wording of the audit report, receives the management letter and hears details that never reach the ears of the shareholder. That places auditors under commercial and personal pressures that sit uneasily with their impartial role, particularly at a time when accountancy firms have become more business-oriented, marketing-driven and competitive with one another. Privately, auditors will talk about the fear of being sued or of losing the client at least as much as about whether they agree with the treatment of the accounts the directors request. (*FT*, 7 January 1993)

David Tweedie has continued with his auditor jokes – "What's the difference between an auditor and an airport baggage trolley? The trolley has a mind of its own!" – *after* the introduction of the new regime (*FT*, 12 July 1994).

Criticism

The role of auditors may in fact be more complex than trolley jokes suggest (see Chapter 18). Nonetheless, auditors have come in for criticisms by shareholders as a result of some Panel investigations. There was a massive shareholder outcry, expressed particularly by individual shareholders, when Trafalgar House's pre-tax profits of £122.4 million for the year ending 30 September 1991 were in the following year, after a

Panel investigation (PN13), reduced by £102.7 million. The company's auditors, Touche Ross, which had not qualified the accounts, were described by one shareholder as the "directors' poodle" (*FT*, 12 January 1993) and were subsequently replaced.

Professional support for the Panel and the ASB has also been questioned over disciplinary proceedings. Auditors who do not qualify accounts subsequently criticised by the Panel are automatically referred to their professional regulatory body, usually the ICAEW Investigations Committee (FRRP, Working Procedures, para. 45). So far, no action has been taken against such auditors. Touche Ross was referred to the Committee over Trafalgar, but no disciplinary action was taken against them. The view was that there had been "honest differences of opinion" .

The lack of disciplinary action generally by professional bodies has been put down to the problem of lack of evidence – a by-product of the confidential nature of Panel investigations. Since September 1993, however, "such detailed information as appears appropriate" (para. 45) has been provided by the Panel to the professional body in the event of disciplinary proceedings – and there has still been no action by the profession.

Clash of views

This may, of course, simply be the result of concluding there were "honest differences of opinion" . This is an important reminder that while a *lack* of whistleblowing by auditors *may* point to a conflict of interest, it may also point to a conflict over law: of which more later. However, either way, it raises questions about the appropriateness – from the Panel's point of view – of relying on auditors to refer cases to them. The Panel may not be able to rely on auditor whistleblowing to produce the cases *it* believes should be investigated.

Time after time we see the Panel requiring adjustments of accounts which have *not* been qualified by auditors but which found their way to the Panel via some other route. On only seven occasions out of the first 42 did auditors qualify accounts on the same grounds as the Panel's concerns (Ultramar, PN4; Shield, PN6; GPG, PN12; S.E.P. Industrial Holdings, PN15; Warnford Investments, PN18; Newarthill, PN37; and M & W Mack, PN46). On four other occasions the accounts were qualified on other grounds (Brandt *et al.*, 1997:43). On many occasions, therefore, unqualified accounts have been found by the Panel to be defective, in need of remedial action and even subject to the threat of court-ordered revision.

Six feet under

Auditors, perhaps on the advice of technical partners, may have a subtler impact too. Their advice may make it *less* likely that anyone else will blow the whistle on companies. Interviews suggest that the very difference of opinion between Panel and the big accountancy firms on several key cases has resulted in professional advisers suggesting companies disclose *less* in their accounts.

As Sir David Tweedie observed, "where they used to leave a foot sticking up out of the grave everything's six feet down now" – though he warned too that auditors take a risk if they take this approach. They cannot so readily rely on the defence that they did try to give some warning to readers of accounts.

Directors

New law requires directors to expressly declare that they have prepared the accounts in accordance with applicable accounting standards. And if they have departed from either standards or statutory provisions, as they might legitimately do using the 'the true and fair override', they must also disclose this (CA 1985, ss.226(5), 227(6); Sched. 4, para 36A). In other words, potential areas for monitoring are to be flagged for the Panel to investigate.

DEPENDING ON COMPLIANCE TO ENFORCE COMPLIANCE

But, what if this is not done, or not done clearly? There is a certain irony in tackling non-compliance and creative compliance by way of rules requiring companies to disclose their non- or creative compliance. Might there not in turn be non-compliance or creative compliance with those secondary rules?

An example is Breverleigh Investments (PN20) and its 1992 consolidated accounts. The assets and liabilities and results of Breverleigh's subsidiary were not included in the accounts (contrary to the requirements of the Companies Act and SSAP 14) and a cash flow statement was not provided (contrary to FRS 1). But, not only were the accounts *not* qualified by the auditors (though their report did draw attention to the non-consolidation), the directors also failed to record these departures from requirements. They did not even include a statement that the accounts had been prepared in accordance with applicable accounting standards as required by the Companies Act.

This latter problem was specifically addressed by the Panel in 1991/92 when it wrote to 240 listed companies which had similarly failed to comply with the new Companies Act 1989 requirement. But there might also be subtler means of meeting the requirement to reveal departures without giving much away.

Understated Disclosure

The UITF has tried to ensure that the nature and impact of departure are spelt out so that both the departure and its significance are flagged. UITF Abstract 7 ('True and Fair Override Disclosures'), for example, spells out how use by directors of the 'true and fair override' should be disclosed. It tackles the "tendency for some companies to understate rather than emphasise the significance of what they have done", failing to give adequate explanations for the departures, failing to specify what exactly was departed from and failing to quantify the effects:

> In some cases it has not been clear from the notes to the accounts whether the directors consider that they have departed from a

> specific statutory rule and that the true and fair view override is being invoked. (UITF Statement, 17 December 1992)

Abstract 7 should make it clearer and less ambiguous when the override has been used – if companies fully comply with it – but what if they don't?

Ernst & Young have shown how practice varies amongst companies. Severn Trent, for example, in its 1997 accounts, disclosed that it had deducted from the cost of fixed assets grants and contributions received relating to infrastructure assets. The company also indicated that this treatment was not in accordance with Schedule 4 of the Companies Act and that the departure was necessary to give a true and fair view. It also gave the effect of this departure. Ernst & Young note that the company has given

> the information required by UITF 7 where the 'true and fair override' is used to depart from the detailed requirements of the Companies Act.

But they added a warning:

> However, many companies that use this approach do not agree that it is a departure from the Act, and thus do not make the disclosure. (1997:1056)

In these circumstances, how can the Panel police such non-disclosure and enforce UITF 7? We seem to be into an infinite regression of depending on compliance with regulations to enforce compliance with regulations.

This kind of self-reporting (although auditors are involved at a later stage) is inherently problematic in a reactive system. This is particularly so when the strategy of directors in creative accounting is not to *depart* from specific rules on the grounds of giving a true and fair view but to *comply* with specific rules – but fail to give what others would see as a true and fair view. This is *not* subject to any statutory flagging requirement. Indeed how could it be? After all it is not a matter of justifiable *non*-compliance, but, the directors would claim, simple compliance with the rules. The Panel might, of course, disagree, but the directors would not be under any obligation to blow the whistle on themselves, so would the Panel pick it up?

That is not, however, the only problem. Even if the whistle is blown there is another limitation to the effectiveness of an exclusively reactive system.

CASE-BY-CASE

Reactive systems operate on a *case-by-case* basis. Cases enter one-by-one and are dealt with one-by-one. Problems identified in one case are not followed up in others unless they too are brought to the Panel's attention. Sir Neil Macfarlane, chairman of Associated Nursing Services, presented his company as just one of many engaged in the same practice. He predicted that "any of the hundreds of companies" which had entered sale and leaseback transactions may find themselves falling foul of the Panel (quoted in *FT*, 19 February 1997). There had been a "small industry in such schemes" in the late 1980s and early 1990s and they had been "aggressively marketed by finance houses" . The ANS action was "aimed at the reappearance of such schemes in niches in several sectors" (*FT*, 19 February 1997).

Yet, no such companies have 'fallen foul' of the Panel, at least in public. Regulators may "hope" that the Panel's inquiry into ANS will "finally stop schemes designed to improve gearing . . . by removing property assets from the balance sheet" and which also improve earnings per share, and indeed it may. The problem is the Panel will not *know* unless it checks. The reactive approach adopted by the Panel may mean that a major source of 'known' creative accounting will go unchecked.

The Panel may be reactive by necessity, but need it be *exclusively* so? Few agencies would claim to police 100% of their populations 100% of the time. A proactive strategy need not aim at blanket coverage. Agencies may opt for random sampling or, more likely, at targeted monitoring, concentrating resources on what are believed to be potential trouble spots. The threat of even selective scrutiny of accounts by an enforcement agency can help deter.

Proactive Reviews

When the Panel *did* undertake a proactive 'scrutiny of company accounts', it showed that 240 companies were failing to comply even with the new Companies Act requirement to state whether their accounts had been prepared in accordance with applicable accounting standards. Would a similar scrutiny of companies in the aftermath of other new accounting requirements reveal similar non-compliance?

One body that does regularly review company accounting practices is *Company Reporting*. In 1997, two years after UITF 13 on employee share ownership plans (ESOPs) came into effect, it found that of 507 reports analysed, while practice was moving into line with UITF 13, *fewer than half* met UITF 13's minimum disclosure requirements:

> The majority of companies are failing to make sufficient disclosure in their financial statements to enable analysts to understand the full nature and scope of ESOP trusts. (August 1997:3)

Many companies disclosed some details of their ESOP trusts but not in their audited financial statements as Abstract 13 requires.

It seems clear that, at the least, the Panel should proactively monitor the implementation of *new* Financial Reporting Standards and UITF Abstracts. When *Control Techniques'* (PN22) 1992 accounts were enquired into by the Panel, a "classification error" was "brought to light". The accounts had wrongly shown the cash impact of the disposal of two subsidiaries. The reconciliation from operating profit to net cash flow from operating activities included the element of working capital of the businesses sold. The effect was to incorrectly show the company with a net inflow before financing of £100,000, while the amended version showed it with a net outflow of £1.14 million for the year (*FT*, 27 September 1993). The error had not been picked up by Coopers & Lybrand, which did not qualify the accounts, but claimed

> It was a complex standard being applied for the first time. A technical error was made but it wasn't material and has been corrected. There was a mistake. Everybody accepts that. (*FT*, 27 September 1993)

Selective investigation might encourage the quicker 'take-up' of new requirements.

Conclusion

It is quite unusual for an enforcement agency to adopt an *exclusively* reactive strategy. We have shown how the detection and discovery of potentially defective accounts is affected by this. Sir Sydney Lipworth, referring to the "sharp falling-off in the Panel's current caseload" in 1997 echoed the words of Peter Goldsmith:

> Unless failures to follow the rules are escaping the Panel's attention, *which has not been demonstrated to us*, the conclusion appears to be that the level of compliance has risen. (FRC, 1998:14, emphasis added)

He added:

> if there are those who feel that the Panel is missing things I would urge them to draw to the Panel's attention the identified specific failures they believe to have escaped enquiry. (*Ibid*)

But it may not be enough to rely on others to tell the Panel what it is missing. The Panel may have to look for itself. The reactive approach may not be enough. Indeed the *deterrent* effect of the Panel is likely to be reduced if the chances of detection are thought to be slim.

No policing can ever be 100%, no resources ever adequate. Yet the resources available for the new regime may be *too* inadequate if they make even the *threat* of selective proactive scrutiny impossible. Opting for a purely reactive approach seems particularly unsuited to the task of controlling creative accounting. There is something paradoxical about depending for detection on disclosure when the basic problem *is* inadequate disclosure, depending on motivated whistleblowers when those most likely to know the whistle should be blown are least likely to be motivated to blow it.

However, there is more involved than resources. The Panel has rejected the proactive approach on other grounds. Edwin Glasgow believed the Panel "shouldn't be a police force looking for trouble". A proactive approach would give the wrong message to companies. It would not be right to go out 'looking for people to shoot'; it would convey the 'wrong flavour'. The Panel does not want its relationship with companies to be confrontational and intrusive but consensual and co-operative.

In short, the reactive approach is not just a matter of necessity but a matter of choice. It is an integral part of the Panel's broader policy of enforcement. We'll look at that in Chapter 4.

4
Investigation and Action

What about those cases that *are* drawn to the attention of the Panel? What is the Panel's policy on enforcement? The Panel's approach bears all the hallmarks of what has been described as a 'benign big gun' strategy: the enforcement agency "speaks softly" while carrying very big weapons (Ayres and Braithwaite, 1992:42). The idea is to secure compliance 'voluntarily' rather than through confrontation and sanctions, but to have the necessary sanctions there to 'encourage' 'voluntary' compliance.

INVESTIGATION PROCEDURES

First, Panel procedures. When what the Panel regards as a *prima facie* case is made, it writes to the company concerned. In this letter the Panel normally outlines its concern, for example, that an accounting treatment appears to be contrary to a particular statutory or accounting requirement.

The company replies in writing. Sometimes the process ends at this point – the Panel drops the matter, perhaps understanding the company's position. If the Panel wishes to proceed further it writes again and there are likely to be rounds of correspondence, followed by a private meeting. The company is invited to "come along with whomever you like", though, at this stage, the attendance of auditors and accountants rather than lawyers is preferred by the Panel. It is an opportunity for further 'fact-finding' and explaining. Again the process may end at this stage. The Panel may be satisfied with the company's explanation. Conversely, the company may see the Panel's view and agree a remedy.

If there is still deadlock after this meeting, the Panel is likely to write again to the company in more direct terms. The Panel here is getting, in the former Secretary's words, "more serious". It states that it is not convinced by the company's explanation and asks the company "what it is going to do about it". If a further round of correspondence does not produce a resolution there is another, more formal, meeting: "the last chance saloon".

Prior to this meeting the Panel will virtually always have taken legal advice from independent counsel. It might also have gone to an independent firm of accountants (for example, to get an opinion on GAAP). If there are still "different minds" at the end of this meeting, the Panel writes a "14-day letter" to the company: unless there is good cause, we will have to go to court. Again, this may lead to a resolution.

Ultimately, the Panel informs the company that it proposes to issue a writ on a particular day and time. So far, no case has gone beyond this stage. The case would be heard in the Chancery Division of the High Court. That is when the two sides "go to war".

BENIGN

The Panel has stated in its working procedures (para 5) that it will seek to *negotiate* a solution – "to operate by discussion and persuasion as far as possible" – rather than threaten to impose one. It will only seek recourse to the court "when the possibility of voluntary agreement has been properly explored" (*ibid*). But while Glasgow described litigation as very much a "last resort", he added (*Accountancy*, April 1993:36), "Where there are abuses we will not have the slightest concern about litigating."

The Panel's softly softly side is reflected in its working procedures which stress co-operation, confidentiality and informality.

Co-operation and Confidentiality

The Panel's decision is its "view" not a "ruling", and "no-one is obliged to accept our views" (Glasgow, *Accountancy*, April

1993:35). To facilitate an atmosphere of co-operation, the Panel will

- "strive to avoid any public comment on individual cases (actual or potential) until they are in the public domain" (para. 12); and it will
- "not normally make any announcement about an enquiry before it makes an application to the court. Nor will it confirm or deny that a particular company is under enquiry." (para. 39)

According to Glasgow, the Panel seeks to guarantee "absolute confidentiality" to anyone coming to discuss an issue. Great importance is placed on

> preserving commercial confidentiality . . . it does not disclose details of cases it has examined where it is concluded no remedial action is called for. Nor does it disclose details of any of its enquiries while they are in train. (FRC, 1997:13)

Glasgow and Goldsmith note that not a single leak has been attributed to the Panel. Great care is taken to preserve secrecy, with companies given code names. This approach, Glasgow says, has allowed companies to present commercially sensitive information to the Panel which satisfactorily explained the particular accounting treatment, e.g. an enormous contingent liability, disclosed but not specified as a potential legal liability, public acknowledgement of which might undermine the position of the company.

Informality

The Panel's policy is that it

- "strives hard to operate as informally as possible." (Glasgow, FRC, 1997:53)

When the Panel revised its procedures in 1993 it included

- "greater provision for cases to be handled informally in the early stages, including greater scope for preliminary and informal meetings with Panel officials and members." (PN23)

This revision drew on the

- "practical experience of the Panel's first two years of operation." (PN23)

The procedures state that hearings and meetings held by the Panel will operate in an informal way and not seek to follow a court-like procedure (although companies may be represented by Counsel or other professional advisers and the requirements of natural justice will be fully observed) (para. 8). The Panel encourages the company to be accompanied by its auditors (para. 9). They are always invited and it is "very rare for the auditor not to attend". The Panel's strategy is further demonstrated by its approach to its press statements which it issues when some remedial action is required. As we shall see, what the Panel sees as "corrective remedial action" can be achieved in ways other than actual revision of accounts.

Diplomacy

The Panel's policy is to publicise cases where remedial action is required (and occasionally where it is not: "for the information and guidance of others" – Ultramar, PN4). It does so via Press Notices. However it rarely does so *unilaterally*. Indeed, it has become increasingly common for the company concerned to "put the requisite information into the public domain" (Glasgow, FRC, 1997:54–55).

Typically the company issues its own announcement and, if it is issuing an Interim Statement, Preliminary Results Announcement or even its new set of accounts, the Press Notice and the Announcement are co-ordinated so that they take place on the same day. On only one occasion in recent times (Butte Mining, PN43) has the Panel issued a Press Notice without any concurrent company action and, perhaps not surprisingly, this was a case in which the Panel demanded revision of the defective accounts in question and it was a second 'offence'.

Allowing companies to issue their announcements or press notices concurrently with its own reduces the impact of the Panel's actions. The related press reports tend to focus on the other events, further reducing the impact of the Panel's intervention (Brandt *et al.*, 1997:39). However, these arrangements may be acceptable to the Panel.

They may be part of a 'diplomatic' approach, which allows companies to 'save face' and avoid the admission of 'wrong-doing'. But it may be 'gun boat diplomacy' if the Panel can manage the degree of stigma it wishes to attach to the company and its directors and use it as a weapon. It can publicly accept the directors' 'good faith' or it can give quite a different signal. In practice, companies have discussions with the Panel over the wording of its Press Notices. And so far, the language of Press Notices for the most part conveys an image of voluntary agreement and consensus.

Consensus

According to the Press Notices, directors "agree" with the Panel; the Panel "welcomes changes" made by the directors who "voluntarily" alter their accounting policies and practices. The image is almost of the Panel responding to rather than initiating changes (see Appendix 5 for details). When faced with what it sees as questionable practices, the Panel tends not to publicly berate or criticise the directors. This became clear, relatively early on, when the Panel was faced with what it saw as the defective profit and loss account in British Gas' accounts.

British Gas (PN14)

The Panel was concerned by the company's presentation of its change of financial year end from 31 March to 31 December 1991. The Group profit and loss account showed the results from 1 January to 31 December rather than from 1 April – i.e. from the end of the last financial period. The profit and loss account thus included a three-month period already included in the previously published profit and loss account. The effect was to boost pre-tax profits by £1 billion, from £496 million to £1.47 billion. The company did present a profit and loss account for the group for the nine-month period to 31 December in the notes to the accounts. But the Panel did not regard this as meeting the provisions of the Companies Act either as to its location or its content. Nor did it contain the relevant earnings per share figure.

The publicised account of the investigation was an essay in consensus:

> The Panel has *discussed* the matter with the directors of the company and their auditors and *accepts* the directors' assurance that there was no intention to mislead and that the company had acted in good faith.

The directors undertook to ensure that the 1991 comparative figures in the company's 1992 accounts covered the period 1 April 1991 to 31 December 1991 in compliance with the statutory requirement.

The typical public portrayal of Panel investigations, whatever really went on behind the scenes, is one of Panel, directors and sometimes auditors engaged in a collaborative dialogue.

Pentos (PN28)

In the Pentos case, for example, the Panel was concerned with the adequacy of the information provided in the 1992 accounts about the company's accounting treatment of reverse premiums received in respect of property leases. Reverse premiums are used by landlords to attract potential tenants. The Panel discussed the matter with the directors and the company auditors. The directors decided to explain their accounting policy more fully in the company's forthcoming accounts. But, according to the Panel, they also

> *shared the Panel's view* that it would be helpful to bring forward the company's clarification of its accounting policy and information in respect of amounts included in the 1992 accounts. (PN28)

Accordingly, the directors themselves issued a public statement giving the information.

Agreed Remedial Action

Of course, other language may be employed in Press Notices too: for example the Panel has been "minded" to make an application to the court on several occasions. So far though, all remedial action has been 'agreed' with the directors themselves. Even when the Panel has sought revision it has not relied on its own formal legal authority to ask the courts to enforce this. It has preferred instead to cajole or 'persuade' directors to use powers *they* have to revise accounts. So, in the first case of revision, Penrith Farmers' & Kidd's (PN19), it was concluded "by *both* the company and the Review Panel", because of the extent of the additional information needed to be provided, that it could best be contained in a Supplementary Note (emphasis added).

Voluntary Revision by Directors

Strictly speaking, the formal power of the Panel is to apply for court-ordered revision of accounts under the Companies Act s.245B. But, at the time of writing, it has not used this power. Where remedial action is required, the Panel normally accepts adjustment in the company's next set of accounts. Where it demands revision, the Panel has made use of the "very useful change" (Glasgow, FRC, 1996:31) introduced in the Companies Act 1989 – 'Voluntary revision' – under which directors are empowered to issue a correction if it appears to them that the accounts do not comply with the requirements of the Act (Companies Act 1985, s. 245). This can be achieved either by the reissue of the full accounts or by the issue of a corrective Supplementary Note dealing just with the issue in question. If the revised accounts are a replacement of the original, the directors are obliged to state, in a

> prominent position, the respects in which the original accounts did not comply with the requirements of the Act and any significant amendment made consequential upon the remedying of these defects. (See Appendix 2)

Of course, just how 'voluntary' such revisions – and indeed, other forms of "corrective remedial action" – are when the Panel is threatening legal action – is a moot point.

BIG GUN

The new financial reporting regime certainly claims to carry a 'big gun': the "nuclear explosion of going to court" (Sydney

Treadgold, Panel Secretary, quoted in *Accountancy*, December 1996:40). Edwin Glasgow has described the Panel's statutory power to apply to the court for a declaration that accounts do not comply with the Act as a "draconian power" (FRC, 1996:31; repeated in FRC, 1997:54). And while the Panel may speak 'softly' to companies during investigations, the new regime has also told them of its willingness to go to court if it has to.

Iron Fist in Velvet Glove

According to Malcolm Samuels, director of accounting and tax at Courts, one of the companies investigated by the Panel (PN33),

> The initial approach is very softly softly. But you are made to feel very much that you are in the wrong, and unless you can prove otherwise you are going to jolly well have to kowtow to their views or else. (Quoted in *Accountancy*, December 1996:41)

"The iron fist in the velvet glove" was how he described the Panel (*ibid*).

Both Sir David Tweedie and Edwin Glasgow have expressed their determination to stamp on abuses. Tweedie has claimed that he "wants a hanging case" to show the new regulatory order means business and has teeth. So far the Panel has not taken a company to court although on a number of occasions it has "come very close indeed to doing so" (Glasgow, FRC, 1997:54). Glasgow has warned that this

> has not been due to any lack of determination on the Panel's side – rather the opposite. We never threaten what we are not prepared to carry out. (FRC, 1996:31)

And "in some instances the necessary steps have been at an advanced stage" (PN45). In the Butte Mining case in 1996 (PN43), for example, "Counsel had been instructed and the necessary papers prepared" (FRC, 1997:54). This is typical of the 'benign big gun' approach – adopting a conciliatory style, protective of the company so long as it complies with the agency's requirements, but threatening if required to secure compliance.

Going to court is a real threat in more ways than one. Not only might the company end up having to revise its accounts, there is also the question of costs. Companies may back down simply to avoid the costs associated with being investigated, costs which will rise as the case gets closer to court.

War Chest

The Panel has a 'war chest' – a legal costs fund of around £2 million should it need to take court action (FRC, 1995:13; FRC, 1996:9). These funds cannot be used for any purpose other than taking steps to ensure compliance with and to investigate departures from statutory accounting requirements including applicable accounting standards (FRC, Group Accounts, 31 March 1995, Note 3: FRC, 1996:47). According to Sir Sydney Lipworth:

> The existence of this fund is a signal to the world at large that the Panel would not be deterred by lack of funds from court action it felt it necessary to pursue, and may be one reason why the Panel has not found it necessary so far to resort to the court. (FRC, 1996:9; he repeated this view in FRC, 1997:15)

In 1997, the Panel spent up to £250,000 instructing counsel in two cases. So the Panel is geared up for legal battle and with senior lawyers as chairmen of both the Panel and the FRC, and funds set aside for litigation there are resources and expertise to back it up.

By contrast, some companies may not have the resources needed to fight a case in court – or want to use them for this purpose. One company that came close to the courts told us the costs of courts and revision would have been into six figures. Some companies that have backed down before the Panel have justified it publicly on grounds of resources and cost effectiveness. Butte Mining backed down after several months of Panel investigation (PN43). According to Christopher Dawes, finance director, the company had to accept the Panel's decision because "we weren't prepared to spend money to go to court" (*Accountancy*, November 1996:15). According to Butte chairman, David Lloyd-Jacob, in a letter to shareholders, challenging the Panel in court

> would be a waste of money . . . and there seems to be no alternative but to send you new accounts, with a qualified audit opinion, and leave you to form your own views. (Quoted in *Accountancy*, December 1996:11)

According to the Supplementary Note sent to shareholders, "The Company does not have the money [to fight the threatened legal proceedings] and no benefit could accrue to shareholders."

Directors' Liability

Companies, of course, may have significant resources they can mobilise too. But, under the Companies Act s. 245B(4), the costs of a court case and also any reasonable expenses incurred by the company in preparing the revised accounts may fall *not* on the company but on some or all of the directors responsible for drawing up the defective accounts. Unless directors can show they were not directors at the time, or took "all reasonable steps to prevent" the accounts being approved they shall be "taken to have been a party to their approval". Early on in the new financial reporting regime, Sir Ron Dearing, first FRC chairman, reinforced this when he wrote to the chairmen and company secretaries of all 2500 listed companies reminding them that the Companies Act 1989 had "significantly widened the liability of directors in relation to a company's accounts" (*FT*, 25 July 1991).

These provisions theoretically expose directors to a serious *personal* financial risk and may prove to be a real deterrent. The cost of preparing and circulating revised accounts to the 600 or so shareholders of Penrith Farmers' & Kidd's (PN19) may not have been significant – the cost was estimated by David Hibbert, the company secretary, to be between £200–300 (*FT*, 6 April 1993). But when there are thousands of shareholders or even, as in the case of British Gas (PN14), millions of shareholders, the cost would be substantial. Tweedie regards directors' liability as important. When directors have it pointed out to them that *they* may have to pay "they blink a bit".

In practice, directors may find ways to pass the costs of compulsory revision on to the company. It is interesting that the chairman of Butte Mining, as we just saw, put it in terms of the *company* not being able to afford to go to court. Nonetheless, 'voluntary revision', clearly paid for by the company, would eliminate this personal financial risk and therefore become an attractive option.

But the big gun directors face is not only the threat of compulsory revision of accounts by the courts (with its potentially adverse affects on EPS, gearing and reported profits) and the associated costs, including the risk of personal liability to directors. There may be adverse consequences as a result of the litigation process itself. There may be other costs which may deter directors from going to court, even if they genuinely believe they have a good case.

Collateral Damage

Those directors that do have the heart – and the support of legal advice – to resist the Panel may still fear being taken to court. Most will fear the adverse publicity which it might generate and which they cannot easily control. For an indeterminate time, the company will be uncertain as to the outcome. Trafalgar House's chairman and group chief executive told shareholders that "in order to avoid the delays and uncertainties which would have resulted from prolonged litigation, your Board agreed to make certain changes". According to a comment in *The Times* (16 October 1992) Trafalgar's

> climbdown shows that even the largest companies will succumb to the threat of bad publicity. Trafalgar's board could not afford to be seen in the spotlight of a court appearance while it was locked in talks with Hong Kong Land, its new shareholder.

Research also points to the potential deterrence role of adverse publicity. According to Fisse and Braithwaite (1983), who looked at adverse publicity 'crises' arising out of allegations of corporate wrongdoing in large American corporations, individual executives regarded their personal reputation in the community and their corporate reputation to be priceless assets.

If this is the case, there are clear risks involved in resisting the Panel should it lead to adverse publicity – the effect on share price, the unwelcome investor concern and scrutiny of company stewardship, the invitation to potential predators will all threaten reputations. Reputation also forms part of the assessment for a credit rating with Standard & Poor's and Moody's. Glasgow himself believes that "the service of a writ will do irreparable damage".

Future Relations

There can also be concerns among companies that confronting the Panel will affect relations with it in the future, or relations with other regulators. This may be particularly the case in regulated industries – finance, insurance, utilities. One corporate counsel told us this was the key weight in the balance in deciding whether to confront the Panel or not.

These fears can strengthen the Panel's position. Fear of adverse publicity, reputational loss, difficult regulatory relations in the future can themselves become sanctions and deterrents.

Arsenal of Weapons

To sum up then, the softly softly approach of the Panel is supported by a variety of weapons:

- the threat of compulsory revision by the courts;
- the adverse effects of revision on EPS, gearing and profits;
- the costs of litigation;
- the costs of revision;
- the threat of personal liability of directors;
- the adverse publicity and the uncertainty associated with litigation.

Voluntary Compliance

In the face of this arsenal of weapons it may be not at all surprising that "in all cases to date the company in question had adopted a voluntary solution that the Panel found acceptable" (FRC, 1996:31). But this raises a question. If companies decide to 'comply voluntarily' is it because they believe the courts would require them to revise their accounts, would agree with the Panel that the accounts as they stand do not comply with the law? Certainly some have taken this view. As Graham Pomroy, group financial controller at BET in 1993, put it:

> When we got the note from the Panel which set out in black and white why they were not happy, it was a bit of a bombshell . . . I don't think anyone will take them to court. I don't think you will stand a dog's chance. (Quoted in *Accountancy*, December 1996:40, 42)

But it may also be that it is other weapons in the arsenal – the side effects of being taken to court – that decide the issue. Companies may feel the *practical costs* are too high. There is too much to lose by fighting. Agreeing to revise accounts now or in the future may be simply a calculated decision in the face of what are seen as unacceptable costs.

Glasgow frequently reiterated the strong line the Panel was prepared to take:

> I should emphasise that the Panel will not hesitate to insist on a formal reissue or corrective note if it believes it to be appropriate. (Glasgow, FRC, 1996:31)

This is not actually within the Panel's *legal* enforcement powers. The only legal authority the Panel has is to ask the courts to enforce revision. But it may be a realistic portrayal of the Panel's *practical* powers. The Panel can, as one official put it, use its power to "lean on a company".

The Panel is then a force to be reckoned with. The threat of the court may be a very significant weapon – on legal or practical grounds. Certainly the Panel can point to a number of 'wins', where an application to the court was imminent.

Trafalgar House (PN13)

After the well-publicised 'climbdown' by Trafalgar House, *The Times* commented that the Panel had the "look of a big game hunter in the financial jungle" with Trafalgar House its "biggest trophy so far" (*The Times*, 16 October 1992). To Sir David

Tweedie it was the Panel's "defining moment". What happened in this case?

In 1992, the Panel investigated Trafalgar House's 1991 accounts. Trafalgar House had reclassified certain commercial properties owned by itself and some associates from current assets to fixed assets in its balance sheet. The group had suffered a loss of £102.7 million on the valuation of these properties. If treated as current assets, the loss would have been deducted from the profit and loss account. The effect of the reclassification was to turn what would have been a £19.7 million pre-tax profit in 1991 into a £122.4 million profit. Put the other way round, if Trafalgar acceded to the Panel request, it would have virtually wiped out Trafalgar's 1991 profits. Trafalgar's auditors, Touche Ross, backed the decision to adopt the company's new accounting policy.

In July 1992, the UITF issued Abstract No. 5 which indicated how companies should deal with similar circumstances in their accounts for accounting periods ending on or after 23 December 1992. The UITF was concerned that there was a

> possibility that companies could avoid charging the profit and loss account with write-downs to net realisable value arising on unsold traded assets. This could be done by transferring the relevant assets at above net realisable value, as a result of which any later write-down might be debited to revaluation reserve. (UITF 5, Transfers from Current Assets to Fixed Assets, July 1992, para. 2)

The deficit on the Trafalgar House revaluation – £68 million – was indeed taken to revaluation reserve.

But UITF 5 was not in effect for Trafalgar House's year to 30 September 1991. The Panel investigated Trafalgar House, its directors were banned from dealing in the company shares, but they refused to restate the figures.

The Panel threatened to take the company to court, barristers were placed on standby, but the hearing was avoided at the last moment when an agreement was struck. The Panel quite clearly claimed victory. According to its press release (PN13):

> On the basis of independent legal and accounting advice the directors of Trafalgar House have hitherto not accepted the Review Panel's view on the two principal matters in contention.

> The Review Panel has therefore been minded to make an application to the court under section 245B of the Companies Act 1985 for an order requiring the directors of the company to prepare revised accounts. However the directors of the company have now undertaken to make appropriate changes and adjustments in the accounts of the company for the year ended 30 September 1992 to meet the Review Panel's concerns, and on this undertaking the Review Panel will not be proceeding with the section 245B court application.

Trafalgar House adopted the requirements of UITF 5 in its 1992 accounts and restated its 1991 comparative figures.

Butte Mining (PN43)

The Panel was concerned about the treatment in Butte's 1995 accounts of shares in Gem River Corporation (GRC) which Butte had received in consideration of services it had rendered to GRC. The issue was the extent to which a profit on the transaction should be included in the profit and loss account at the balance sheet date, given that the tradability of the shares was subject to restrictions.

In the accounts as published, a profit had been included in the profit and loss account on the whole transaction. In the Panel's view, profit should only have been included on the shareholding that had been realised at the time the accounts were completed.

At that date the remaining shares were subject to an Escrow agreement prohibiting their trading on the Alberta Stock Exchange, on which they were listed, until certain conditions relating to the success of a GRC mining operation were fulfilled and certain periods of time had elapsed. Consequently, in the Panel's view the ultimate cash realisation of these shares could not be assessed with reasonable certainty and profit should not have been recognised on this element.

The amounts involved were significant. The directors informed the Panel that, as at present calculated, the effect of the revision required by the Panel would be to translate the figure presently published as *profit* on ordinary activities before and after taxation – £339,000 – into a *loss* – £628,000 – that is, a reduction of £967,000.

But this is what they agreed to do. The directors undertook to prepare and issue as soon as possible a revision, in view of which "the Panel has refrained from undertaking proceedings under section 245B of the Act".

Associated Nursing Services (PN44)

There were two matters at issue in this second investigation of ANS, both of which turned on whether the accounting treatment reflected the substance of the transaction as required by FRS 5. The company's 1995 *and* 1996 accounts were involved in the investigation.

The first matter concerned quasi-subsidiaries. ANS had entered into joint ventures with two partners and had treated both joint ventures in the two years' accounts as associated undertakings. One case involved a 'deadlocked' joint venture with a bank. In the Panel's view, the financial and operating policies of the joint venture were substantially predetermined by underlying agreements; and through its interest in the joint venture ANS gained benefits arising from the net assets of the company such that it had control.

The other case involved a venture capital arrangement with five capital venture funds set up through an intermediary. In the Panel's view the financial and operating policies of that company were again substantially predetermined by underlying agreements. Although in that case ANS held only a minority of the ordinary share capital, the investor's interests were effectively limited and the Panel took the view that ANS gained benefits arising from the net assets of the company such that it had control.

In both cases, therefore, the Panel regarded the substance of the arrangements was such that the companies were quasi-subsidiaries as defined by FRS 5. Consequently they should not be accounted for by the equity method but treated, as FRS 5 requires, as though they were subsidiary undertakings. Under the company's accounting treatment, only the company's share of the net assets of the companies in question was reflected in the consolidated balance sheet. In accordance with FRS 5, by contrast, the full amount of their assets and liabilities should be included in the consolidated balance sheet with appropriate changes to the consolidated profit and loss account.

The second matter involved a complex sale and leaseback transaction. This involved a 25 year lease, renewable for a further 25 years, and a call option held by ANS. In the Panel's view, the nature of the transaction was such that not all the significant rights or other access to benefits relating to the asset in question and not all the significant exposure to the risk inherent in those benefits had been transferred to the purchaser. Consequently, in accordance with FRS 5, an asset should have remained on the consolidated balance sheet and the sale proceeds should have been included in borrowings, with consequential profit and loss adjustments.

The Panel had "extended discussions" with ANS over these matters and following these, the directors undertook to prepare and issue as soon as possible a revision of the accounts for both years. The Panel welcomed their decision "thereby avoiding a Panel application to the court under section 245B of the Companies Act 1985".

Guardian Royal Exchange (PN49)

In accordance with the Companies Act as amended to implement EU Directives, Guardian Royal Exchange's insurance subsidiaries set aside in their accounts "equalisation reserves" (equivalent to provisions: to smooth fluctuations in loss ratios in future years or to cater for special risks). The law requires them to be treated in individual insurance company accounts as charges against profits and as liabilities. In the December 1996 consolidated accounts, however, the directors excluded these amounts. They considered that these reserves should not be treated as a charge against profits and as a liability so as to achieve consistency of treatment with Guardian Royal Exchange's other subsidiaries where the creation of equalisation reserves was not required.

The effect, as disclosed by the company in its 1996 accounts, was that had the liabilities in question not been excluded from the consolidation, pre-tax profit of £651 million would have been reduced by £33 million and earnings per share of 48.7p by

2.76p. The exclusion also resulted, as the Panel put it, in "liabilities being understated and shareholders' funds of £2,306 million being overstated by £75 million".

In the Panel's view, specific Companies Act requirements, as they apply to insurance companies, were not complied with. Although the directors strongly contested the Panel, they agreed to do as the Panel required. The "necessary steps" for a court application had, in this case, been "at an advanced stage."

Conclusion

The Panel may have developed a strategy which works. The 'benign big gun' model has been advocated as the enforcement strategy most likely to secure compliance in business settings (Ayres and Braithwaite, 1992). This model may be particularly relevant in financial reporting where the scope for honest error, justifiable deviation or just plain difference of opinion is acknowledged as a reality. Accounting involves a good deal of subjective judgement. Glasgow has acknowledged that

> The grey areas are a real problem. We are dealing with what are necessarily very sophisticated rules, designed to meet the needs of a huge variety of industries and commercial concerns. There is bound to be room for honest debate and difference of opinion. (*Accountancy*, April, 1993:36)

A strategy that seeks to avoid confrontation could also be seen as good for the regime as a whole. The ASB and Review Panel are striving to achieve consensus. Tweedie is concerned to avoid a 'backlash' where changes he and the ASB want in accounting practices clash with particular interests in industry and commerce. Mary Arden QC has also argued that acceptance of an accounting standard in practice will strengthen the likelihood that the court will hold that compliance is necessary to meet the true and fair requirement. As Tweedie has also said: given the need to win in court if standards were challenged, the ASB had to ensure that its proposals enjoyed "broad support" in the financial community (*The Times*, 28 February 1992). The significance of market actors' acceptance of the regime is acknowledged also by Edwin Glasgow: "we can only function with the support and respect of the City generally" (CBI conference, 15 June 1993).

So the Panel may be adopting a 'benign big gun' strategy and this may augur very well indeed for the new regime in the battle against creative accounting. The 'benign' aspect may make sense both for the case in hand and strategically, and the Panel may indeed be a 'big gun'. Though there has as yet been no resort to the court, it may be that the threat of court action, and all that implies, is enough. The threat of the court may be a very big weapon indeed. The Panel may be destined to win without ever going to court, and to ensure that all the cases of what it sees as defective accounting – and detects – are dealt with appropriately.

But this also begs some questions. First, what exactly does the Panel mete out as appropriate treatment? What kind of 'wins' are being chalked up in the Panel record? We'll look at this in Chapter 5. Second, what if companies don't concede? For the benign big gun strategy to work, the big gun threat must be seen to be real. In Chapter 6 we'll delve a little deeper into the factors that might affect the reality of the big gun threat.

5
The Message is Medium

Panel enforcement is recorded publicly in its press notices – 49 cases to date. These are *not* a full record of Panel *investigations*. Panel policy (in line with its emphasis on confidentiality) is not to disclose information on cases where "no specific remedial action has resulted" (Glasgow, FRC 1997:55) – though in fact a few such cases were the subject of press notices in the early years. As policy has developed, however, it is usually cases where remedial action has been required that have been publicised, although it is clear policy that *all* such cases *are* publicised: it is "standard practice" (Goldsmith, FRC, 1998:63; Working Procedures, para. 41). There have been 45 to date. The Panel's press notices then, represent tangible evidence of what the Panel has actually *done* in terms of requiring remedial action.

Deterrence

The Panel's press notices are seen by the Panel as having a wider role too. The aim is not simply to record outcomes but to provide "information and guidance", and according to Goldsmith, to deter:

> Such press statements serve the very important function of drawing attention to accounting practices that the Panel has found not to comply with the requirements of the Act, *with the object of deterring others*. (FRC, 1998:63; emphasis added)

In other words, press statements form part of the Panel's

general enforcement strategy and are intended to give a clear message. But, what exactly *is* the message so far conveyed by the Panel through this medium? Could the message the Panel is actually giving have the opposite effect?

RECORD REVIEW

First, what kind of corrective action has been required? What kind of 'compliance' has been secured?

Seeking remedial action means that in the Panel's eyes – though not necessarily in the company's – the accounts are defective. Yet, Appendix 6 shows that of the 45 cases of remedial action, only seven cases have involved revision of any kind. The accounts have been fully revised on just three occasions (Newarthill, PN37, Butte Mining, PN43 and Associated Nursing Services, PN44). On three other occasions, accounts were partially revised by the issue of a Supplementary Note (Penrith Farmers' & Kidd's, PN19, Butte Mining, PN30 and H & C Furnishings, PN53). Burn Stewart Distillers' 1996 accounts were amended to give additional disclosures via a circular sent to shareholders (PN47). In other words, as Glasgow himself admitted, "in only a minority of cases" has the Panel required corrective action "in the form of a formal reissue or corrective note" (FRC, 1996:31).

Glasgow notes that the Panel has sometimes been criticised for not insisting more frequently on the reissue or formal corrective note route. The Panel is "very conscious of this criticism", an official told us, and acknowledges the strong logic that lies behind it. According to the statutory model, requirements should be followed and a true and fair view should be presented. If accounts are defective, "their correction should be widely and speedily disseminated" (Glasgow, FRC, 1997:55). And there is a clear procedure available to remedy the defect via court-ordered revision of accounts or via voluntary revision by directors (see Chapter 2 and Appendix 2 for details). In short, if accounts are defective or unsatisfactory they do not give a true and fair view and they should be put right. Unless everyone who received the original accounts is informed of the shortcomings, the goal of true and fair accounts may not be realised.

Instead, Panel policy so far has overwhelmingly been to accept directors' assurances that they will comply with the Panel's view *in future* rather than insist on a retrospective revision of the accounts held to be faulty. On no less than 39 of the 49 occasions where press statements have been issued the Panel has settled for obtaining assurances from companies that their accounts will in future conform to the Panel's interpretation. Typically, this will involve an adjustment of the comparative figures in those accounts. This is true of even 'big trophy' cases like Trafalgar House.

Trafalgar House: Another View

Though Trafalgar House was a high profile company, it was not such an unlikely target. Its accounting policies had been commented upon adversely for some time in the press. In Terry Smith's 'blob guide', Trafalgar House was the joint second worst company for creative accounting. When the company reclassified certain current assets into fixed assets there was "an outcry in the City and the press at the time because the new classification flattered the profit and loss account" (*FT*, 16 October 1992). The *FT* scathingly described the practice as "British financial engineering at its finest."

Yet the Panel did not insist on revision of what it and others saw as defective accounts. In its Press Notice on the case, the Panel explicitly drew attention to the fact that Trafalgar House was issuing separately its own Press Notice. While the emphasis in the Panel's notice was on 'big gun' rhetoric – its intention to take the company to court if the directors insisted on their view – the emphasis in the company's Press Notice was on the facts:

> As a consequence of the agreement the Company will restate the 1991 comparative figures in its 1992 accounts to comply with the requirements of Urgent Issues Task Force Abstract No. 5 issued on 22nd July, 1992. As a result the 1991 comparative figures will show deficits on revaluation of properties of £102.7 million as a charge to the profit and loss account rather than to reserves.

> In addition the company will revise its policy on ACT which is expected to result in an increase of £20 million in the tax charge included in the 1991 comparative figures and an increase in the write off in the 1992 accounts.

Effectively, therefore, Trafalgar House's message was that it agreed to implement UITF 5 earlier than it would otherwise have been obliged to do (though only in the comparative figures of the next year's accounts) and to amend *future* treatment of ACT.

DILEMMAS OVER DELAY

Requiring adjustment of comparative figures in future accounts may simply reflect the reality that by the time defects are spotted and investigated, it is time for the next set of accounts to be published. The Panel recognises that

> Since the concern of the Panel is the possible need for revision . . . the matters it deals with will normally call for speedy action, and the Panel's procedures must therefore be quick. (Working Procedures, para. 4)

In practice, it has found it difficult to live up to this aim. Accounts are by definition post hoc; they report on the past year; they have to be prepared, and directors have up to seven months after the end of the financial year to publish them; detection and investigation take time; delay is inherent.

The average time between the end of the financial period investigated and a Press Notice release is 13 months. The longest period so far was in excess of two years (PN51); the second longest was 22 months (PN44), and there have been several at 15–16 months. Brandt *et al.* (1997:39) measured the time between directors signing the accounts and the Panel's Press Notice (up to PN45). The shortest interval was 174 days; the average 310; and the longest 397. In all, seven cases took more than a year. Where accounts have actually been revised, the average period of delay has been higher: 15 months.

Playing for Time

Delays may be the result of failure to blow the whistle promptly after accounts are published. But the investigation process can also last several months as in the case of Butte Mining in 1996. Tweedie believes companies themselves engineer delays – 'the chairman is out of the country' – until it is close to the next accounting date, then argue for a change in the comparatives rather than revision.

Despite the delays in practice, the law still expressly provides that revision shall *not* take into account assets and liabilities, income or expenditure arising *after* the date of the original accounts. Glasgow too believes that there have been occasions when the delay in company responses "has been purely a matter of tactics. We intend to be increasingly intolerant of such tactics in future" (FRC, 1997:53).

But how intolerant can the Panel be? It may hit problems of delay itself. Its chairman may be 'out of the country' at a crucial time. Its members are all part-timers. There is the question of how quickly they can meet again.

Fairness

In any case, the Panel may find itself in a difficult position when it comes to hurrying companies along. There is concern about *companies* bringing in the courts against the Panel – in a judicial review of *how* it investigated and reached a decision, over whether fairness and due process were observed. So far "companies have played the game on that" as one regulator put it, but the threat is always there.

According to Glasgow,

> It's a matter of striking a balance between the fundamental right of fairness and the public interest. A company has to have the benefit of the doubt if it asks for adjournment.

Counsel for one company which did consider judicial review told us the directors decided against because their concern was with the substance of the matter. But others might use judicial review as a delaying tactic itself. In the meantime the threat of it is likely to stop the Panel from being too intolerant of delays. Even the 14-day letter, the "last chance" for directors to avoid a court application, can in practice turn into a 28-day letter.

BENIGN STRATEGY?

Delay may be unavoidable but the decision not to require revision is still a matter of choice on the part of the Panel. Companies *could* be required to revise past accounts regardless of timing. Indeed this could be quite a deterrent. That the Panel has chosen not to do so might provide further evidence of its 'benign big gun' approach. Companies are treated non-punitively first time round, given time to 'come into compliance'.

Licensing non-compliance

There is a price, however. Indeed this policy means that, for the year in question, what the Panel sees as creative accounting, with its attendant manipulation – of EPS, gearing, profits and the like – is in effect *licensed* by it. The early examples illustrate this well. The first two companies publicly reprimanded by the Panel had used accounting practices which, according to Sydney Treadgold, Panel Secretary, "flattered their earnings per share" figures (*FT*, 29 January 1992).

Ultramar (PN4)

The Panel was faced in this case with a company which had departed from SSAP 8 and whose accounts were perennially qualified. For several years, Ultramar had boosted its earnings per share by treating its advance corporation tax (ACT) as a part of the cost of dividends rather than as a tax charge as required by SSAP 8 in relation to irrecoverable ACT. Ultramar argued that most of its revenue came from overseas which meant that there was only a small, strictly UK, tax charge against which to offset the ACT, and that was unfair to the earnings figure. It also argued that it fully disclosed what it had done.

The outcome of the case was that the Panel received written assurances from the directors that the company's accounts for the *following* year would be presented in accordance with SSAP 8. In fact, Ultramar was taken over by LASMO and ceased to circulate audited accounts. Shareholders thus were *never* provided with information compiled in compliance with SSAP 8.

Williams Holdings (PN5)

Williams Holdings boosted its earnings per share in its 1990 accounts by treating exceptional items as if they were extraordinary. Again, this was fully disclosed in a note to the accounts: the auditors did *not* qualify them, but the Panel disagreed. Still, all the Panel required from the directors was a promise of future compliance; a written assurance that the 1991 accounts would meet these requirements, stating that the profit and loss account did not comply with Companies Act requirements and that the earnings per share statement was not in accordance with SSAP 3 requirements; and another written assurance that the failure of the company to disclose fully the names of undertakings acquired and sold, as required by the Companies Act, would not be repeated. The directors gave both the written assurances requested and said that they would not do it again.

Smoothing the Picture

Adjusting the comparative figures will correct the impact of creative accounting on ratios and profits in the *new* accounts – but not in the old. For the past accounts, the objectives of creative accounting have already been accomplished. Adjustments in the comparative figures will *not* therefore remove the benefits of creative accounting designed to escape borrowing restrictions, avoid shareholder control or enhance management performance (and pay).

Requiring only future compliance can also permit clever adjustments to be made. When Newarthill's accounts eventually adopted the accounting policy demanded by the Panel, its earnings per share actually *rose* by 89.5p, an increase of 371.37%

(Brandt *et al.*, 1997:34): "However, had Newarthill adopted the accounting policy in earlier years, EPS would have been reduced" (*ibid* 36). EPS can change for many reasons, but it does illustrate the problem: could the requirement to adjust comparative figures in future accounts actually serve to *conceal* the defect and its effects? While compulsory revisions have to be highlighted "prominently" and voluntary revisions will be circulated to shareholders, future adjustments may be missed. Panel investigation may then be a way of *smoothing* the transition from creative to compliant accounts and protecting the directors from proper corporate accountability.

Accountability

Around a third of companies required by the Panel to take some action did not acknowledge the Panel's involvement in their subsequent year's accounts (Brandt *et al.*, 1997:44). Unless shareholders diligently *check* the prior year's accounts they will not be aware that the figures have been adjusted. Of course, Press Notices are issued, so shareholders might be alerted. But the proper vehicle of accountability, the accounts themselves, might be less than transparent. What's more, the consensual nature of Press Notices, and directors citing costs or other reasons for not challenging the Panel, may neutralise accountability issues implicit in Panel action.

Season of Goodwill?

Another danger of a policy of future compliance is that directors may see Panel strategy as an opportunity for a *season* of creative accounting free from the costs of revision. One of the aims of the new regime is clearly to tackle creative accounting. The problem the regime is addressing, though, is *creativity*, often dynamic creativity. All creative accountants need is a *season* in which to exploit rules, loopholes and gaps in regulations.

The new regime often draws parallels between creative accounting and creative tax avoidance. The doyens of 1980s tax avoidance, Roy Tucker and Ron Plummer of Rossminster, knew the Inland Revenue would eventually spot new devices and that the next Budget would suppress them. But that did not matter. All *they* needed was the time *until* new rules came into force. Every device needed only 'a season'. By the time of the next Taxes Act, a new device would be in place.

The new approach in financial reporting acknowledges dynamic creativity as a problem. Yet the Panel's enforcement policy could be read as giving to creative accountants the season they require. This could *encourage* the search for short-term gains, to stay one step ahead.

Cat and Mouse

The Panel's enforcement policy could be seen as *inviting* a cat and mouse game. As each device is caught by the Panel, but only a future adjustment required, creative accountants have time to identify a new device for next time. As one device is made redundant, another can take its place. The directors of Warnford Investments (PN18) had been reluctant to comply with SSAP 19, in the company's December 1991 accounts, and show its only freehold property at open market value. Since the company only owned one property, its value would have been clearly identifiable if disclosed in the accounts. The company was negotiating to sell it, so the directors cited commercial confidentiality as justification for departing from SSAP 19. The Panel rejected this. According to Sydney Treadgold, "Reasons of commercial confidentiality can never really be justification for departing from accounting standards" (*FT*, 3 April 1993). But while the directors agreed to comply with SSAP 19 in future, they still "managed to escape revealing the value of the property by re-allocating it to a subsidiary" (*FT* 3 April 1993). By April 1993, the property had still not been sold.

This Year, Next Year, Sometime, Never . . .

The strategy of requiring compliance in the future may well be appropriate in some regulatory settings. Most regulatory agencies adopt such a strategy (Hawkins, 1984), and 'forgiving' firms which plan to co-operate in the future can lead to a progressive improvement – pollution may be cleaned up over time – via a commitment to comply. Demanding instant compliance may be counter-productive: the world cannot be put to rights overnight. Tweedie concluded in the FRC's first report:

> Perhaps [the Board's] most important task – and that for the new system generally – is to encourage and secure a change of climate in financial reporting, away from the tendency of a minority to use creative accounting and towards financial reporting that is genuinely balanced, helpful and informative. (FRC, 1991, para. 5.45)

In financial reporting though, accounts may *never* be cleaned up. New creative accounting may replace old and accounts may always be defective in some way.

Second Time Around

This suggests that if the Panel is to be gentle first time around, it cannot afford forgiveness with second offenders. However, that is far from straightforward when all the same issues of 'grey areas' and 'honest differences of opinion' could be as applicable the second time around as the first. This is not an easy area for tough enforcement. However, there is some evidence that the Panel sees forgiveness as a concession to *first* offenders. Recidivists may have a different experience.

Butte Mining was a recidivist – it had to revise its 1993 accounts by way of Supplementary Note issued as part of its 1994 accounts (PN30). The Panel also expressly demanded that the Note be circulated not only to those entitled to receive the 1994 accounts but also those entitled to received the 1993 accounts. When the directors resisted revision of the 1995 accounts in the second case (PN43), the Panel was at an "advanced state of preparation" (FRC, 1997:59) of legal proceedings under s. 245B when the directors made a "last-minute undertaking" to revise.

Associated Nursing Services was investigated twice, and though it was cleared the first time, it was required to revise second time around. When ANS first encountered the Panel in 1992 (PN11) it agreed to change its accounting policy in the future, which it did. It also claimed to 'introduce' FRS 5 – a below the waterline effect. But during its 'season' of licence it did some creative accounting, or at least that was how the Panel saw it in 1997 (PN44) when Associated Nursing Services came before it again. The Panel was not so co-operative the second time. Associated Nursing Services was required to revise *two* years' sets of accounts.

ANS and Butte were of course not only relatively easy targets – one using an off-the-peg scheme, the other ultimately involved in convictions for fraud – but they were relatively small fry. Would the same line be taken with big fish? This is another issue that has been raised on the Panel's record.

MINNOWS OR WHALES?

The Panel is clearly concerned about the view which has been expressed that it focuses too much on small fry – 'minnows' rather than 'whales'. Nearly half of the companies about whom investigations have been disclosed in Public Statements have been relatively small companies with turnovers below £100 million. Eight smaller companies would have been excluded from the Panel's jurisdiction on grounds of size had they not been public limited companies (Brandt *et al.*, 1997: 31,35). Sutton Harbour Holdings, investigated by the Panel in 1995 (PN42), had a turnover of only £2 million in 1995–96 (*FT*, 25 July 1996). The 'significant' cases in which accounts have actually been revised – Butte Mining (twice) and Associated Nursing Services for example – involved smaller companies.

Between July 1991 and June 1992, the Panel wrote what Tweedie called a "ferocious letter" to 240 listed companies that had failed to comply with the requirement introduced by the Companies Act 1989 to disclose whether their accounts had been prepared in accordance with applicable accounting standards, to give particulars of any material departures from them and to state the reasons for such departures. Directors complied with this requirement to disclose their compliance with the Act.

No revision was required – not surprisingly. Failure to disclose *compliance* as opposed to *non*-compliance must be low in the scale of misdemeanours, though the Panel did describe this as a "key financial reporting requirement" (PN2). However, when it came to a 'tiny' company and a lapse little further up the scale – failure to *explain* its compliance with the Act – the Panel did require revision.

Penrith Farmers' & Kidd's (PN19)

Penrith, in its 1992 accounts, properly restated the 1991 comparative figures to comply with statutory requirements. The accounts failed, however, to give the particulars and reasons for these adjustments, another statutory requirement. As a consequence of Panel action, the directors issued a Supplementary Note to the Accounts providing this information.

The Panel clearly does regard compliance with this kind of provision as something it wants to investigate and remedy. But the Panel also acknowledges that the adjustments did *not* affect Penrith's reported profits or the balance sheet totals and that the sums themselves were *not* significant. It is therefore somewhat unclear why a revision – the first ever – was required. The message might be that the Panel not only targets small fry, it also tackles trivial matters. And this has indeed been another source of complaint.

TRIVIAL PURSUITS?

In the Chrysalis Group case, the directors undertook to make adjustments, following a Panel investigation, which "will have no effect on the reported total net assets of the group" (PN26). This led Nigel Butterfield, group finance director, to describe the case as a "storm in a teacup" (*FT*, 30 November 1993), which is precisely how Blake Nixon, GPG's UK executive director, had earlier described the issue for which his company had been criticised by the Panel (PN12; *FT*, 8 October 1992).

Intercare (PN27) was investigated by the Panel for its treatment of items in its 1992 cash flow statement and its non-compliance with FRS 1. The company amended the statement in its 1993 accounts. According to Gary Vicary, finance director,

> It's irritating. This was basically a small technical misclassification. It has no impact on the profit and loss account or the balance sheet and there was full disclosure in the accounts. (*FT*, 29 January 1994)

The Panel's view is that "we would never take on a case if we didn't believe it was really misleading". What's more, it is obviously a useful defence for a company to neutralise a complaint as trivial. Still, agencies need to be wary of creating a reputation for pursuit of the trivial – or having such a reputation created for them. The more readily a Panel investigation can be shrugged off as a trivial technicality, the less significant its deterrent power will be.

THE MESSAGE

The reality is more complex than these complaints suggest. The Panel *has* tackled large companies and it has tackled issues with very material sums involved. The largest companies so far have been British Gas (PN14) and the Royal Bank of Scotland (PN21). Arguably sums in the British Gas case were material – profits were boosted by £1 billion by 'double counting' a three-month period – while those in the Royal Bank case were not – although the directors' argument that the amount involved was not material was rejected by the Panel.

Though no big company has had to revise its accounts, big companies have been threatened with courts and court-ordered revision. When the Panel threatened to take Guardian Royal Exchange (PN49) to court, it was hardly dealing with a 'minnow'. As we shall see later, it was requiring a treatment which GRE strongly contested but which the directors agreed to adopt in future.

At the same time, there are disquieting comments, such as Ernst & Young's, that "the Panel has still to establish its credibility in policing the more difficult areas of UK GAAP" (1997:23). We will look at some "difficult areas", and why they are difficult, later.

Compliance?

What of the Panel's record on securing compliance among those companies it detects, and defines as engaging in defective accounting? Simply stated, if securing compliance by correcting defective accounts is the measure, the Panel's policy is not as successful as is claimed.

What message does this convey? A cynical reading might be: put it right after the event, with, to be sure, adverse publicity to manage, and perhaps legal costs if you resist the Panel's challenge, but *with* the benefits of a season of goodwill, and *without* the costs of revision. And perhaps – though we have yet to see this for sure – be careful next time.

This is not to say there is no deterrent message. No one wants to be investigated by the Panel, or publicly required to take corrective action, of whatever sort. And there may be knock-on consequences. To return to Trafalgar House, the shareholders there took a very 'big gun' approach. Both directors and auditors came in for criticism. Heads rolled. The auditors had to stand down. Indeed if Trafalgar House has been claimed as a hanging case, it was the shareholders who really did the hanging, not the Panel.

Of course the Panel's intervention may have been the necessary catalyst for shareholder action. Trafalgar was coming in for highly publicised criticism for creative accounting at just this time. Terry Smith's 'blob guide' came out in 1992 with Trafalgar House ranking joint second by number of "dubious accounting methods used" (*FT*, 16 August 1992). But it may have taken the endorsement of the Panel to set off action. The Panel may well have been the key in a chain of events which made for a message of deterrence for others.

But the message was ultimately the shareholders'. What if the shareholders had not reacted as they did? In many other cases there has been no such reaction.

Softly Softly

The dominant approach to date has been softly softly, not just in the style of enforcement, but in the terms enforced. This might be justified as part of a long term strategy. What is important is to secure a long-term *ethos* of compliance not short-term punishment. Many researchers have supported this approach. Perhaps the Panel should be seen as only part of an armoury of control which includes active corporate governance (and more, as we see in Chapter 18).

Others, of course, might see it as under-enforcement of law, with the much-vaunted power to revise accounts remaining largely symbolic. Or as special treatment for 'white collar' breach of law. It might be seen not just as softly softly, but as soft.

And there may be other issues involved. The Panel may, in any circumstances, choose a softly softly approach as the best strategy. It may also be, however, that there are practical pressures encouraging such an approach. Sanctions no tougher than agreeing to do better next year may be the *price* of securing voluntary agreements. And voluntary agreements may be important for the new regime. There may be structural tensions underlying the big gun threat.

6
A Risky Strategy?

The biggest threat of the Panel is to take a company to court if the directors refuse to adopt a 'voluntary solution'. The first letter from the Panel reminds companies of the Panel's right to make an application to the court. Litigation is threatened "on more occasions than might be expected" (Glasgow, *FT*, 28 September 1993).

But how far can the Panel go in wielding its biggest weapon? Is Edwin Glasgow's claim that "where there are abuses we will not have the slightest concern about litigating" realistic? And if it is realistic for the *Panel*, is it *wise* for the regime as a whole?

First, let's look more closely at Panel finances.

FINANCING THE BIG GUN

The 'war chest' may not be quite as strong as first meets the eye. The first three-year tranche of financing for the FRC began in March 1990. In the first two years, each of the three sources of funding – the accountancy profession, the government and the City – contributed £1 million, much of it towards building up the £2 million 'fighting fund' for the Review Panel to pay for litigation. Since the Panel did not go to court, the amount due from the sectors was reduced to £2 million between them in the third year. According to the Group Accounts (FRC, ASB, FRRP) for the year ending 31 March 1995, the Legal Costs Fund grew by a net £21,000 (£30,000 income less £9,000 for the costs of the Review Panel investigations). In the following year it declined by £13,000 (£6,000 income less £19,000 for Review Panel investigations).

Note how the cost of Panel investigations had more than doubled even though the number of cases substantively considered was rising only slightly (see Appendix 4). This trend was even more marked in 1997 with a sharp fall-off in the Panel's overall caseload (from 64 in 1996 to 37 in 1997), but with the cost of Panel investigations in the year to March 1997 rising from £19,000 to £259,000, due to "costs incurred in preparation for an application to the court in respect of two cases" (Lipworth, FRC, 1998:7). As a result, income from FRC sponsors rose sharply in 1997–8 (FRC, 1999).

For the time being, Panel funds appear healthy. But how far would the war chest go if there really was a war? How would the FRC replenish it in an 'emergency'? What if there were more than two cases going to court, as nearly happened in 1997? What if companies were prepared to go to litigation in every case? The size of the war chest may influence the credibility of the Panel in taking on both minnows and whales in court; it may also affect its selection of cases to fight and to concede.

Tweedie acknowledged that litigation can "wear you down". If companies do settle, even at the last minute, the Panel cannot recover its costs from the directors or the company, as it most likely would if it won in court. If it lost, of course, it could find itself liable for the company's legal costs as well as its own. Tweedie hopes that, if necessary, the DTI would step in with financial support: "They wouldn't let us lose for the wrong reasons".

There might be more than the other side's legal costs to consider. If the publicity surrounding a court case is seen as damaging to a company, might the Panel find itself facing claims for damages?

This issue, indeed, might filter back to investigation in general. If word of a Panel investigation were to leak out, with adverse effects on a company, whose practices were then found to be bona fide, might the Panel find itself open to claims for compensation? The emphasis the Panel places on confidentiality may reflect not just a co-operative approach but a need to protect the Panel by protecting the company from publicity.

There are issues other than finances involved, though. Should the Panel have "not the slightest concern" about litigation?

Standing back from the 'cut and thrust' of specific cases we can see potential tensions in the big gun threat.

PERSUADING THE COURTS

Once a company contests the Panel's view, what is involved is not just enforcement but enforceability. To win in court the Panel will have to persuade the judges that the accounts are defective. The repeated threat of taking a company to court fosters an image of Panel success as inevitable. But the court is not a rubber stamp. The reality is that the Panel's view would be just as much on trial as the company's.

Would the courts agree with the Panel's interpretation of regulations, of the true and fair view? Glasgow acknowledged financial reporting is beset by "grey areas". Sir David Tweedie recognises even his 'hanging case' may lose in court (*Accountancy*, July 1992).

Close-Run Things

It has been suggested in several of the cases where the company has in the end conceded to the Panel, that the Panel's case was far from cut and dried. What the Panel saw as defective accounting, the company contested was perfectly legal, and had expert legal and accounting opinion to back it.

Many companies taken to task by the Panel have accepted the Panel's requirements only under public protest, and without conceding their activities were illegitimate. Caradon (PN34) claimed that the issue in its case was a "grey area" and that the way in which it had accounted for non-equity reflected "reality and common sense" (*FT*, 9 November 1995). But the company agreed to amend its accounting policies in its September 1995 Interim Statement and in future accounts. Ultramar and Williams Holdings both claimed their accounting treatments gave a fairer view. The Panel was accused of taking action "on a technicality".

Trafalgar House (PN13)

Trafalgar House stated that it did not mind going to court on legal grounds. It insisted it had not breached regulations. It had refused the Panel's request as a result of "independent legal and accounting advice". Trafalgar "came bristling with legal and accounting opinions" as one leading regulator put it. The auditors, Touche Ross, did not qualify Trafalgar's accounts. Indeed, after they had ceased to be Trafalgar's auditors, Touche Ross took the unusual step of writing to shareholders and stating that criticism of their auditing of the 1991 accounts had been unjustified:

> We did not, at the time of signing the report, and we do not now, believe there was any material departure from the then existing accounting standards.

This view has, it said, been supported subsequently "by leading counsel and another leading firm of chartered accountants" (*Accountancy*, June 1991:17). Since the accounts had not been qualified, Touche Ross (and four Trafalgar House directors) were automatically reported to the ICAEW Investigations Committee, but no disciplinary action was taken against them: there was "no case to answer" (*FT*, 13 August 1993).

Such statements may, of course, be defensive measures in the face of public criticism and a potential negligence action or disciplinary proceedings. Nonetheless, in Touche Ross's case, the ICAEW Investigations Committee stated that "honest differences of opinion are not suitable subjects for disciplinary action" (*Accountancy*, September 1993:12). It noted that

> both sides' positions were supported by a substantial body of professional opinion and it is by no means certain that [the Panel's legal] proceedings would have succeeded. (*Ibid*)

Referring to the Trafalgar case, Brian Singleton-Green, the editor of *Accountancy*, described the Panel's action as "daring stuff . . . If the case had gone to court, it's anyone's guess what would have happened" (*Accountancy*, December 1992:117).

Butte Mining (PN43)

And Trafalgar House is not the only example of a company who claimed its treatment was perfectly legal. Another was Butte Mining which was forced to revise its 1995 accounts despite its claim, backed by auditors Cooper Lancaster Brewers, that it had done nothing wrong:

> We took a lot of advice regarding company law and accounting standards over the issue and we still don't agree with the Panel's position. (Michael Chartres, CLB partner, quoted in *Accountancy*, December 1996:11)

Indeed, the auditors actually qualified the revised set of accounts Butte was required by the Panel to send out to its shareholders:

> In our opinion the consolidated financial statements as restated in the Supplementary Note do not give a true and fair view of the state of the Company's and Group's affairs as at 30 June 1995 or of its results for the year ended on that date . . . In our opinion the Original financial statements gave a true and fair view of the state of affairs of the Group and the Company at 30 June 1995 and of the Group's profit for the year then ended.

The Panel referred the firm to the ICAEW's disciplinary procedure for so doing.

Other companies have taken the same line. According to Malcolm Samuels, director of accounting and tax at Courts, "We had been advised by our auditors that what we did was OK. We felt we had a case which they wouldn't see" (quoted in *Accountancy*, December 1996:41). Guardian Royal Exchange was taken to task for an approach supported in *Accountancy* as "entirely logical in terms of accounting concepts" (Whewell, February 1998:82).

Practical Pressures

Would these cases – and there have been many others – have won or lost in court? One leading accountant who has been involved with Panel cases both as auditor and expert, observed that, though all companies so far investigated had "caved in", it "wasn't because they believed the court would go against them". Indeed, "my reaction was that the company would win". Leading counsel in one case put the odds at 80% to win: "It's very unusual for counsel to give odds like that". Indeed, he said, "if you see it from the inside, the Panel is not always on strong technical grounds".

Several cases have reached "the courtroom steps". In the end, all have settled without going to court. Directors have agreed to go along with the Panel's view. They have not, however, conceded the case on legal grounds. They have put it down to the practical costs of a court case.

Pleading practical pressures can sometimes be a convenient justification for backing down on what is presented as a strong case but felt to be a weak one. Auditors may rise to the defence of their clients to protect their own reputation. And it's easier to talk of a strong case after settlement when it is safe from challenge in court. "You can put on an immensely impressive front after you've climbed down" as Glasgow put it.

But what if directors were prepared to contest the Panel in court? It might seem that companies have more at stake in going to court then the regulators. If they lose, after all, directors face personal liability for costs. They may be held responsible by shareholders for adverse effects on the company. All stakeholders in the company may have a great deal to lose. For the Panel, this is just one case among many, with, it would seem, far less at stake. There might, however, be a great deal at stake if the Panel were to lose in court.

THE RISK OF LOSING

For the new regime, the stakes in any particular case go beyond that case alone.

Demonstration Effect

If the courts were to find against the Panel, others might be encouraged to challenge it too. It would make the Panel's policy of settling out of court harder. Losing may not only affect the case in hand but encourage others to challenge the Panel, to accuse the Panel of behaving badly in not accepting the company line.

Precedent

What's more, court decisions can have more than one function. They not only determine the specific issue involved but can set precedents, the higher the court, the more authoritative the precedential value. Court decisions can be used as the basis of legal arguments in the future.

When regulators take a company to court over what they see as unacceptable creative accounting, what's going on is a battle for the *definition* of what unacceptable creative accounting is. It is a battle for where the authoritative line is to be drawn between the acceptable and the unacceptable, between what is true and fair and what is not, in any particular situation.

Panel defeat in court could open the floodgates for creative accounting. It would undoubtedly lead to copycat use of the techniques endorsed by the court. It would also, if past form in other areas is anything to go by, encourage a reading of the decision for guidance on what other techniques might be considered to be similar cases. Similar cases, it would be argued, require similar treatment. If the judges found accounting policy X to be on the right side of the law, policy Y, with its parallels with X emphasised, should be treated in the same way – whatever the Panel's view.

One lost case on one technique could prove the thin edge of the wedge.

Higher Stakes

It may be not just a case, or even a series of cases, that is at stake but the key legal weapons of the new regime themselves. A case might focus on some very specific technical issue, but the underlying issue may be something more fundamental. It may be that issues fundamental to the new regime's claim to strength are ultimately being tested.

In a clash between specific rules and general principles, which are to be complied with? When and how far should a true and fair view be equated with specific rules, when and how far should it override them? What is the status of accounting standards? To lose on such issues would be a massive blow to the new regime. It would expose the Panel's legal weapons as less powerful than they might seem. "A daft judge could kill a standard" as one regulator put it. The risk of this might cool the Panel's enthusiasm for litigation. There is much more at stake than losing a single case.

THE RISK OF WINNING

Of course the Panel might win. It is easy to see the advantages of a win in court. The company would lose; others would be deterred; the image of a powerful regime would be supported. The Panel's legal power – at least in the particular area tested – would be endorsed and its practical power to secure settlement in the shadow of the courts in future, enhanced. But, unfortunately for the Panel, in a context like creative accounting, even winning can carry problems with it.

Winning but Losing

A victory might not be unambiguous. Court decisions, as we have seen, are potential precedents. When looking for a legal basis to justify specific activities lawyers look to past cases. They look for similar situations, advantageously treated, with which they can draw parallels, and argue similar treatment is appropriate. Or they construct structures which can be argued to be similar to situations advantageously treated in the past. But they can also work to distinguish their case from cases that failed in the past, or to construct structures which can be argued to be different. Either way, past cases – case law – can be mined for material from which to construct arguments to justify practices in the future. These arguments may be in the spirit of the decision or they may simply use the words to justify practices within the letter but not the spirit.

In short, precedent is not just a problem for regulators if they lose. Whether they win or lose, the decision is likely to generate material that can be used to justify creative accounting.

Court cases on financial reporting have been rare even before the new regime, though it is worth noting than even an unreported magistrates' court case – of no authoritative precedential value, the *Argyll* case in 1981 – was used extensively as legal justification for off-balance sheet financing in the 1980s, even though the directors *lost*.

Argyll

The directors of Argyll invoked the true and fair override to include in the company's December 1979 group balance sheet a company, Morgan Edwards, it did not actually own until March 1980. It was not a subsidiary under existing statutory regulations.

However, the directors claimed that they effectively controlled it: "the world regards Argyll and Morgan Edwards as one company" was how one director put it in court (Ashton, 1986:3). Consolidation, they argued, would reflect economic substance and provide a true and fair view of the group's financial status. The auditors accepted this approach, but they also drew attention to it, which may explain why the Department of Trade intervened and brought a prosecution in the magistrates' court (Ashton, 1986:9).

The regulators of the day won and the directors were convicted. But this decision, and the Department of Trade statement that followed in support, were then exploited. *Argyll* was extensively cited to argue that any group business that did not meet the statutory definition of a subsidiary *must* be kept off a group's balance sheet. Even the true and fair override could not be used to bring them into the accounts. After all, hadn't it just been stated by court and government that the true and fair requirement could not override the specific statutory provision? Solicitors such as Ralph Aldwinckle, then of Linklaters and Paines (subsequently a member of the Review Panel), argued that the law, under the Fourth Directive, would simply not allow the true and fair override to be used to set aside the statutory definitions (Aldwinckle, 1987).

This view was not without its critics. David Tweedie and James Kellas, both then of Peat Marwick, urged the opposite view – the requirement to give a true and fair view should override the rules for orphan subsidiaries (Tweedie and Kellas, 1987). But the point was never tested in court. Instead there was created a 'working rule', a shared assumption for practical purposes of management and auditors' decision making, on what the law 'was', and how it could be used.

The *Argyll* case became a charter – or, as one commentator put it, a "rogues' charter" (Atchley, 1986) – for one of the most effective techniques of creative accounting of the 1980s. A magistrates' court case would rarely have such an impact. But this one – an oasis in a case-less desert – provided eminently usable material from which to construct new forms of creative accounting and justify them.

Unintended Consequences

If the Panel goes to court, more authoritative rulings than *Argyll* would be brought into play. And, as the *Argyll* case demonstrates, the consequences are not necessarily as anticipated. Decisions may be used in unexpected ways. A decision intended to prohibit one form of creative accounting may end up justifying another. Winning could have unintended consequences.

Looking for Guidelines

It is not just judicial decisions themselves that are valuable material for case building, but the reasoning used, the distinctions made, the boundaries drawn. The *Curtain Dream* case (1990) had parallels with some of the issues of form and substance central to FRS 5. It centred on the issue: when is a sale not a sale?

Curtain Dream

In determining the nature of a transaction, according to Mr Justice Knox, "it is the substance of the transaction that has to be looked at and not just the form." This is an approach that may benefit the Panel if it is seeking to enforce the principle underlying FRS 5. Nonetheless, the judgement in *Curtain Dream* (1990) gives guidance on how to manipulate the findings of the court.

The court identified the particular features of the transaction which affected its characterisation as a financing transaction rather than an outright sale. First, neither party was able to withdraw from the global transaction; there was an 'indissoluble link' between the parties; the destiny of the goods involved was predetermined. Secondly, the judge also identified what features in the parties' relationship were important. There was an overall agreement to establish a credit line and several references to that fact; there was an interest rate specified (LIBOR = 1% p.a.); and, most important of all, there was "an exact degree of mutuality".

The court's 'substance over form' approach meant that the structure failed to achieve its purpose. But the decision of the court provided others with guidance on how to construct similar transactions to avoid what the court defined as unacceptable and fit with what is by implication acceptable.

A Sting in the Tail

In the same way then, judgements on creative accounting, even judgements which come out in favour of the Panel, might have a sting in the tail. Decision and reasoning may be used as a new basis for claiming techniques of creative accounting, carefully tailored to the case, are 'perfectly legal'.

Courting Disaster

The role of court decisions as precedent might be doubly significant for the new regime in financial reporting. One of its key approaches has been to focus on broad definitions, such as 'actual dominant influence' in the Companies Act definition of subsidiaries, and on general principles such as the need to give a true and fair view, or, in FRS 5, to report the substance of transactions.

These are all ways of countering the problems experienced with detailed rules which then provide a cookbook of criteria for avoidance. The government refused to define 'actual dominant influence' in the statute. It also declined to take the option in European law to define when the true and fair override could be used. The ASB declared a preference for framing its standards as principles not rules. In all cases the reason was the same. Detailed rules and precise definitions were too easy to avoid.

Once courts come into play, however, there is every prospect that narrower definitions with authoritative backing will begin to emerge. Cases that go to court will involve some specific situations and a judgement will be made on how that specific situation is to be treated. Then there will be another specific situation and another, until a whole body of specific treatments – or specific rules – builds up. Court decisions may gradually provide the detailed rulebook the legislators and regulators were seeking to avoid precisely because it was seen as facilitating creative accounting.

For a regime bent on regulating through principles not just detailed rules, going to court could be courting disaster.

The threat of court-enforced revision of accounts, with directors liable for costs, is a major innovation for enforcement in the new regime. Along with the attendant collateral damage to reputation and share price this is a significant sanction for both directors and companies. Edwin Glasgow, himself, has described it as "a draconian power" (FRC, 1996:31). But in an area like creative accounting there are particular tensions underlying the role of the courts. These underlying tensions could adversely affect the enforcement process in two ways.

Winning the Battle or the War?

First they could affect the *consequences* of enforcement. Bringing the courts into play could mean short-term success but long-term problems: success with the individual case but an undermining of the structure of control more generally. It could mean winning the battle but losing the war.

THE OZ FACTOR AND ENFORCEMENT

Secondly, where regulators are aware of these underlying tensions, they may lead to a reluctance to use the courts. Tensions can become dilemmas. The court is the big gun to brandish at companies, yet for the regulators as well as the company it involves risks. This means there are attractions for the Panel as well as for the company in settling out of court.

Courts and judges are often thought to play a vital role in making and enforcing law. But, like the Panel, they can only react to cases brought before them. The court's role can be managed by keeping cases out of court. Either party can do this by 'settling out of court', as several companies appear to have done 'at the last minute'. The Panel can do it too. And it may be tempted to if it feels the court's decision has implications not only for the case in hand – win or lose – but for the future. The Panel's policy of treating the courts as a last resort may prove strategic not just to reap the benefits of persuasion rather than enforced compliance, but to avoid the risks for the new regime in going to court.

The 'Oz factor' might come into play in affecting the Panel's enthusiasm for litigation, or even for risking enforcement at all in 'tricky areas'. The power of the Wizard of Oz lay in not exposing the mortal behind the image. For the Panel, there may be more power in the projected image of a big gun, never used, than one which falls short of target, or reaches too far, when fired.

Impact

Though the Panel has clearly been prepared to go to court in a number of cases, it must have breathed a sigh of relief when companies conceded. However, settling out of court can have its price. Would those companies have conceded if the Panel had been demanding revision of accounts, with the costs and high profile with shareholders and others that would involve? Might a policy of seeking compliance in future and a change of comparatives reflect not only a policy of keeping companies on side in the long run, but the risks inherent in a tougher approach?

The fact that the big gun of the courts can backfire raises other questions. Could the 'court as last resort' policy give too much negotiating power to companies?

Negotiated Justice

It takes two to settle. What if a company refuses to settle but insists on a zero sum – the case is dropped or it goes to court? The Panel has insisted that it will not hesitate to litigate if a company refuses to act on what the Panel sees as 'abuses'. But can it afford to, in terms of both immediate costs and wider implications? Might companies play on these potential concerns? Big companies in particular, with credible war chests of their own, may be in a strong negotiating position.

The threat of the court has tended to be discussed as though it is only a weapon for the Panel. It may also in reality be a weapon for the companies the Panel is seeking to bring into compliance. The reality of the threat of the court may then prove more complex than the big gun rhetoric of the Panel suggests.

Collateral Damage as Control

However, the *rhetoric* may be all the Panel needs. The threat of the draconian power may be enough to ensure companies concede to the Panel. As we saw in Chapter 4, there are very real practical disincentives to directors taking on the Panel in court – concern over costs, of the use of shareholders' money for little return, fear of adverse publicity, concerns that delays and uncertainty might affect sensitive deals. According to Lex, in the *Financial Times* (16 October 1992), the Panel was "lucky that it was adjudicating on Trafalgar – one of its most high profile victims – at such a vulnerable stage in its history". The company was "under siege" from Hong Kong Land which sought to increase its stake in it via a tender offer, defended by Trafalgar House.

The significance of practical pressures rather than legal strength or weakness may be the reality of how law so often works. The evidence to date suggests that if the corrective action the Panel requires is not too demanding, a company will go along with its recommendations. Panel enforcement policy may succeed not through the courts but in the shadow of the courts, and by diplomacy rather than by war.

From Enforcement to Enforceability

But what if it doesn't? What if a company is prepared to contest the Panel in court? To bring its draconian power into play the Panel will have to prove regulations have been breached. In a contested case *enforcement* powers are subject to *legal enforce-*

ability. Indeed, contesting the Panel in the courts or out of them, means taking it on on legal grounds. At the end of the day, the big gun the Panel needs is not the sanctions that may follow a court case, but a case the courts will sustain. The hurdle it has to overcome is the company's argument that its accounts are perfectly legal. It is to this battle of legal arguments that we turn in Parts III and IV.

PART III

ENFORCEABILITY: LOOKING FOR LOOPHOLES

7
From Enforcement to Enforceability

Policing creative accounting is not so much a matter of 'whodunnit' – but 'whodun' *what*. The key issue is whether what was done was lawful or not. And that is not always straightforward, even – or perhaps especially – under the new regime. Talk of stronger enforcement of the law glosses over the fact that 'the law' is problematic. What is the law? What does it mean? How does it apply in this particular case? Indeed, what *legally* speaking is creative accounting?

Soundbite

The battle to control what the regulators see as unacceptable creative accounting is also a battle for the *definition* of what unacceptable creative accounting is. Creative accounting is a nice soundbite but what exactly it is may not be obvious. One person's creative accounting is another's carefully considered judgement; one person's device to deceive is another's legitimate management tool; one person's systematic understatement of profit is another's application of the prudence concept. Nor is motivation any clearer.

Good Faith and Law

Companies may look to the law to decide what they ought to do or to assess what they might get away with doing. They may believe in good faith that their approach is legally the right one. They may take a more pragmatic approach, adopting what they see as a not unreasonable reading of law or regulations, which suits their interests. They may see themselves as sailing close to the wind – or even in their own judgement as on the wrong side of the line, but find some basis for arguing a case in the hope of getting away with it. All, however, are likely to present their arguments as in good faith.

Distinguishing genuine good faith from a presentation of it is not easy to do. In both cases the same evidence is produced – pointing to statute and standard, to auditor support, to accountants' and barristers' opinions. Supporting opinions might be easily found, or they might have been accomplished only after extensive 'opinion shopping'. Only the supporting opinions, not the adverse ones, or the shopping for them, will be disclosed. Good faith may be presented, but not in good faith.

Whether companies are arguing in 'real' good faith or not, however, the issue is the same. Are regulations breached or not?

Creative equals Defective

The new regime has tried to introduce regulations that will bring what it sees as creative accounting into the net of defective accounting, which can then – at least in theory – be forcibly revised. But how powerful are the new weapons? Are they immune from the challenge of creative accounting? In the practices of the 1980s we can identify a number of grounds on which companies could claim accounting practices, which the regulators considered 'creative accounting', were nonetheless 'perfectly legal'. Can companies still find such grounds even under the new regulations. Can they still argue their practices are immune from enforcement? Can companies still try to challenge enforcement on the grounds of legal enforceability?

Examining the scope for such arguments is pertinent not only for companies seeking to use them, but for regulators seeking to detect and control them. The precise reach of the new regulations has not yet been tested in the courts. Quite what is and is not to be caught in the net of defective accounts, in the eyes of the judges, as opposed to the Panel, is not yet known. There may be scope for contested views even on quite fundamental issues.

Perfectly Legal

The new regime wants an emphasis on principles, but there are still, as we shall see, many detailed specific rules in the new regulations. The ASB sees the principles as what really count. But will the judges? Might companies point still to specifics in their requirements to argue that their accounts comply with what standards or statutes demand? Statutes and standards are there after all, to say what is true and fair. Following them must surely be perfectly legal, they would say.

Perfectly Illegal

Or might companies just as readily argue they have followed principles, that they have reported substance, they have given a true and fair view? It is the Panel's notion of true and fair, the Panel's notion of substance, that is wrong.

Might companies even challenge the *legitimacy* under law of the new standards? Might they argue the requirements of the regulators are 'perfectly *illegal*'?

Challenging the New Weapons

In this part and the next we will examine the weapons available to the Panel to try to capture creative accounting, from the perspective of those interested in circumventing them, and we will consider how the Panel might respond. In Part III we will explore 'perfectly legal' arguments, in Part IV the 'perfectly illegal' approach. We will focus especially on FRS 5, designed to ensure the substance of transactions and not just their legal form is reflected in accounts, on changes in the Companies Act and on the overriding requirement to give a true and fair view.

The Companies Act was modified, and FRS 5 introduced, by regulators aware of the dangers of loopholes in the law, and keen to try to close them off. But what if directors, their advisers – and the banks which are so often behind new smart devices – continue to look for them? As Sir David Tweedie joked, "some people read our standards more carefully than we write them!" In Part III we will consider whether the Companies Act and FRS 5 still leave scope for companies to seek out loopholes.

The Principled Approach

The Panel's response may be equally technical, arguing that the company's construction of the law – *con*struction perhaps – is wrong. Under the Tweedie approach, however, the Panel might also be expected to respond by pointing to more basic principles in statute or standard, and calling for compliance with them. The Panel might be expected to challenge 'creative compliance' as non-compliance, because it does not comply with the true and fair view or the requirement to report substance. The accounts are therefore still defective.

Companies may, however, have a riposte to this approach. Legal strategy is often to have several, possibly conflicting, lines of attack on hand. If one line fails, it does not necessarily mean retreat but the introduction of another. Even if the technical case founders on the principled response, the principled approach itself might also be vulnerable to challenge. We will explore this and responses to it in Part IV.

LOOKING FOR LOOPHOLES

The search for loopholes has traditionally followed a number of strategies. The basic approach is to search the words of statute, standard and, if it exists, case law to find material on which to argue a practice is 'perfectly legal'. What kind of material is sought out and used?

Gaps

The first strategy is to look for what is not there, to seek out gaps in regulation, to point out simply that there is no statute or standard that expressly prohibits the company's approach. This can be summed up as the 'where does it say I can't do that' approach.

The ex-files

Another version of the gap approach is to seek out *express* gaps, what we'll call the 'ex-files' of law and regulation. Lawyers look for express *exclusions* and argue 'the law expressly says this activity falls beyond its remit. It is therefore obviously beyond the remit of regulators.'

Gaps can be found *within* a statute or standard in express *exemptions*. Sometimes there are express rules acknowledging that legitimate *exceptions* may occur. The basic rule is for the 'ordinary', but other rules allow for extraordinary situations too.

A classic avoidance technique, then, is to structure activities in a way that can be *argued* to locate them in excluded, exempt or exceptional categories. We consider how companies might seek out gaps and 'ex-files' in the new regulations in Chapter 8.

Out of bounds

Another strategy is to scrutinise definitions and construct structures that fall beyond the defined reach of the regulation. The classic case in the creative accounting of the 1980s was the orphan subsidiary. In substance it was a subsidiary but in legal form it was not. It fell beyond the statutory definitions of a subsidiary, beyond the bounds of law.

The orphan subsidiary has been a key target of the new regime's new weapons. Is it dead? Or can legal arguments still be constructed to justify off balance sheet corporate structures? (Chapter 9)

Working to rule

The orphan subsidiary and many other techniques of creative accounting have been based on claims of compliance with the letter of specific rules. The new regime hopes to counter this with regulations based on principles rather than specific rules. FRS 5 is a keystone of this approach. But can FRS 5 still be scrutinised for opportunities for 'working to rule'? (Chapter 10)

Literal compliance

Literal compliance is key in working to rule. The question arises: can literal compliance also be claimed in relation to *principles*? Might even the requirement in FRS 5 to report substance be used to justify creative accounting? (Chapter 11)

Brief 'n' Counter

In the chapters that follow we demonstrate how these strategies might be applied in the new regime of financial reporting regulation. We explore bases on which legal arguments might be constructed in a bid to pre-empt or counter intervention by the Panel, to challenge the legal enforceability of the Panel's view, and to claim immunity from control.

Whether they would succeed or fail – with the Panel or in court – is another matter. We look at the factors affecting that – and what it means – in Part V.

8
Find the Gap and the Ex-Files

Are there 'gaps' in the arsenal of new weapons? Might some of these be exploited by directors keen to find 'perfectly legal' means of enhancing their accounts?

THE GAP: WHERE DOES IT SAY I CAN'T?

There certainly remain areas where there is no specific regulation on how companies should report particular types of deal or event. The new regime's approach of basing standards on general principles was intended to provide a means of filling the vacuum; the general principles could be applied to the specific situation to determine the true and fair treatment. The Panel took this approach in the RMC case.

RMC (PN51)

Subsidiaries of RMC had been fined in 1995 for breaching Orders of the Restrictive Trade Practices Court. The fines, together with legal costs, totalled £4.97 million, but were not disclosed in the Group's 1995 consolidated accounts. They were deemed not material in the context of group pre-tax profits in excess of £350 million. There was no specific statutory or accounting standard requiring disclosure.

The Panel argued that payment of the fines, though not quantitatively significant

> was an important matter that ought to be brought specifically to the attention of the users of the accounts because of the nature and circumstances of the fines. While this was a matter of judgement, in the Panel's view this was a material matter, the special nature and circumstances of which were such that its materiality needed to be determined primarily by reference to its qualitative aspects.

The directors agreed to provide further information about the fines in the Directors' Report accompanying the Group's 1997 accounts. But, what if they had resisted?

In 1995, Sir David Tweedie expressed his fears about a "resurgence" of companies taking a "where does it say that I can't do this?" attitude (FRC, 1996:25). This approach, he says, would be contrary to the spirit of the new regime. The fact that he is worried about this attitude means that, new regime or not, companies may continue to take this line. RMC could certainly have done so, there being no rule requiring disclosure. But how would such an argument have fared?

There are hints that such a line could be successful – even without venturing into the courts. There have certainly been instances of the Panel investigating a 'gap' treatment but taking no action vis-à-vis the company. Instead of passing judgement on the way the company has reported the deal, enforcing its own view of what would be true and fair, or applying the principles for reporting the substance of transactions in FRS 5 – two of the key weapons of the new regime – the Panel has chosen to drop the case and pass the issue on to the standard setters for guidance. This is what it did with Pentos (PN28). New rules, of course, affect accounts in the future, but for a company that is quite different from facing enforced revisions now.

If gaps in the regulation are treated by the Panel as beyond the remit of its enforcement powers, directors may be encouraged to 'find the gap' in regulations, and argue their chosen treatment is 'perfectly legal': 'where, after all, does it say I can't?' In the same FRC report in which Tweedie voiced these fears, Edwin Glasgow again referred to the 'grey areas' where there is "some genuine uncertainty or divergence of practice". And while a "clear contravention" of the Act or accounting standard

> plainly falls within the Panel's remit . . . Where the ground is less certain it is a very important function of the Panel to draw such matters to the attention of the Accounting Standards Board or, where appropriate, other regulators (FRC, 1996:33)

and not, the implication is, to deal with it themselves. If the ASB or UITF comes into play, the gap may be temporary, but it still provides an opportunity.

Temporary Gaps: or Pre-Implementation Licences

The inevitable lag between recognising an issue and implementing a regulation to deal with it can provide a temporary gap, or indeed, be treated as a *pre-implementation licence*. UITF 13, for example, provided an interpretation of FRS 5 in respect of ESOPs, on the basis that clear guidance was required. But it did not come into formal effect until 22 June 1995 although 'early adoption' was encouraged. While some companies responded positively to this invitation to early adoption, others did not, despite FRS 5.

Courts, for example, brought back sale and leaseback properties on to its 5 March 1995 balance sheet following the implementation of FRS 5, but chose not to change treatment of its ESOP despite the imminence of UITF 13. It continued to treat its guarantee of £4 million on account of borrowing by its ESOP as a contingency. Conrad Ritblat, the property agency, similarly continued to treat its guarantee as a contingency in its 31 May 1995 accounts. It 'beat' UITF 13 by just three weeks.

The UITF was clarifying a grey area. It was clarifying what should be done, and therefore removing the scope for companies to claim the most amenable treatment was the right one. However, ironically, the delay before implementation was treated by companies as licensing them to choose their own method *until* the new rule came into effect. It provided a basis for arguing other treatments were *not* ruled out until the express date. Where does it say I can't *now*?

This will not necessarily work with the Panel, however. The Panel might argue that an imminent UITF rule merely endorses what true and fair reporting now should be. The Trafalgar House case might be seen in this light.

THE EX-FILES: THE TRUTH IS OUT THERE

Rules within regulations on exclusions, exceptions and exemptions are all grist to the mill of legal argument. We'll call these the 'ex-files'. The argument is that the truth is out there, or, more prosaically, the true and fair view lies *outwith* or *beyond* the normal rules.

Exclusions – FRS 5

Faced with apparently powerful weapons against creative accounting, such as FRS 5, one strategy is to look for express exclusions from them. The argument is that express exclusions are clearly beyond the remit of enforcement.

FRS 5 "sets out principles that will apply to all transactions", says paragraph (d) of the summary of the standard. But in fact FRS 5 does not apply to all transactions. It expressly excludes a number of particular kinds of transaction from its scope (unless they are a part of another transaction that does fall within the scope of FRS 5):

- forward contracts and futures;
- foreign exchange and interest rate swaps;
- contracts where a net amount will be paid or received, based on the movement in a price or an index;
- expenditure commitments and orders placed, until the earlier of delivery or payment; and
- employment contracts (FRS 5, para. 12).

The ASB is, as we go to press, producing a standard on 'Derivatives and other Financial Instruments: Disclosures' (see FRS 13, 1998), so some of these transactions will be expressly regulated in future. In the meantime, however, such transactions have been employed to enhance accounts in a 'perfectly legal' way – 'perfectly legal' at least so far as FRS 5 is concerned, because these areas are expressly excluded from it.

Some companies, BP and Grand Metropolitan for example, have anticipated the standard on derivatives, but others have not. And, according to Martin Scicluna, chairman of Deloitte and Touche, companies like financial instruments because they resemble *icebergs*: "The risks that companies assume in taking on derivatives remain mainly off-balance sheet, under the water" (*The Times*, 18 September 1997).

Other exclusions in FRS 5 have been problematic too. Take expenditure commitments, for example. According to Isobel Sharp, professional standards partner at Binder Hamlyn (as was), the exclusion of expenditure commitments in particular "is perhaps the most damaging in terms of taking transactions outside FRS 5" ('A Question of Substance', *Accountancy*, December 1994:138). Although there is a rationale for the exclusion – to avoid bringing on to the balance sheet items which would fall within the FRS 5 definition of liabilities, for example, orders for raw materials placed by the year end for delivery in the new year – it "works widely". It could be used "to overturn custom and practice and the conventional application of the accounting principles of matching and prudence", for example, making provision for future major expenditure commitments – such as overhauls of aircraft or dry-docking of ships – which do not meet the definition of liabilities.

In *Johnston* (1994) – a case on tax – the taxpayer airline company provided for the accruing costs of major engine overhauls (which were required by the Civil Aviation Authority as a condition for obtaining a certificate of airworthiness). The High Court acknowledged that the accounts were drawn up in accordance with the 'ordinary principles of commercial accountancy' and therefore, in the absence of any statutory restriction, were to be accepted for corporation tax purposes as a true statement of the company's profits for the relevant period. It would be ironic if the exclusion of expenditure commitments from FRS 5 was used to justify a reversal of such practice. In the event, this particular route has now been plugged (FRS 12), but the search for exclusions might bear fruit elsewhere.

Exclusions – FRS 2

FRS 2 takes a similar approach to FRS 5. In paragraph C of the summary, it states that it applies "to all parent undertakings", even those that do not report under the Companies Act (unless prohibited by statute from so doing). Two paragraphs later though it states that under both the Companies Act and FRS 2 certain parent undertakings are excluded from preparing consolidated financial statements:

- its group is small or medium-sized and not an ineligible group (i.e. its members are a public company or body corporate empowered to offer shares or debentures to the public; a banking institution; an insurance company; or an authorised person under the Financial Services Act 1986);
- the parent is a wholly owned subsidiary undertaking and its immediate parent undertaking is established under the law of an EU member state. (Exemption is conditional on compliance with certain further conditions set out in the Companies Act s. 228(2); and is lost if the company has securities listed on any EU member state Stock Exchange);
- the parent undertaking is a majority-owned (50%+ of the shares) subsidiary undertaking and meets all the conditions for exemption in ss. 228(2) and 228(1)(b).

Such a parent undertaking should state that its financial statements present information about it as an individual undertaking and not about its group. This statement should disclose the reason why the company is not required to prepare group accounts as stated (Companies Act 1985, Sched. 5 para. 1(4)).

Exclusions – FRS 9

Although we have focused here on express exclusions such as those in FRS 2 and 5, exclusions can be found de facto too. A good example of this is FRS 9, on Associates and Joint Ventures. The scope of FRS 9 is very wide: it applies to "all financial statements that are intended to give a true and fair view" (para. 2). But, FRS 9 *effectively excludes* investment funds in respect of their portfolio investments; not expressly, but via para. 50:

> for consistency, the stake is properly accounted for as an investment according to the method of accounting applied to other investments within that investment portfolio rather than as an associate or joint venture, even if the investor has significant influence or joint control.

So, while investment funds apply FRS 9 to investments through which they carry out investing activities, they do not do so to those investments held as part of their investment portfolios. While "this effectively sanctions long-standing practice in at least some sections of the investment trust industry" (Ernst & Young, 1998 (FRS 9):7), it also opens a potential escape route from consolidation.

Exceptions

The true and fair override is an express licence in the Companies Act to depart from, rather than comply with, specific legal requirements, in "special circumstances" (CA, ss. 226(5); 227(6)). This escape route from compliance with specific regulatory requirements is adopted for accounting standards too, in "exceptional circumstances" (Foreword to Accounting Standards, para. 18).

Although Sir David Tweedie saw the true and fair override as a valuable weapon for regulators, to overrule devices which complied in form but not in substance with the law, the Companies Act actually frames the override as available to *directors* to depart from rules where they believe compliance with them would not give a true and fair view. And in the 1989 Companies Act the DTI changed the words of the statute in order to make the override more readily available. So, scope for departure is available, albeit in special or exceptional circumstances.

In the 1980s this route was used by directors and, it has been suggested, allowed through by auditors too often and on too lax a basis. Hence the requirement in the Companies Act 1989 (reinforced by UITF 7) that departures from statutory or accounting standards requirements be flagged, and the Panel's specific interest in monitoring them. Using the override is therefore likely to be open to scrutiny. That does not mean that the 'exceptions' route is necessarily ruled out as a base for justifying creative accounting. It simply means it is less likely to slip through without investigation, but that in turn might stimulate the pursuit of a different style of legal argument. We will explore this in Part IV.

Exemptions

Regulations that expressly *include* specified types of transaction or structure may, at the same time, specify exemptions. Such express exemptions may be another valuable source of material for arguing an accounting treatment is 'perfectly legal'. The Companies Act, we have seen, provides what can be seen as weapons to counter the specific device of the orphan subsidiary: it provides weapons with the potential to counter creative accounting in general by requiring a true and fair view; but the statute that does that also sets out express exemptions. Could companies find ways to fall into these exemptions then claim immunity from Panel enforcement?

The current Companies Act provides exemptions from the rule that all subsidiary undertakings of the parent must be included in the consolidated accounts. The parent shall exclude subsidiaries where their activities

> are so different from those of other undertakings to be included in the consolidation that their inclusion would be incompatible with the obligation to give a true and fair view. (s.229(4))

'Shall' is strong, mandatory, wording, and good material for legal argument.

There are also permissive exemptions. Subsidiary undertakings *may* be kept out where

- the interest of the parent company in the as yet unconsolidated subsidiary is *held exclusively for subsequent resale* (s. 229(3) (c));
- inclusion is not material for the purpose of giving a true and fair view (s. 229(2));
- the information necessary cannot be obtained without *disproportionate expense or undue delay* (s. 229(3)(b)); or
- *severe long-term restrictions* substantially hinder the exercise of the rights of the parent over the assets or management of the subsidiary (s. 229(3)(a)).

ACHILLES' HEELS?

The Companies Act was implementing European law, the Seventh Company Law Directive. The Directive was controversial and the finished product was not what the European Commission had originally wanted.

Its original approach strongly opposed special cases and exemptions, which it saw as an opening for "abuse" (Commission of the European Communities, 1976). However, the final version of the Directive contained a range of exemptions, special cases and exclusions. These could be pointed out to justify omitting subsidiaries which would detract from group accounts.

In the wake of the 1989 Act, *Company Reporting* drew attention to many companies using these exemptions, often implicitly or explicitly questioning this practice. Wiggins, the property development group, for example, in 1990 revalued downward its investment in its South Quay development and the development was sold to a special purpose vehicle, a subsidiary under statutory definitions, financed with only limited recourse to Wiggins. This subsidiary showed a net liability of £42 million for 1991. This was disclosed in a note to the group accounts. However, since the terms of the finance package were such that the company is "severely restricted in its freedom of action relative to the South Quay development" the accounts were not consolidated on the basis of the statutory exception (*Company Reporting*, November 1991:10; *Accountancy*, December 1991).

FRS 2

Nowadays companies would have to take into account, in the search for express exemptions, not just the Companies Act but also FRS 2. FRS 2 gives guidance on group accounting under the new Companies Act. So far as express exemptions are concerned, it does two things. Some exemptions, permitted by the Act, it makes mandatory. For example, under the Act companies "may" exclude subsidiaries where severe long-term restrictions substantially hinder the exercise of the parent's rights over the assets or management of the subsidiary undertaking or where the parent's interest is held exclusively with a view to subsequent resale. In these situations FRS 2 requires non-consolidation. The express exemption has therefore been firmed up – for good reason: it was argued that it would be misleading to include such a subsidiary.

The ASB's second tactic was to try to counter abuse of the exemptions by limiting the situations in which they could be involved. It did this by providing guidance on the application of statutory exemptions based on 'substance over form', commercial reality and effects in practice. For example, 'severe long-term restrictions are identified by' their effect in practice rather than by the way in which the restrictions are imposed (para. 78(c)).

But both tactics have potential shortcomings. In particular, might companies construct a way of falling into exempt categories in situations not intended by the ASB? If they could show severe long-term restrictions or if they could construct a situation of being exclusively held for resale, FRS 2 *requires* non-consolidation.

Severe Long-Term Restrictions

According to FRS 2, echoing the terms of the Companies Act, 'severe long-term restrictions' refer only to restrictions on the exercise of the rights and interests held by or attributed to the parent "by reason of which the parent undertaking is defined as such . . . and in the absence of which it would not be the parent undertaking" (FRS 2, para. 25; CA, s. 229(3)). In other words, FRS 2 and the Act are looking to restrictions on the control a parent has over its subsidiary undertaking via its holding of a majority of voting rights, control of the board of directors, dominant influence (by virtue of a control contract or the memorandum or articles of association) or sole control of voting rights pursuant to an agreement with shareholders (CA, s. 258).

More recently, however, the ASB in FRS 9 has given a different interpretation which may be exploited:

> In some cases an investor may qualify as the parent of an entity under the definition of a subsidiary in FRS 2 (for example by holding a majority of the voting rights in that entity) but contractual arrangements with the other shareholders mean that in practice the shareholders share control over their investee. In such a case the interests of the minority shareholder amount to "severe long-term restrictions" that "substantially hinder the exercise of the rights of the parent undertaking over the assets or management of the subsidiary undertaking". (para. 11)

And, as FRS 9 reminds us in a footnote to para. 11:

> subsidiary undertakings where there are severe long-term restrictions of this sort are required by paragraph 25 of FRS 2 to be excluded from consolidation.

Accordingly, the subsidiary undertaking should be treated as a joint venture under FRS 9.

Ernst & Young describe this as "a surprisingly loose interpretation of FRS 2 and the law" (1998:13) but "presume that the ASB has had the benefit of legal advice that its wider interpretation is sustainable" (1998:14). In any case, they illustrate how FRS 9 can be exploited to take advantage of the statutory exemption option, which FRS 2 makes mandatory:

> Suppose, for example, that a parent company enters into a shareholders' agreement with a minority shareholder of a subsidiary that the subsidiary, absent mutual consent for change, must operate solely in the UK, not diversify its product range, not spend more than £1 million on new plant, and not declare a dividend beyond a certain level.
>
> Such an agreement places significant commercial restrictions on the parent's freedom of action while leaving unaffected its voting rights. (Ernst & Young, 1998:14)

Ernst & Young see this as an opportunity for creative accounting. We'll look at this in more detail in Chapter 9.

Exclusively Held for Resale

In FRS 2 the phrase used in the Companies Act s. 229(3)(c) – interest held exclusively with a view to subsequent resale – was refined to

- "an interest for which a purchaser has been identified or is being sought . . .";
- ". . . and which is reasonably expected to be disposed of . . .";
- "within approximately one year of its date of acquisition" (para. 11a).

But, the exemption could still be problematic, particularly in the context of takeovers and acquisitions. There were many examples in the late 1980s of highly leveraged buy-outs undertaken in order to 'unbundle' the target company, that is to sell off non-core divisions either to strengthen the company or merely to repay some of the debt incurred. We have seen how orphan subsidiaries have been used in the past in take-overs to keep the potential risks for the parent off the balance sheet.

Could the 'exclusively held for resale' exemption be invoked to the same effect and with the same dangers? Could a massive acquisition be kept off the balance sheet on the basis that it is only being held for resale? Certainly, prior to FRS 2, News International justified excluding acquisition Harper Collins (UK) from its group accounts in 1991 on this basis (*Company Reporting*, November 1991:12). Hawker Siddeley excluded a 90% owned subsidiary as it was "actively held for resale", with a letter of intent pointed to as evidence (*Company Reporting*, June 1991:16).

There are other problems in practice. How is 'a reasonable expectation of disposal within approximately one year' to be proved or disproved? Bunzl excluded subsidiaries in 1989 on the grounds of a decision to sell, although they were still unsold, and still recorded as current assets, in 1990 (*Company Reporting*, June 1991:16).

Different Activities

FRS 2 also mentions this statutory exemption. But it does not provide guidance, nor does it attempt to change the mandate placed on directors to exclude subsidiary undertakings from consolidation where their activities

> are so different from those of other undertakings to be included in the consolidation that their inclusion would be incompatible with the obligation to give a true and fair view. (CA s. 229(4))

The ASC had considered tightening up this exemption by restricting the circumstances in which subsidiaries should be excluded. It did so by reference to the Companies Act and its recognition of two categories of company for accounting purposes: ordinary companies and banking and insurance companies. Banking and insurance companies are still required to comply with the main accounting requirements of the Companies Act, but they draw up their accounts in accordance with Schedule 9A, which provides substantial exceptions from the normal disclosure rule.

ED 50 proposed that a company could be excluded from consolidation if it was a banking or insurance company, and the parent was not or vice versa. But potential for abuse remained. As Ernst & Young put it (in a letter to the ASC, 15 October 1990):

> we agree that it is necessary to draft such rules with great care to ensure that they do not present new opportunities for companies to avoid consolidation in appropriate circumstances.

What the ASC had actually done in its proposal, instead of *limiting* the scope of the exemption, was to *clarify the route* and method of escape from consolidation, and thereby provide the material for creative compliance. As Coopers & Lybrand Deloitte pointed out (in a letter to the ASC, 15 October 1990), the exemption proposed in ED 50 "could still be open to abuse". It would be relatively easy for a finance subsidiary which is closely related to the trade of the group to take a small number of deposits and therefore get authorisation from the Bank of England as a banking company. So further rules – and material – would be needed to limit this abuse.

In the end, the ASB in FRS 2 decided that it was not possible to identify any particular contrast of activities where the necessary incompatibility with the true and fair view generally occurs. But the ASB did emphasise how exceptional cases of this sort are. And the statute itself reminds directors that the provision does not apply

> merely because some of the undertakings are industrial, some commercial and some provide services, or because they carry on industrial or commercial activities involving different products or provide different services. (CA, s. 229(4))

The statutory test therefore is stringent and the ASB endorses this. But, the exemption remains on the statute book, despite the ambitions of the European Commission and the practice in other countries such as the USA.

According to the European Commission:

> group undertakings will not be permitted to be excluded from consolidation where their activities are very different from the

> normal activities of the group. A diversity of activities within a group is not in itself a valid reason for permitting undertakings to be excluded from consolidation. (Commission of the European Communities, 1976:26)

The Commission was not alone in its concern over the opportunities for abuse afforded by such exemptions. In the USA, exclusion of a subsidiary on the grounds of different activities is no longer allowed. American companies had used this opportunity to remove liabilities from their balance sheets. In 1987 the FASB consequently introduced SFAS 94 which declared:

> The managerial, operational and financial ties that bind an enterprise into a single economic unit are stronger than the differences between its lines of business . . . differences between the varied operations of a group of affiliated corporations that constitutes an economic and financial whole do not preclude including them all in consolidated financial statements. These differences also do not make the equity method a valid substitute for consolidation of majority owned subsidiaries.

This statutory exemption, according to Ernst & Young in 1990, "has been applied too frequently in the past" (Letter to the ASC, ED 50, 15 October 1990). But FRS 2 has not changed the position one iota. Companies may therefore continue to use this and other exemptions as in the past. The Independent Broadcasting Association (IBA), for example, in its 1990 accounts excluded its *wholly owned* subsidiary Channel Four Television on the grounds of dissimilarity, although *Company Reporting* commented that the Channel 4 operation was "of paramount significance" to the IBA (6 December 1990:4). Northumbrian Water Group in its 1991 accounts excluded its subsidiary Three Rivers Insurance on the grounds that its activities were so different and cited s. 229(4) in support. The acquisition was recorded as an investment of £0.2 million and the notes to the accounts stated that no further details were provided "because the directors are of the view that the information is not material" (*Company Reporting*, September 1991:9). Similarly, the 1990 *Doctus* accounts did not consolidate a 51% subsidiary, *Kingsmark Travel*, which cost £117,000 and had reported net assets of £10,444; it was treated as a fixed asset investment. Kingsmark itself lost £39,556 for the year in question. Despite this, the subsidiary was excluded from the group's accounts on the grounds of "the insignificant amount involved" (*Company Reporting*, March 1991:21).

FRS 5

In FRS 5 the ASB has set out to extend the requirements of group accounting beyond the Companies Act. But at no point does it *prevent* companies from using one of the express exceptions in the Companies Act. Companies might stand on the argument that FRS 5 does not affect exceptions expressly allowed, or indeed required, by statute. They would find support for this in the fact that, in the making of FRS 2, the regulators acknowledged they could not remove statutory exceptions. If FRS 2 could not overrule a statutory provision, how could FRS 5? The ASB's Foreword to Accounting Standards too declares that

> Where accounting standards prescribe information to be contained in financial statements, such requirements do not override exemptions from disclosure given by law to, and utilised by, certain types of entity. (para. 15)

IN CONTENTION

The Panel might, of course, argue that the statutory requirement to give a true and fair view extends to challenging what it sees as artificial or misleading uses of express exceptions. The fact that the ASB could not come up with general rules on when different activities should and should not be excluded from group accounts, does not mean the Panel could not argue a company's treatment does not make for true and fair accounts in its particular case. Such arguments might lead in turn to counter-arguments – but we'll see more on these later.

9
Out of Bounds

Another classic strategy of creative compliance is to scrutinise definitions and criteria in statute and standard to try to construct relationships or forms of transaction that fall *beyond* them – out of regulatory bounds.

The classic example of the 1980s was the orphan subsidiary – a key target of the new regime. Has the orphan subsidiary been defeated by the new regime? Or could parallel structures still be dreamed up with an arguable case that they belong not on, but *off*, the group balance sheet?

THE ORPHAN SUBSIDIARY

Before the 1989 Companies Act it was remarkably simple (with hindsight) to construct a company that to all intents and purposes was a subsidiary, but fell beyond the Companies Act definitions. Under the Companies Act a company B was a subsidiary of A – and B's state of affairs and profit or loss had to be included in A's consolidated accounts – if:

1. A controlled more than half in nominal value of B's equity share capital; or
2. A was a member of B and controlled the composition of B's board of directors (Companies Act 1985, s. 736).

A could hold 49% of B's equity share capital, and have a friendly bank hold another 2%, or its minority of shares could have the majority of votes which is how the Savoy Hotel famously resisted being taken over for so long. The Savoy's B class shares controlled by the Wontner family since 1953 carried 20 times the vote of the A shares.

A could control only the minority of the board, but still control the vote, say, by ensuring, through its shares structure and voting rights, that its four directors had two votes each to the other five directors' one each. And hey presto, there was an orphan subsidiary. There were much more complex ways of achieving this too.

Companies with such structures left off their balance sheets could argue they were in perfect compliance with the law – *creative* compliance perhaps, not quite what the legislators had in mind when they constructed their definitions, but compliance nonetheless.

This argument succeeded, in practical terms, under the old regime. Orphan subsidiaries were used by many large companies without audit qualification. There were no cases of the DTI prosecuting companies for excluding orphan subsidiaries – the only prosecution, indeed, was for exactly the opposite. In the *Argyll* case in 1981, as we've seen, the directors were prosecuted for *including* in their group accounts a subsidiary company which was acquired after the end of the financial year in question but prior to publication of the accounts. This made the case for *excluding* any company falling outside statutory definitions even stronger.

The New Regime

The task of changing the regulations to bring such structures onto the balance sheet was tackled in stages:

- via the Companies Act 1989, which implemented the Seventh Directive;
- via the ASB's guidance on the application of the Companies Act in FRS 2 (1990); and
- via FRS 5 in 1994.

Directors and their advisers, searching for arguments to justify keeping potential subsidiaries *off* the balance sheet, would have to look carefully at all of these regulatory instruments to spot potential loopholes. The new regime is counting on this not being an easy task. Certainly there are layers of obstacles to overcome:

1. new definitions of a group relationship, requiring consolidation of 'subsidiary undertakings' in a wider range of specified situations than before;
2. anti-avoidance measures dealing expressly with the more obvious routes to control beyond the reach of these definitions;
3. a statutory 'catch-all' definition of a subsidiary, based on the broad criterion of 'actual dominant influence';
4. FRS 5's 'catch-more-still' requirement that *quasi-subsidiaries* be consolidated too.

That does not mean the creative financial engineer will be daunted.

New Definitions

To argue they fall beyond the remit of statute and standard, directors would first have to ensure they were not caught by the new definitions introduced by the Seventh Directive, and implemented by the UK in the 1989 Companies Act (which amended the 1985 Act). The new range of specific definitions of a subsidiary takes in more forms of relationship than the previous Companies Act did. What is more, the Directive and Act apply not just to 'companies' but to 'undertakings'. This wider term includes partnerships and unincorporated trade or business associations, with or without a view to profit (Companies Act 1985, s. 259).

Consolidation of undertaking B is required if undertaking A:

- *holds* a majority of the *voting rights* in B (Article 1(a); implemented in Companies Act 1985 s. 258(2)(a));
- has the *right* to appoint or remove a majority of the members of B's administrative, management or supervisory body and is a *shareholder or member* in B (Article 1(b); CA s. 258(2)(b));
- has the *right* to exercise a dominant influence over B by virtue of a *control contract* or of *provisions in B's memorandum or articles of association* (Article 1(c); CA s. 258(2)(c)(ii) and (i));

- is a *shareholder or member* of B and controls alone, pursuant to an agreement with other shareholders or members, a majority of B's *voting rights* (Article 1(d)(bb); CA s. 258(2)(d));
- has a *participating interest* in B and actually exercises a dominant influence over B (Article 1(2)(a); CA s. 258(4)(a)); or
- has a *participating interest* in B, and A and B are managed on a unified basis (Article 1(2)(b); CA s. 258(4)(b)).

Anti-avoidance Measures

Even as the Act was being drafted, it was not too difficult to think of structures that would still fall beyond these definitions, and some of the more obvious escape routes were closed off in the legislation. For example, the EC Directive required that consolidated accounts be drawn up if A controlled B's board of directors. This requirement mirrored provisions then in existence in the Companies Act 1985, provisions which the UK government knew could be easily circumvented, as we showed above.

So, the government introduced an anti-avoidance provision when implementing the directive. The amended Companies Act declares that the reference in s. 258(2)(b) to the right to appoint or remove a majority of the board of directors

> is to the right to appoint or remove directors holding a majority of the voting rights at meetings of the board on all, or substantially all, matters. (Companies Act 1985, Schedule 10A, para. 3(1), emphasis added).

As is so often the case though, even 'better' rules, though necessary, are unlikely to be sufficient in the face of creative thinking.

What, for example, if A controls B's board on substantially all trivial matters, while C controls it on one or two key matters? In the view of Arthur Andersen & Co (letter to the ASC, ED 50, 15 October 1990), as drafted the Companies Act could be used to "create a loophole". For example, A and C could set up a board in which C controls the director who has the power on one important matter, and A controls all the other directors who have power on trivial matters. C controls but A consolidates under the terms of the Act.

A 'Catch-all' Definition: Actual Dominant Influence

There was another layer to the Seventh Directive's definitions. It offered member states the option of a much broader definition, which the DTI, anxious to do something about off-balance structures, took up. This definition tried to capture the essence of the parent–subsidiary relationship, rather than any specific form it might take. This was seen as the 'actual exercise of dominant influence', by one undertaking over another, by whatever specific means. It is easy to see why Coopers and Lybrand Deloitte described this as "potentially a 'catch-all' clause" (Nailor, 1990).

However, that potential was limited by the addition of another clause. An undertaking did not necessarily become your subsidiary if you actually exercised dominant influence over it. It had to be included in the group only if you also held a 'participating interest' in it.

Participating Interest

A participating interest means:

> an interest held by an undertaking in the shares of another undertaking which it holds on a long-term basis for the purpose of securing a contribution to its activities by the exercise of control or influence arising from or related to that interest. (s.260(1))

This is a broad definition.

In addition:

- the Act stipulates that a shareholding of 20% or more shall be presumed to be a participating interest;
- the definition includes more than actual shareholdings. It would include, for example, an interest which is convertible into shares, or an option to acquire shares or any interest in them, even if their shares are not issued until the conversion or exercise of the option (s. 260(3));
- the ASB in FRS 2 has defined 'on a long-term basis' broadly: it means held other than exclusively with a view to subsequent resale (para. 10) – and we saw in Chapter 8 how carefully

'held for resale' was drafted (para. 11). Indeed, in FRS 9, the ASB has gone further and clarified that the issue of whether an investment is held for the long term is determined by reference to the date of acquisition, rather than the balance sheet date. In other words, once it is treated as being held on a long-term basis, it should continue to be so treated, even if disposal is expected (FRS 9, para. 43).

MORE ACHILLES' HEELS?

Notwithstanding the broad drafting however, the effect of the participating interest provision is still to confine the application of 'actual dominant influence'. Even if an undertaking does actually exercise a dominant influence over another it will not be a parent for the purposes of s. 258(4) unless it also has a participating interest in it. Herein lies another Achilles' heel for financial engineers to exploit and some possibilities have been pointed out by practitioners.

According to BDO Binder Hamlyn (letter to the ASC, ED 50, 15 October 1990), for example, it would be feasible to "design shares which carry votes and have all the economic rights of equity but which do not meet the legal definition", and so avoid a finding of a participating interest. Similarly, it has been suggested, an entity may make a loan to another entity in its start-up years when it is in a loss-making situation and only establish a participating interest relationship once the new entity has started generating profits. In other words, it may have a dominant influence but no participating interest at the early stages (ICAEW Memorandum on ED 50, 15 October 1990).

'Actual Dominant Influence'

The suggestion is that 'participating interest' might be worked on to find a way of getting beyond the scope of the Act. So too might 'actual dominant influence'. FRS 2 was produced on the invitation of the government to the accounting regulators to provide guidance on the application of the Act in relation to consolidation. It emphasises the *de facto* nature of 'actual dominant influence': "The actual practice of dominant influence is identified by its effect in practice rather than by the way it is exercised" (FRS 2, para. 7).

But there has still been close scrutiny of the words of the Act and FRS 2 for ways to 'orphan' subsidiaries. The words 'actual exercise' have been seized on, for example. Though their purpose was to include *de facto* – 'actual' – control, rather than merely legal forms of control (voting rights and the like), the words have been used to argue for exclusion of subsidiaries if there is no 'actual', i.e. current, active control, over them (The Law Society, 1990 ED 50:4).

'Dominant influence' has also been defined and this may prove a base for arguing particular structures fall outside the rules.

The Dangers of Definitions

The DTI was aware of the dangers inherent in defining a broad 'catch-all' concept like 'dominant influence'. Indeed in the Companies Act 1989, Parliament deliberately left it undefined:

> Any definition of the term will encourage attempts to avoid the provision by artificial constructions with the intention of escaping from the letter of the definition. (Lord Strathclyde, HL Deb. vol. 503, col. 1018)

The government made sure it remained undefined even though it had to implement – and define – another version of 'dominant influence' from the Seventh Directive: dominant influence pursuant to a control contract or company 'by-laws' (Article 1(c); Companies Act s. 258(2)(c)(ii) and (i), Schedule 10A para. 4(1)). The statutory definition of 'the right to exercise a dominant influence', in this context, is as follows:

> an undertaking shall not be regarded as having the right to exercise a dominant influence over another undertaking unless it has a right to give directions with respect to the operating and financial policies of that other undertaking which its directors are obliged to comply with whether or not they are for the benefit of that other undertaking. (Companies Act 1985, Schedule 10A, para. 4(1))

This definition significantly limits the scope of the 'dominant influence' in that part of the Act. As the Law Society Company Law Committee observed, it means that an undertaking will not be regarded as having the right to exercise a dominant influence over another

> unless it has a right to give directions on the operating and financial policies and the directions are such that the directors are obliged to comply. (Comments on ED 50)

The government did not want 'actual dominant influence' in the broad definition of a subsidiary undertaking limited in this way. It therefore ring-fenced 'actual dominant influence'. Not only did it refuse to define the term, but it expressly declared that this definition of 'dominant influence':

> shall *not* be read as affecting the construction of the expression 'actually exercises a dominant influence' in section 258(4)(a). (Schedule 10A, para. 4(3), emphasis added)

It was left to the accountancy regulators to provide guidance in accounting standards as to the meaning of the concept. The ASB did this in FRS 2 and FRS 5 but, arguably, in a way, via its definitions of 'actual dominant influence' and 'control', that invites the 'artificial constructions' the government said it wanted to pre-empt.

Financial and Operating Policies

The ASB has defined 'the actual exercise of dominant influence' as:

> the exercise of an influence that achieves the result that the operating and financial policies of the undertaking influenced are set in accordance with the wishes of the holder of the influence and for the holder's benefit whether or not those wishes are explicit. (FRS 2, para. 7(b))

'Control' of an entity is defined as the

> ability to direct the financial and operating policies of that entity with a view to gaining economic benefit(s) from its activities. (FRS 5, para. 8; FRS 2, para. 6)

The main problem (for the regulators) or opportunity (for directors and their advisers) in both these definitions is the reference to the phrase (echoing the statutory definition of dominant influence): "financial and operating policies". In 1987, the DTI proposed to require consolidated accounts where the parent had the ability to determine the financial or operating policies of the subsidiary. It favoured this formulation rather than "the financial and operating policies of the subsidiary" which it saw as a "weaker" formulation (although it welcomed views on the pros and cons of the alternative) (DTI, Consultative letter to CCAB Bodies on the Implementation of the Seventh Directive, 30 October 1987). In the end, of course, the government avoided giving any definition at all.

What the ASB has done is not only to provide a definition – something which the government thought could weaken the concept – but it has done so in terms that the statute specifically avoided, that the DTI regarded as weak and that many commentators specifically warned against. Arthur Andersen & Co, for example, in response to ED 50, recommended that the wording should be financial or operating policies "to prevent the direction of one but not the other being used to create a loophole" (Letter to the ASC, ED 50, 30 November 1990).

The new regime may have set new, tough hurdles for creative accountants. But it has also provided material from which to argue ways out of regulatory control.

FRS 5: Quasi-subsidiaries

There is yet another regulatory layer for directors to circumnavigate: FRS 5. This could be expected to herald the end for orphan subsidiaries. It directly attacks the 'out of bounds' approach and it specifically attacks what it calls "quasi-subsidiaries": "vehicles" that are subsidiaries in substance, "though not fulfilling the [statutory] definition of a subsidiary" (FRS 5, para. 7).

Note the use of the word 'vehicle'. Even the statutory concept of 'undertaking' has been widened by the ASB in FRS 5. It had been suggested, for example, that a trust might be argued to fall beyond the boundaries of an 'undertaking'. The FRS's definition of quasi-subsidiary could include both.

Yet it has been argued that there remain ways of falling beyond the remit of the Companies Act, FRS 2 and even FRS 5. The deadlocked joint venture is one key device that has been suggested.

DEADLOCKED JOINT VENTURES

A deadlocked joint venture is a device in which neither potential parent exercises day-to-day control – or actual dominant influence – because the policies of the joint venture are predetermined. Several versions of the deadlocked joint venture can be constructed. The basic model is as follows: companies A and B create joint venture company C. A and B control half the voting rights and directors' voting rights of C, so neither has a majority. Company C is 'deadlocked,' that is, the ability of A or B (or any other 'external' agent) to exercise any day-to-day control over the policies of C is excluded.

So far as the Companies Act (and FRS 2) is concerned, the argument for keeping the deadlocked joint venture off the balance sheets of both 'parents' is that it falls beyond both the specific and the general definitions of a subsidiary:

1. it matches none of the specific definitions;
2. it falls beyond the wider requirements to consolidate. In particular, though both 'parents' have participating interests, neither, it is claimed, actually exercises a dominant influence.

What of FRS 5?

FRS 5

Deadlocked joint ventures are explicitly addressed in FRS 5 via the detailed guidance for identifying the existence of quasi-subsidiaries. This includes criteria for determining whether a vehicle gives rise to benefits that are in substance no different from those that would arise were the vehicle a subsidiary:

- regard should be had to the benefits arising from the net assets of the vehicle (para. 32);

- evidence of which party gains these benefits is given by which party is exposed to the risks inherent in them (para. 32);
- in determining whether the reporting entity controls a vehicle, regard should be had to who, in practice, directs the financial and operating policies of the vehicle (para. 33);
- the ability to prevent others from directing those policies is evidence of control (para. 33);
- the ability to prevent others from enjoying the benefits arising from the vehicle's net assets is evidence of control (para. 33);
- where the financial and operating policies of a vehicle are in substance predetermined, contractually or otherwise, the party possessing control will be the one that gains the benefits arising from the net assets of the vehicle (para. 34);
- evidence of which party gains these benefits is given by which party is exposed to the risks inherent in them (para. 34).

FRS 5 thus specifically addresses the issue of control and the deadlocked vehicle in paragraph 34: where the financial and operating policies of a vehicle are in substance predetermined, contractually or otherwise, the party possessing control will be the one that gains the benefits arising from the net assets of the vehicle. Do these provisions capture the deadlocked JV company? Perhaps, but even after FRS 5, as Glasgow put it, "blatant schemes were being flogged. They were so rigged they were absurd".

Just Handle With Care

Indeed a 1994 manual on property development promoting the deadlocked joint venture as "essential" where the wish was to keep the business off balance sheet, stated that deadlock was a direct response to the Companies Act and accounting standards:

> The effect of CA 1989, and accounting standards which have followed it, is such that the management of a JVC must be far more carefully structured than in the past if it is important to the co-venturers that the JVC's borrowings remain off their respective balance sheets. This is because the Act concentrates on the substantive control of a company rather than on technical ownership . . . if the avoidance of consolidation is an objective, then the JVC must be deadlocked and care should be taken to ensure that this is in fact so. (Darlow *et al.*, 1994:26)

How could this be done? The manual recommended routes. There should usually be an equal number of directors from each parent with equal voting rights; it was important that the chairperson should not have a casting vote. The directors would be under a duty to manage the JV in accordance with the Memorandum and Articles of Association and these may be very specific in their requirements. There might be detailed provisions regarding the financial and operating policies of the JV; limits placed on directors' decision-making power by a detailed objects clause; express agreement on key decisions in advance and so on. The directors would be under a duty to exercise their powers for the benefit of the JV as defined by the Memorandum and Articles.

The idea was that, while the parents would not be able to direct the financial and operating policies of the JV – i.e. would not be able to 'control' the JV for the purposes of FRS 5 (para. 8) – the directors would be bound to comply with policies predetermined by the parents and contained in the Memorandum and Articles. The need to show independence meant that directors were more likely to be employed and remunerated by the JV itself rather than seconded from the parents; it would be staffed by its own employees rather than those seconded from the parents "in order to ensure non-consolidation" (p. 17).

The idea is to avoid consolidation by avoiding separate control by either co-venturer:

> the provisions of CA 1989 concerning off balance sheet accounting – in particular, the 'dominant influence' provisions – may mean that in the future JVCs will be more autonomous and independent from the co-venturers than they have been in the past. The desire for control must therefore be weighed against the desirability of off balance sheet accounting. (p. 27)

Darlow *et al.* try to tackle the issue of 'control' in search of loopholes. They might, of course, find another hurdle: who gets the benefits?

FRS 5 Works?

Since Darlow *et al.*'s manual, the Panel has successfully invoked FRS 5 to require consolidation of what were claimed to be deadlocked joint ventures. One of the concerns of the Panel in the ANS case was the accounting treatment of two deadlocked joint venture arrangements as associated undertakings rather than quasi-subsidiaries. In one case, in the Panel's view, the financial and operating policies of the joint venture company were substantially predetermined by underlying agreements; and through its interest in the JV ANS gained benefits arising from the net assets of the company such that it had control.

In the other case a venture capital arrangement with five venture capital funds had been set up through an intermediary. In the Panel's view the financial and operating policies were again substantially predetermined by underlying agreements. In this case ANS only held a minority of the ordinary share capital but the investor's interests were effectively limited and the Panel took the view that ANS gained benefits arising from the net assets of the company such that it had control. In the Panel's view therefore the substance of the arrangements was such that the companies were quasi-subsidiaries as defined by FRS 5. So they should not have been accounted for by the equity method but treated, as FRS 5 requires, as though they were subsidiaries. Under the accounting treatment adopted by the company only the company's share of the net assets of the companies in question was reflected in the consolidated balance sheet.

Following extended discussion between Panel and directors, the directors accepted the Panel view that the accounts did not comply with FRS 5. They accepted that the substance of the transactions was such as to require that, in accordance with FRS 5, the full amount of the JV companies' assets and liabilities should be included in the consolidated balance sheet with appropriate changes to the consolidated profit and loss account. They undertook to prepare and issue as soon as possible a revision of the two years' sets of accounts involved.

Deadlocked Joint Ventures Work?

Of course, that success does not prove the deadlocked joint venture argument is over. Bigger fish might have fought harder. The form of the joint venture could have been constructed to provide more 'bullet-proof' arguments. Who knows what the courts would have decided?

There is still expert opinion to back the argument that deadlocked joint ventures can work as legitimate off balance sheet devices. Ernst & Young certainly believe so:

> A 'deadlock' 50:50 joint venture will still be off balance sheet for both parties, but only if the two parties concerned are genuine equals in terms of both their ability to control the venture and their interests in its underlying assets. (1997:944)

Other arguments might come into play. What if the operating and financial policies are split? What if 'parents' A and B share equally the benefits and risks of the JV? What if they are split between A and B? Such a split could arise in the context of a venture capitalist 'parent' who invests heavily – takes risks – in return for a fee (possibly related to the performance of the JV), while the other parent has little risk (beyond the payment of a fixed fee) but stands to gain the benefits. Which one consolidates the JV? Should both – if and when the ASB propose this as a possibility (FRC, 1995:17)? Currently FRS 2 states that not more than one parent can have control as defined in FRS 2 para. 6.

Clearly, an undertaking, such as a bank, offering to consolidate another undertaking by creating a control relationship with it will provide a valuable service to other undertakings which do not wish to consolidate.

Companies Act to the Rescue?

Whatever the ASB decides, though, it might still meet counter arguments. Indeed the Companies Act might be brought in to counter any recommendation of proportional consolidation. The Companies Act does permit proportional consolidation of unincorporated joint ventures, but it explicitly prohibits it for a corporate joint venture (Schedule 4A, para. 19(1)). According to Ernst & Young, this is why FRS 9, on Associates and Joint Ventures, technically abolishes proportional consolidation as an option for virtually all joint ventures (Ernst & Young, A Guide to FRS 9, 1998:6).

In practice, many JVs are likely to be unincorporated. They make take the form of a partnership or limited partnership. This is so for several reasons: the JV is for a single purpose, and incorporation would present an administrative burden; the accounts of a corporate JV must be publicly filed, and this would prejudice commercial sensitivity which may be paramount; non-incorporation also gives the JV partners greater flexibility in terms of utilising tax losses.

But one potential way of circumventing the quasi-subsidiary criteria in FRS 5 would be to use a corporate joint venture and argue against proportional consolidation on the basis of the Companies Act prohibition.

Musical Chairs

Ernst & Young argue another route. Where shareholders in a 'true' 50:50 JV wish to prevent a deadlock, they might take it in turns each year to appoint the chairman (with the casting vote):

> this will mean that the joint venture will be a subsidiary undertaking of each shareholder company every second year. The question then arises, should the undertaking be consolidated, then equity accounted, in alternate years . . . In our view this would clearly be a nonsense and we believe that the appropriate treatment would be not to consolidate on the grounds that there are long-term restrictions which hinder control, but to equity account throughout. (1997:228)

Tay Homes

There are certainly examples of corporate joint ventures which have remained successfully off the balance sheet. Tay Homes, the building and construction company, set up a 50:50 joint venture company with the investment bank Barclays de Zoete Wedd (BZW) to buy show homes from Tay with funds provided by BZW. Tay was charged a licence fee for use of the properties and when sold, profits or losses would be shared 50:50. Yet Tay treated its investment in the joint venture company, in its 1995 accounts, as an associated undertaking despite expressly adopting the now mandatory provisions of FRS 5.

FRS 9

In 1997, the ASB issued FRS 9 on 'Associates and Joint Ventures'. This came into effect from June 1998. In this the ASB implemented the "radical proposal" (Ernst & Young, 1998:5) of its 1994 discussion paper by abolishing proportional consolidation for joint ventures (although it remains an option in effect for joint 'arrangements' that are not 'entities' – i.e. contractual arrangements through which the participants in the arrangement conduct their individual businesses, but which itself has no commercial identity (para. 4)).

Accordingly, under FRS 9, joint ventures should be accounted for using the 'gross equity method'. This method is substantially similar to the equity method, which is the accounting treatment for associates, but the investor's share of the assets, liabilities and turnover must be disclosed on the face of the consolidated accounts. But is this enough?

Under FRS 9 a joint venture is an

> entity in which the reporting entity holds an interest on a long-term basis and is jointly controlled by the reporting entity and one or more other venturers under a contractual agreement . . . A reporting entity jointly controls a venture with one or more other entities if none of the entities alone can control that entity but all together can do so and decisions on financial and operating policy essential to the activities, economic performance and financial position of that venture require each venturer's consent. (para. 4)

In short, joint control, which might result from a shareholders' agreement, would require gross equity accounting treatment rather than consolidation. But Ernst & Young warned (1998:14)

> there is a risk that [FRS 9] may have created an unintended opportunity for off-balance sheet financing. Suppose, for example, that a company sets up a 99%-owned subsidiary with the 1% held by a 'friendly' third party. It then puts in place a shareholders' agreement requiring unanimity on all issues, which the parent is certain will in practice be obtained. On the face of it FRS 9 requires that, as the parent has only joint control in these circumstances, the subsidiary should not be consolidated, so that its borrowings (for example) do not appear as such on the consolidated balance sheet!

While Ernst & Young consider this scheme

> blatant . . . there are bound to be cases more on the borderline. It appears that FRS 9 has readmitted at least the possibility of some of the abuses that the Companies Act 1989, and FRSs 2 and 5, were aimed at eradicating.

PLUS ÇA CHANGE

The orphan subsidiary – in one guise or another – may continue to haunt the new regime. There may still be scope for arranging devices that directors can claim lie beyond the bounds of regulation.

10
Working to Rule

Underlying many techniques of creative accounting is a strategy of what we could call 'working to rule'. This involves focusing literally and narrowly on the words of a rule, and working creatively on it.

We have seen examples of this in both the preceding chapters. A company might construct a form of transaction or corporate structure which can be claimed to fall beyond a rule imposing some disadvantage (such as bringing a debt on balance sheet), or to fit into a rule offering some advantage (such as exemption from that requirement). Being able to point to a clear rule with which one can claim compliance can be presented as a strong argument. The rule, it can be argued, is there to be complied with. The onus is on the Panel to demonstrate why the rule should not be applied. Rules are strong 'material' for creative compliance.

To pursue this strategy, however, one must first find a rule to work to, the more precise and prescriptive the better. One objective of the new regime has been to try to shift away from the detailed specific rules that are so vulnerable to being worked on and used in ways never intended or envisaged by regulators. "I hate rules", says Sir David Tweedie, and the ASB has declared itself intent on basing regulation less on specific rules and more on principles.

By adopting this approach, the ASB hopes to put an end to companies seeing compliance as a matter of ticking off specific rules rather than meeting the objectives and spirit of a regulation. The Hampel Committee on corporate governance has taken exactly the same line – opposing specific rules as leading to a 'box-ticking' approach to compliance.

FRS 5: From Rules to Principles . . .

FRS 5 is the flagship of this approach. Its avowed strength is its claim to be based on, and expressed as, principles. Anxious to stop artificial transactions which comply in form – tick all the right boxes – but not in substance, the ASB in FRS 5 has set out the principle that it is the substance of transactions, their commercial effect, that must be reported, and it stipulates in the preface that the standard should be read in the context of that objective. Does this mean companies will no longer argue on the basis of 'working to rule'? After all, to work to rule, we said, you must first find your rule. How do you work to rule with a principle?

But if FRS 5 sets out the principle of reporting substance, it also sets out a great deal more. It is in the 'great deal more' that grounds for 'working to rule' may be sought.

. . . to Rules?

Expressing a standard's requirements in terms of broad general principles proved difficult to accomplish. FRS 5 took nine years and four drafts (TR 603, ED 42, ED 49 and FRED 4) before it finally reached the standard book. One of the main reasons was repeated criticism that it was too vague, that more detailed guidance was required. The ASB responded to this pressure with guidance and clarification in a number of ways.

By the time the standard-setting process had been completed in 1994, the amount of detail and text material covered had grown to a 137-page "fat booklet" (Robert Bruce, *The Times*, 28 April 1994) comprising:

- FRS 5 (39 paragraphs: Objective – 1 paragraph, Definitions – 9 paragraphs and SSAP – 29 paragraphs, but to be "read in the context of the Objective and the definitions and also of the Foreword to Accounting Standards and the Statement of Principles for Financial Reporting currently in issue" (Foreword to FRS 5));

- Explanation Section (64 paragraphs: "part of the SSAP insofar as they assist in interpreting that statement");
- Application Notes (103 paragraphs: "part of the SSAP insofar as they assist in interpreting that statement");
- Application Notes tables and illustrations (5 tables; 4 illustrations: "an aid to understanding and . . . not . . . part of the SSAP").

The ASB stressed that the basic principles were still what mattered. But in adding detailed guidance of various sorts it may also have introduced, however reluctantly, a hostage to fortune.

Directors and their advisers may don legal blinkers, focus on the specific guidance in the standard and argue it constitutes a set of rules on how to report substance. They may then work on these rules in all the usual ways, arguing they fall inside, or outside their ambit. This was certainly the warning issued by major players as detailed guidance began to creep into the standard.

Warnings

Several commentators argued that the combination of general principles and detailed examples gave confused messages on the scope of the standard:

- "The title and stated objectives of the proposed standard are very broad, but the subsequent discussion is rather narrower." (Ernst & Young, Letter to the ASB, FRED 4, 19 April 1993)

Many commentators left the ASC and ASB in no doubt of what would happen if such material were available:

- Ernst & Young warned of "The danger of any detailed guidance . . . [which] . . . may encourage the development of avoidance schemes" (Letter to the ASC, ED 49, 1 October 1990);
- Touche Ross felt that the detailed application notes "could jeopardise the effectiveness of the standards by encouraging the design of a new breed of transactions specifically designed to avoid the apparent bounds of the standard" (Letter to the ASC, ED 49, 27 September 1990);

- Arthur Andersen in its response to the ASB on FRED 4 saw it as in danger of being "viewed as a set of detailed rules which can be scoured for apparent loopholes, inconsistencies and ambiguities to be exploited in accounting for particular transactions" (Letter to the ASC, 30 April 1993);
- British Gas expressed concern that guidance notes would be used prescriptively, with the examples "setting the standard rather than the underlying principles of the text of the standard", and since they cannot be exhaustive will be used to justify loopholes (Letter to the ASB, FRED 4, 28 April 1993);
- The CBI regarded it as likely to be effective only "as a piece of anti-avoidance legislation" since, more generally, "very detailed rules will allow much greater scope for avoidance through creativity than would broad principles" (Letter to the ASB, FRED 4, 21 May 1993);
- Many others echoed the view that the standard would, as Ernst & Young put it, "be easily sidestepped" (Letter to the ASB, FRED 4, 19 April 1993).

The view that FRS 5 still leaves room for creative accounting has continued long after the publication of the final draft.

In Search of Rules

A number of potential weak points (from the regulators' point of view) or openings (from the creative accountant's) have been, or could be, pinpointed as bases for building 'work to rule' claims to compliance:

- the application notes;
- the requirement to comply with more specific standards;
- the precedent of conceding to statute;
- the criteria for establishing substance.

Financial engineers may come up with many more.

APPLICATION NOTES

The Application Notes demonstrate how to find the substance of transactions in specific cases of consignment stock, sales and repurchase agreements, factoring of debt, securitised assets, loan transfers and, from 1998, the Private Finance Initiative. Essentially they show how transactions might be caught on substance even if not on form. The ICAEW pointed out from the beginning that these might be approached as a 'rulebook', as setting out precise criteria to be complied with or avoided:

> If a strict rulebook approach is encouraged we are unlikely to see in practice situations that exactly match those in the application notes because the originators of such "schemes" will ensure that there are differences.

We can see how this happens by looking at Application Note B, illustration 2.

Building Constructions

This refers to a housebuilder selling land to a vehicle company and providing the vehicle with a subordinated loan. When this was first drafted in 1990, it referred specifically to a loan equal to up to 40% of the consideration. According to the ICAEW, if this example was incorporated into a standard, "people would do it, but with 30% and avoid disclosure by accounting for the transaction as a sale". Ernst & Young commented:

> The danger of any detailed guidance such as this is that it may encourage the development of avoidance schemes (there is evidence that financial institutions are already thinking in these terms). (Comments to the ASC, 1 October 1990)

Thresholds and the 'Big Mistake'

Including precise thresholds such as 40% in the example was inviting trouble. SSAP 21 on leasing has demonstrated that to such an extent that Sir David Tweedie has described it as "a big mistake" (CBI Conference, 15 June 1993). Just like FRS 5, SSAP 21 aims at accounting treatments based on the substance of transactions, specifically, in this case, leases. But it gives guidance too, guidance which refers to specific thresholds. A lease is a finance lease and on the balance sheet where substantially all the risks and rewards are transferred, and:

> It should be presumed that such a transfer of risks and rewards occurs if, at the inception of the lease, the present value of the minimum lease payments, including any initial payment, amounts to substantially all (normally 90% or more) of the fair value of the leased asset. (SSAP 21, ASC, 1984, para. 15)

The presumption based on this 90% threshold can be rebutted, but only in "exceptional circumstances."

This guideline for deciding whether "substantially all the risks and rewards" have passed became an operational rule in practice: an objective 90% test. Thus, according to Ernst & Young, "the 90% test has been widely interpreted as a rule rather than a guide" (1990:714).

A 90% transfer makes the lease a finance lease and on the balance sheet. With less, it is an operating lease and off the balance sheet. Not surprisingly 88% leases have become the norm. As Sir David Tweedie put it: "With a 90% rule they all come in at 88%. If we'd made it 80%, they'd come in at 78%" (CBI Conference, 15 June 1993). Technical Release (TR) 664 (Implementation of SSAP 21 'Accounting for leases and hire purchase contracts', 1987) on the implementation of SSAP 21 on leasing, attempted to influence the practice of treating the 90% test as a firm rule:

> [The 90% test] does not provide a strict mathematical definition of a finance lease. Such a narrow interpretation would be contrary to the spirit of SSAP 21 and SSAPs generally. (para. 5)

Yet accounting for leasing this way continued as routine practice. *Company Reporting* described it in 1992 as "one of the few legitimate off-balance sheet devices". The rule-like status of the 90% test had become established.

Other Criteria

In the final version of FRS 5, illustration 2 was changed to omit precise numerical thresholds. But there were still other criteria to work to, with the aim of constructing devices claimed to fall beyond the 'rules' in the application notes.

KPMG Peat Marwick McLintock suggested (letter to the ASC, 1990) disclosure of a sale and repurchase transactions could still be avoided as follows:

i. Company A develops a property for £6 million and lets it on a long lease at a market rent. The property has a market value of £10 million. A intends to hold the property for the long term, but would like
   a. to raise funds and
   b. realise a profit.
ii. So, A sells the property to company B for £9 million, but has the right to repurchase it for £12 million (i.e. £9 million plus interest less rent received by B) in five years.
iii. If A does exercise its option, B will sell and pay A any surplus over £12 million (net of selling costs). A indemnifies B against the first £3 million of any loss.

Since A retains substantially all the risks and benefits of ownership (it is unlikely that the value of the property will fall below £9 million), the property should be on A's balance sheet. But, A owes B nothing. In law, A only has a £3 million contingent liability, which will not crystallise if property inflation averages 3.7% p.a. over five years. In other words, there is no obligation to repurchase and no, or very little, liability to the other party.

Hard or Soft Rules?

The ASB introduced another hurdle, however, by softening the status of the application notes. The firmer the rule, the more cogent the argument that it sets the reference point for what must be complied with. It might be more difficult to argue this convincingly if the application notes are 'just guidance'.

When introduced, the idea was that the notes "should be regarded as standard in relation to transactions fitting the circumstances they describe" (ED 49, para. 65). The ICAEW warned then that they should not be standard: "If this approach is adopted then it is likely to encourage a strict rulebook approach" (ICAEW Memo, ED 49). In the final version of FRS 5 the ASB changed the words on the status of the Application

Notes to make them less like mandatory rules and more like the illustrations they insist they are:

- "They shall be regarded as part of the SSAP insofar as they assist in interpreting that statement".
- The status of the illustrations had also changed. They were represented in a shaded area of the Application Notes. The tables and illustrations shown in the shaded areas were "provided as an aid to understanding and shall *not* be regarded as part of the SSAP" (Application Notes, p. 51, emphasis added).
- The Explanation Section too, like the Application Notes, has an interpretative role only: both "shall be regarded as part of the statement of standard accounting practice insofar as they assist in interpreting that statement."

Basically, what the ASB is saying is that the Application Notes in FRS 5 are illustrative not exhaustive. Coming up with something that's not on the list will not provide a means of wriggling out of the standard on the argument: 'where does it say we can't do that?' The basic principle – report substance – will catch it.

Hard Rules by the Back Door?

Do these changes remove the grounds on which companies could argue a rulebook approach to the Application Notes? Or will they seek out others? Have grounds for arguing a rulebook crept in by the back door? There may be openings in an express statement introducing the Application Notes, an express general provision in the SSAP, and an express example. These state:

- "observance of the Notes will normally be sufficient to ensure compliance with the requirements of FRS 5" (p51);
- FRS 5 also notes that while it sets out general principles relevant to reporting the substance of transactions

> other accounting standards, the *Application Notes of the FRS* and companies legislation apply general principles to particular transactions or events. It follows that where a transaction falls

within the scope of both the FRS and another accounting standard or statute, *whichever contains the more specific provisions should be applied.* (para. 43, emphasis added)

The implication is that if the Application Notes contain the more specific provisions, they, rather than the provisions of the SSAP, apply;

- This general rule is confirmed in paragraph 45 with a specific example of a sale and leaseback arrangement with an option for the seller/lessee to repurchase the asset. This arrangement is subject to SSAP 21 and Application Note B in FRS 5. According to para. 45, for some lease arrangements, and particularly for those that are merely one element of a larger arrangement, FRS 5 will contain the more specific provisions. But these more specific provisions, it states, are in Application Note B.

These express provisions, it might be argued, elevate the status of the Application Notes and bring their more specific provisions explicitly within the scope of the SSAP. This was what many commentators had warned against and which the ASB had tried to avoid when it changed the status of the Notes.

Certainly there have been examples of companies strictly following the Application Notes, to produce what might be seen as form over substance. *Company Reporting* drew attention to Stagecoach Holdings for example.

Stagecoach Holdings

In its April 1997 accounts, Stagecoach Holdings, the public transport services company, disclosed securitised assets and associated debt. The company had acquired another company, Porterbrook, an acquisition funded initially by a bridging loan but which was refinanced through a bond issue. The bond issue was secured on underlying capital lease rentals receivable by Porterbrook from Train Operating Companies, 80% of which were guaranteed by the UK government. As the bonds were secured on lease rental payments, the risk of default by the Train Operating Companies was transferred to the bondholders, with no recourse to Stagecoach and limited recourse to Porterbrook.

Yet Stagecoach showed both the debt and the assets in the balance sheet although the financial review pointed out that the debt was effectively off balance sheet in terms of the risk to the company. What the company had done though was to strictly follow the letter of Application Note D24 of FRS 5 which required this treatment (*Company Reporting*, October 1997:21).

OUT OF PRINCIPLE

Creative accountants might look to another source in FRS 5 in search of a rule to avoid a principle. FRS 5 acknowledges that transactions and events may be subject to several sources of regulation. It sets out general principles relevant to the reporting of all transactions while other FRSs, SSAPs or statutory requirements also govern the recognition of assets or liabilities and apply general principles to particular transactions and events.

Privileging the Specific

Acknowledging this, as we saw above, paragraph 13 of FRS 5 outlines what a reporting entity should do in the event of a clash or a conflict:

> Where the substance of a transaction or the treatment of any resulting asset or liability falls not only within the scope of this FRS but also directly within the scope of another FRS, a SSAP, or a specific statutory requirement . . . the standard or statute that contains *the more specific provisions(s) should be applied.* (emphasis added)

Paragraph 43 emphasises that the specific provisions should be applied to the substance of the transaction and not merely to its legal form. Nevertheless, the effect of privileging the more specific over the more general provisions may be to encourage creative compliance and the search for loopholes.

We'll look at two examples: leasing and pensions

Leasing

FRS 5 states that "In general, SSAP 21 contains the more specific provisions governing accounting for stand-alone leases" (para. 45). SSAP 21, of course, is the standard with the "big mistake", as Tweedie described it, of the 90% 'test': a very specific provision indeed. Will FRS 5 be undermined by the privileging of this test?

FRS 5 tries to emphasise substance:

> the specific provisions . . . should be applied to the substance of the transaction and not merely to its legal form and, for this purpose, the general principles of FRS 5 will be relevant (para. 43);

> the general principles of the FRS will also be relevant in ensuring that leases are classified as finance or operating leases in accordance with their substance (para. 45).

But, by privileging specific provisions over general, there is a danger that the 90% "objective test" (Mayne Nickless Europe plc, letter to the ASB, 22 March 1993) will take precedence over the emphasis on substance in FRS 5 just as it has done in SSAP 21. As we have seen, *Company Reporting* in 1992 described leasing as "one of the few legitimate off-balance sheet devices" and nothing appears to have changed, despite FRS 5. Peter Holgate (senior accounting technical partner at PricewaterhouseCoopers, a member of the ED 49 Committee and subsequently member of the UITF) stated in 1994 after the introduction of FRS 5 that the rule-like status of the 90% test had become so established that it would not be affected by FRS 5's reiteration of the need to account for substance not form: "The rule continues to be a rule and nothing in FRS 5 changes it" (BRI conference on FRS 5, 15 April 1994).

Interestingly, many companies are putting operating leases on the balance sheet since FRS 5. Indeed *Company Reporting* has observed:

> The number of companies now reclassifying operating leases as finance leases, in apparent contradiction to SSAP21, without any underlying change in the lease arrangements suggests that SSAP21 should be revised so as to exclude the '90% test'. (August 1995:8)

This suggests increased compliance with substance rather than form, though, of course, there may be many reasons other than a sense of regulatory obligation for doing this.

But the issue is: could companies find grounds to argue otherwise? And the answer would seem to be an incontrovertible 'yes'. Ernst & Young state categorically:

> The practical reality is that unless and until SSAP 21 is superseded and the 90% test abolished, preparers should continue to look to that standard when accounting for stand-alone leases that fall wholly within its parameters. (1997: 990)

And as a 1997 manual on the 'Tax and Financial Aspects of Leasing' (Collins *et al.*, 1997) put it: "Until SSAP 21 is altered, leasing will probably continue to be the principal means of obtaining off balance sheet finance in the UK" (para. 3.96).

Pension Funds

FRS 5 used the word 'quasi-subsidiaries' not 'undertakings' to bring such forms as trusts within its ambit. Pension funds – though trusts – could therefore, arguably, fall under the requirement to consolidate quasi-subsidiaries. Several commentators have argued that they should be consolidated, and indeed that to leave them out of the ambit of FRS 5 provides an opening for creativity.

KPMG Peat Marwick described as "superficial" (letter to the ASB, 30 April 1993) the reasoning in FRED 4: that pension funds do not meet the definition of a quasi-subsidiary since independent trustees are appointed to determine major issues of the fund's policy. Ernst & Young similarly questioned whether it was true as a matter of economic substance, as FRED 4 claimed, that employer companies do not have control of pension funds. According to BDO Binder Hamlyn, many pension scheme trusts give the right to the sponsoring employer to appoint trustees:

> so they are not independent in the sense that they are appointed by a third party. Of course, while trustees they must act consistently with their duties as trustees, in substance that is no different from the obligation of the directors of a subsidiary company to act in the best interests of their company rather [sic] the interests of the parent company. (Letter to the ASB, 26 April 1993)

In any event, Ernst & Young argued:

> there is no doubt that the employer is exposed to the benefits and risks of the fund's performance and we think there is a strong case for regarding the fund as a quasi-subsidiary. (Letter to the ASB, 19 April 1993)

ESOPs Fables?

Pension obligations have been likened to ESOPs (employee share ownership plans) by Ernst & Young, and others, and in fact ESOPs have been brought within FRS 5 by the UITF in Abstract 13 (June 1995). According to the UITF, the sponsoring company has *de facto* control. This is despite the fact that ESOP trustees must act at all times in accordance with the interests of the beneficiaries under the trust – the employees. Most ESOP trusts are designed to serve the purposes of the sponsoring company and to ensure that there will be minimal risk of any conflict arising between the duties of the trustees and the interests of the company. There will be nothing to encumber implementation of its wishes in practice.

The UITF distinguishes ESOPs from pension schemes. But to many commentators, the substance of pension schemes and ESOPs can be identical – "the economics of these arrangements are similar". (Ernst & Young, 1997:905) An employer may have to meet any shortfall in the value of the shares in an ESOP trust in the same way as it would have to meet the balance of the cost necessary to provide final salary pensions: "it thus has a direct economic interest in the fund even though the scheme is operated by independent trustees" (Ernst & Young, 1997:905).

With ESOPs on the balance sheet, there would seem to be even more of a case – in substance – for the same principle applying to pension schemes.

Ruling Out

But the rule in FRS 5 of privileging the more specific standard takes pension obligations out of FRS 5. Pension obligations fall within the scope of both FRS 5 and SSAP 24 (ASC, SSAP 24,

'Accounting for Pension Costs', November 1984). SSAP 24 contains the more specific provisions and does not require consolidation of pension funds. Accordingly, FRS 5 declares, "such funds should not be consolidated as quasi-subsidiaries" (para. 44).

SSAP 24 is one of two SSAPs inherited from the ASC and identified by the ASB as most in need of attention; it has been the subject of review. But progress has been "slow and difficult" (Tweedie, FRC, 1998:35). Until it is revised, however, and this has been explicitly recognised by the ASB (FRC, 1996), it is clear that pensions surpluses and deficiencies are accepted by the regulators as legitimately off balance sheet.

This may be used as a rule in FRS 5 on which to base creative accounting schemes. Ernst & Young made no bones about the likelihood of this. Indeed, they observed that:

> The wording of the present draft has already encouraged some banks to devise off balance sheet schemes using trusts which have the ostensible objects of providing benefits to employees and claiming that they are not quasi-subsidiaries because of the analogy with pension funds. (Appendix 1 to Letter to the ASB, FRED 4, 19 April 1993)

They proposed that the standard should say that a pension fund is a quasi-subsidiary.

> If this is not done, a company will easily be able to use its pension fund as the vehicle for off balance sheet transactions. For example it could sell a property to the fund and lease it back as an operating lease; this would take the asset off balance sheet, even though it had not really surrendered any of its economic interest in the property.

Whatever Happened to Substance?

There is another point to note here. FRS 5 privileges the more specific standard (or other guidance) but it also stipulates that the more specific standard should still be applied to the substance of the transaction. Indeed this could be seen as a significant hurdle for creative accounting schemes that rely on literal use of 'rules' in FRS 5 or related standards. What the discussion of the substance of pension schemes would seem to suggest, however, is that the requirement may be easier said than done.

While Ernst & Young, KPMG, BDO Binder Hamlyn and others have argued pensions, like ESOPs, can be seen as in-substance quasi-subsidiaries, the ASB and UITF treated ESOPs and pensions as different in substance. The UITF saw pension schemes as having a longer time frame and being wider in scope "with the result that the obligations imposed by trust law and statute have a much greater commercial effect in practice" (UITF 13 Appendix 1; *Accountancy*, July 1995:144). The ASB analysed pension funds as not under the *de facto* control of the company because of independent trustees. The accounting firms disagreed.

There is clearly scope for argument over what constitutes the substance of a transaction. We will return to this later.

GETTING IN ON THE ACT

Another way to get out of FRS 5 might be to get into a different, more advantageous, category by arguing FRS 5 cannot overrule the Companies Act. Getting in on the Act therefore may be looked to as a way out of FRS 5. Companies might be able to find a rule to justify this in FRS 5 itself, in the ASB'S own concession to the Act over the case of securitisation.

Securitisation

In early drafts of the Application Notes, securitisation vehicles were treated as coming under the requirement to consolidate quasi-subsidiaries. The regulators saw securitisation as a potential problem, as Tweedie said in an interview in 1992:

> it isn't just a banking problem, it's pervasive because it could totally transform companies' balance sheets – they could securitise their head offices, stocks and debtors and argue it is non-recourse. (*Accountancy*, July 1992:30)

The ASB wanted to nip this in the bud. However, the banks lobbied against the proposal arguing that securitised assets should not be consolidated because they were non-recourse. The result was "a sensible compromise" as Allan Cook, technical director of the ASB, put it. Instead of consolidation, FRS 5 allowed for a 'linked presentation' in the accounts if strict conditions relating to recourse were fulfilled. The compromise may have been made with the best intentions. Arguably, however, the effect has been to incorporate, ironically in the very last numbered paragraph of the standard, another Achilles' heel into FRS 5.

FRS 5 and the Companies Act

The ASB's starting point for defining the entities that constitute a group are the provisions of the Companies Act 1985. Since the quasi-subsidiary does not come within the statutory definition of a subsidiary, it is "not part of that group" (para. 102). But, it should still be consolidated "in order to give a true and fair view" (ASC, ED 49). Thus, FRS 5 requires the assets, liabilities, profits, losses and cash flows of any quasi-subsidiary to be included as if they were those of a subsidiary (FRS 5 Summary, para. m).

In paragraph 102 of FRS 5, the circumstances in which a linked presentation of a quasi-subsidiary will be appropriate are explained. Again the true and fair requirement is cited in support:

> Where an item and its finance are effectively ring-fenced in a quasi-subsidiary, a true and fair view of the position of the group is given by presenting them under a linked presentation.

But, within two sentences the ASB declares:

> where the item and its finance are *similarly* ring-fenced in a subsidiary, a linked presentation may not be used. This is because the subsidiary is part of the group as *legally* defined . . . The subsidiary would be consolidated in the normal way in *accordance* with companies legislation and a linked presentation would not be used. (emphasis added)

The effect is to allow a linked presentation in a securitisation which employs a quasi-subsidiary but not if it employs a 'statutory' subsidiary undertaking.

This interpretation of the Companies Act could, of course, be challenged. The Act allows not only the provision of additional information by a company in order to present a true and fair view but also, in special circumstances where compliance with provisions is inconsistent with the requirement to give a true and fair view, it requires the departure from specific provisions. It might thus be possible (and Clifford Chance did suggest this in a letter to the ASC, 15 January 1993) to use a linked presentation for both, since they are in substance the same and it could be argued that the circumstances are special. In FRS 5, however, the ASB has not only sacrificed the goal of standardisation in financial reporting but, more significantly, it has undermined the regulatory strategy of requiring the reporting of the substance of transactions. And it has done so apparently not because of "pressure from preparers" but "in response to legal advice" (Touche Ross, response to FRED 4, 29 April 1993).

In short, it heeded the criticism that the provisions of FRS 5, despite their emphasis on reporting substance, cannot take precedence over specific statutory requirements. This has led to the clearly unsatisfactory result, from the ASB's point of view, that the accounting treatment of a quasi-subsidiary would be different from an identical in-substance subsidiary undertaking, what KPMG Peat Marwick in its comments on FRED 4 described as making "no sense" (Letter to the ASB, 4 May 1993).

A Precedent to be Used?

It has also arguably set a precedent, or conveyed a rule, that FRS 5 cannot overrule the statute, and specifically that the true and fair argument cannot be used to bring statutory subsidiaries under FRS 5. Further support for this 'rule' could be brought to bear by referring to the views of the DTI. Essentially it has taken the line that where the statutory rules are clear they should be adhered to despite the views of the standard-setters:

> The DTI has indicated that it believes the true and fair override is not available to be used in deciding not to consolidate B if A does not control B but where A meets any of the objective tests (a–d) of s. 258 in the Act to identify the parent of the subsidiary (B). (Crichton, 1990)

Scope for Creative Accounting?

What emerges from this compromise is a potential loophole the implications of which may not be lost on the innovative financial engineer:

- A quasi-subsidiary is defined in FRS 5 as a vehicle that does not fulfil the Companies Act definition(s) of a subsidiary.
- Thus, any 'vehicle' which does fulfil that definition would be "consolidated in the normal way in accordance with companies legislation" (FRS 5, para. 102) by its 'parent undertaking'.
- Such a vehicle might then be in the accounts of the 'legal parent' but not those of the 'substantive parent'.
- During the standard-setting process the ASC and ASB expressly rejected the idea that there could be two parents of a (quasi-) subsidiary. It is interesting to note that this notion is being reconsidered (FRC, 1996). Until it is changed, however, there can be only one parent. This might provide an opportunity to choose which it should be.

Could this situation allow a 'friendly third party', C, which does not mind having a vehicle, B, on its balance sheet to take it on as a statutory subsidiary undertaking and so get it off the balance sheet of A? Could it pay to fit into a statutory definition of a subsidiary and a statutory exemption rather than fall under the quasi-subsidiary provisions? There are fewer exemptions for a quasi- than for a statutory subsidiary undertaking.

And could all of this be justified with the argument that there is a rule against FRS 5 overruling the statute? If so, compliance with the Companies Act provisions will allow non-compliance with those of FRS 5, even though the subsidiary may give rise to benefits for another entity that are in substance no different from those that would arise, were the vehicle a subsidiary.

What is quite clear from interviews is that special purpose vehicles are currently being constructed to take creative advantage of the ring-fencing rule. "Ordinary corporate activities" as one corporate counsel put it, "are being repackaged as securitised assets".

ESTABLISHING SUBSTANCE

Finally, there is guidance on how to establish what the substance of a transaction is. The basic principle in FRS 5 is the principle of reporting substance. This is not, however, left as a bare injunction, to be met in any way accountants may think fit. To help preparers of accounts exercise their judgement appropriately, this basic requirement is filled out with further principles on how to determine substance.

In particular, there are criteria for identifying and recognising assets and liabilities in substance. These take the form of principles; they do not stipulate specific thresholds, detailed prescriptions or the like. But the issue is: could these principled criteria still be used to justify keeping assets or liabilities on or off the balance sheet in ways which the regulators might consider inappropriate?

Identification and Recognition Criteria

To 'determine' the substance of transactions, FRS 5 paragraph 16 declares: "it is necessary to identify whether the transaction has given rise to" new or changed "assets" or "liabilities". Assets and liabilities are defined and criteria provided to assist in their identification:

- *assets* are rights or other access to future economic benefits controlled by an entity as a result of past transactions or events (para. 2; see too ASB Statement of Principles, para. 3.5). Evidence of an asset is given if the entity is exposed to the risks inherent in the benefits, taking into account the likelihood of those risks having a commercial effect in practice (para. 17). This means that companies cannot escape disclosure merely by excluding or removing loss-making quasi-subsidiaries;
- *liabilities* are an entity's obligations to transfer economic benefits as a result of past transactions or events (para. 4; see too Statement of Principles, para. 3.21). Evidence of a liability is given if there is some circumstance in which the entity is unable to avoid, legally or commercially, an outflow of benefits (para. 18).

In the GRE case, where the Panel wanted 'equalisation reserves' included in the group accounts, the company (and others) could point to this definition to argue that they were not liabilities and should be excluded.

FRS 5 also deals with the question of what to do when the substance has been determined. Disclosure is not automatic and there are further criteria to assist preparers decide whether or not to recognise the assets and liabilities in the balance sheet. Where a transaction results in an item that "meets the definition of an asset or liability" it should be disclosed on the balance sheet if there is sufficient evidence of its existence and the item can be measured at a monetary amount with sufficient reliability (para. 20).

Sufficient Reliability

In effect, then, there is a series of 'tests' to determine substance, all of which may be susceptible to creative compliance. One route might be to have items whose amounts cannot be measured with 'sufficient reliability'. When it comes to liabilities the ASB has argued 'less reliability' will do: it is more important to reveal risks than to omit them despite insufficiently reliable measurement. Nonetheless even here 'a reasonable estimate' of the amount is still required for recognition.

It is not difficult to envisage techniques being developed to ensure that the monetary amount of items (which might previously have been measurable with reliability) cannot now be reliably measured, even via a reasonable estimate. One potential device was outlined by an accountant who subsequently became a member of UITF: the monetary value of the financing elements of 'earn-outs' or other deferred consideration depends on future, unpredictable, events (Peter Holgate at 15 April 1994 Conference on FRS 5). While such liabilities may be significant, they are 'vague' and can thereby escape disclosure under these 'literal' interpretations of para. 20:

- the item should *not* be disclosed *unless* its monetary amount can be measured with sufficient reliability; or
- the item should *not* be disclosed if its monetary value *cannot* be disclosed with sufficient reliability.

The issue of risks versus rewards/benefits is, as we have seen, vitally important when it comes, for example, to the treatment of deadlocked joint ventures.

Principles Ruled Out?

What these examples suggest is that there may be scope for arguments that the principles of FRS 5 are either defined or limited by 'rules' within it. Companies may challenge regulation by seeking them out and working to rule.

11
Substance Abuse and Counter Strikes

How can you 'work to rule' with a principle, we asked in Chapter 10 – and concluded that one way is to find rules to *substitute* for the principle. There is another way. Even a principle may be scrutinised for literal meaning and used to justify creative accounting techniques.

CREATIVE COMPLIANCE WITH SUBSTANCE

This approach can be illustrated by experience in the USA of 'in-substance defeasance'.

In-substance Defeasance

In-substance defeasance is a device to remove debt from the balance sheet. Even though the debt has not been repaid, it is acknowledged as 'extinguished' and officially *allowed* to remain off the balance sheet.

In the 1980s, in the USA, this situation could be accomplished by a company purchasing virtually riskless government securities and placing them in an irrevocable trust. The sole purpose of the trust would be to meet the cash payments due on a company's debt. The company would thereby be freed from making any further payments on the debt as long as the cash flows on the trust's riskless assets matched those promised on the company's debt. In *substance*, therefore, it was argued, the debt would be eliminated, even though in law the liability remained. The debt could then be taken off the balance sheet by off-setting the trust investment against the liability. The purchased securities were also removed from the balance sheet. In the USA, this was expressly permitted under SFAS No 76 in 1983 (FASB, 1983).

However, defeasance was then extended as a basis for creative accounting. Wall Street bankers developed 'instantaneous in-substance defeasance' (Rosenblatt, 1984). Newly issued debt rather than existing debt was defeased in a form of arbitrage transaction. For example, a US corporation could borrow DM100 million at 8% and use it to buy DM100 million German government security yielding 8¼% in trust to cover the debt *and* create an excess. Not only would the debt be extinguished; a gain was also recognised.

UK Defeasance?

Debt defeasance has also been used as the basis for creative devices in the UK. Securities would be bought in at an amount below the book value of the existing debt. If, for example, a company had £100 of debt with a coupon rate of 5% and interest rates generally were 10%, the company could expect to buy £100 worth of government securities to service the debt for about £50. Tweedie was one of the first to draw attention to this practice in 1988:

> It has not escaped the notice of companies that the income statement can benefit when their debt is retired at a time when market interest rates are at a level higher than those existing when the debt was first issued. (Tweedie, 1988)

In this example, a company will have removed £100 debt, but only £50 cash from its balance sheet. So it can record a gain of £50 in its income statement.

There has been some question as to whether defeasance is lawful under the offset provisions of the Companies Act. It would be ironic if the requirement to report substance in FRS 5 were to be used to legitimise substance-based creative compliance. Responding to FRED 4, and the proposals on 'linked presentations' (which were subsequently introduced to FRS 5) Coopers & Lybrand asked for clarification as to how defeasance should be accounted for since "It appears that the proposals in the draft FRS may for example allow in-substance debt defeasance, which has so far been regarded as illegal in the UK" (Letter to the ASB, FRED 4, 30 April 1993).

Derivatives

The approach might be tried in other contexts too. In 1998, the ASB issued FRS 13, its "first instalment" on rules on derivatives (Ernst & Young, FRS 13, 1998:6), requiring both narrative and numerical disclosures. If, as seems likely, in a subsequent standard it adopts a 'substance' approach to the recognition and measurement of devices such as forward contracts and futures and foreign exchange and interest rate swaps, a problem similar to the defeasance example may occur. Companies use such instruments to hedge against risks but also to take speculative positions to make gains. The dangers became apparent in 1998 with the exposure of the 'hedge' fund, Long-Term Capital Management.

The US Solution

Ron Paterson of Ernst & Young, in his book on FRED 4, 'Off Balance Sheet Finance' (1993), also looked at defeasance in the UK context. In his view, defeasance would only be possible if the lender was a party to the defeasance agreement "which will generally not be the case" (p. 104). A substantially similar position now operates in the USA.

The FASB, in the USA, tackled creative compliance with defeasance regulations in 1984. It indicated that the practices which emerged were not what it intended with SFAS No 76; it accordingly introduced a specific rule. The proximity of the borrowing and the acquisition of securities it argued suggested that these arrangements were 'borrow-and-invest' activities, rather than the true elimination of debt; so, they should be reported as borrowing and investment rather than defeasance (FASB Technical Bulletin No. 84–4, 'In-Substance Defeasance of Debt', issued October 1984). In other words, instantaneous in-substance defeasance should be left *on* the balance sheet.

More recently, SFAS 76 has been withdrawn and replaced by SFAS 125 ('Accounting for Transfers and Servicing of Financial Assets and Extinguishment of Liabilities', FASB, June 1996). Under this, debt is considered extinguished when *either* the debtor pays the creditor and is relieved of its obligation for the liability *or* the debtor is legally released as the primary obligor under the debt, either judicially or by the creditor. A major difference between the old and the new regulation is the role given to the creditor. Under SFAS 125, it is no longer possible to have extinguishment of debt without the creditor becoming aware that it has occurred.

Acknowledging Defeat?

The perceived need for a regulatory response, however – first, producing a specific rule to plug the loophole, then changing the regulation more generally – was a clear acknowledgement by the regulators that they accepted the device as legally effective, as falling beyond the ambit of their then control. The example demonstrates also how even a broad principle-based approach, such as the requirement to report substance, may be used creatively to achieve objectives *not* envisaged or approved by regulators. It demonstrates how even a regulation based on reporting substance might be used to justify creative accounting.

Will the broad concepts in the new UK financial reporting framework be approached in the same way?

12
The Panel Strikes Back

There is then a whole range of ways of looking for loopholes – searching for gaps, ex-files, boundaries, rules, even finding form in substance by treating the words of principles literally.

Arguing a practice is perfectly legal does not, of course, necessarily mean that argument is accepted – however persuasively the letter of the law is pointed to in support. The Panel might challenge the company's defence in either, or both, of two ways.

Battling Over the Small Print

It might respond in kind, taking just as technical an approach, reading the regulations just as narrowly, but coming up with a different answer. The Panel might disagree with the way the company has read and applied the small print of the law. Or it might point to different small print – different words, provisions, criteria, rules – to argue the Panel's view, not the company's is 'perfectly legal'.

The Panel might, however, as well or instead, confront the company on more 'substantive' grounds. It might accept the company has complied with the small print but not with the principles of statute or standard. It might invoke the wider weapons of the law to 'look through' the technical arguments or to 'override' them.

LOOKING THROUGH LOOPHOLES

The Panel might turn to FRS 5 to argue that however accurate the company's technical analysis of the legal form of a transaction is, it is not what counts. It is the substance that counts for accounting, and the substance requires a different treatment altogether. In terms of *form* the treatment may be perfectly legal; in terms of *substance* it is not.

Overriding Technical Compliance

Or the Panel might invoke the true and fair override to argue that even acknowledged compliance with the small print is not enough if the result is not true and fair accounts. The Companies Act *expressly* requires companies to *depart* from specific rules if it is necessary to give a true and fair view. So does the ASB's Foreword to Accounting Standards. There are ex-files the Panel can draw on too to argue technical compliance is not necessarily enough. Looking for loopholes and pleading the result is perfectly legal won't do.

Filling Gaps

And that goes for 'gaps' too. The where-does-it-say-I-can't-do-that argument won't do, the Panel could respond. There may be areas where there are no specific rules. But there is a general rule: give a true and fair view. The treatment you have chosen, in the absence of specific rules, the Panel might argue, does not result in true and fair accounts. It is still therefore in breach of the law.

Practice and Promise

This kind of approach would be exactly what we might expect of a regime geared to principles, substance and the spirit of the law. Has the Panel taken this approach in practice?

The Panel has looked through form to substance in ANS, though, if we were to be pernickety, we'd have to note that the Panel appears to have been applying a 'rule' in FRS 5 – the who-gets-the-benefit criterion set out in paragraph 34 – rather than just the bare principle of finding substance. Still, the substance approach has been used to look through the loophole of at least one form of deadlocked joint venture. Arguments over companies departing from rules have also involved discussions of the substance of the deals involved.

The Panel has rejected directors' views of what constitutes a true and fair view in the absence of rules. It has used 'true and fair' to fill gaps. Indeed the Trafalgar House case could be seen as a gap-filling exercise. When it set out to investigate Trafalgar, the Panel was not in fact requiring Trafalgar to anticipate a UITF abstract but imposing what *it* saw as true and fair accounting. There was then no UITF abstract to anticipate. It seems that Chinese walls between the ASB/UITF and the Panel were operating embarrassingly effectively. The Panel was pursuing Trafalgar, and the UITF pursuing the kind of practices for which Trafalgar was attracting publicity, at the same time without realising it. In the RMC case, the Panel has been seen as filling gaps in the law to the point of making "a major extension to the true and fair view requirement" (Brian Singleton-Green, *Accountancy*, June 1998:3).

The true and fair override has not yet been used to reject the claim of compliance with rules. On the contrary much corrective action has been about bringing companies back into line *with* rules. Given the structure of whistleblowing this might not be surprising. One of the Panel's routine flags for investigation is directors' declarations of departures from rules in order to give a true and fair view. The Panel has on several occasions rejected directors' departures. It has not, however, *enforced* departures itself on the basis that technical compliance with rules does not give a true and fair view.

Nonetheless the promise of the new regime is that principles, purposes and substance can be brought into play to counter creative accounting based on narrow, literal and technical readings of regulations that do not result in true and fair accounts. Recent cases – ANS and RMC – could be taken as signs of both the kicking in of FRS 5 as a new weapon of control, and a more assertive deployment by the Panel of the true and fair requirement. Might directors defending themselves on the basis of loopholes find their efforts confronted by a no-nonsense approach by the Panel?

Certainly, the rhetoric of the Panel is very much in line with this. Glasgow put it like this:

> Where we are firmly of the view that accounts are not true and fair, we will not be deterred from taking action by the fact that there is room for forensic argument as to technical compliance with a particular SSAP. (FRC, 1992:24)

A Second Front

How might companies respond then? They might simply accept that the new weapon, substance over form, and the old one, the overriding requirement to give a true and fair view, with an agency now to enforce it, have emerged triumphant.

If directors see a practice as 'blatant abuse' they had hoped to get away with, or if they think others might see it in this light, they might be reluctant to let the case go to court. In an era where substance over form is being pressed by the regulators, directors might not want to expose themselves to comment that, technically legal or not, this is not playing the game; it reflects an approach that is artificial and opportunistic.

One barrister distinguished his client's case from others based on arguments over form and substance. He could, he said, "understand why the directors of those companies did not want to defend in court the treatments they had adopted".

However, if the 'technically perfectly legal' argument is rejected by the Panel, or ruled out by directors themselves, there may be a series of 'second front' arguments on which to attack. Directors might challenge the *judgement* of the Panel, or they might challenge the *authority* and *reach* of the new weapons themselves. We look at these issues in Part IV.

PART IV

ENFORCEABILITY: CHALLENGING THE REGULATORS

13
Whose Substance is it Anyway?

FRS 5, with its focus on substance not form, tackles head on the claim that technical compliance with the literal word of regulations makes a practice 'perfectly legal'. But what if companies contest the Panel's view of what constitutes substance? Companies could argue they *have* reported the substance of transactions. It is the Panel that has got it wrong. The issue becomes: whose substance is it anyway?

THE SMELL TEST

According to Sir David Tweedie: accounting should be intuitive. He talks of the smell test: "if it doesn't smell right, it's wrong". He and others have advocated a 'common-sense' approach to the interpretation of accounting standards. In FRS 5, this means applying economic and commercial criteria to determine the appropriate accounting treatment. Throughout FRS 5 and its accompanying notes, the emphasis on 'commercial effects' of transactions is repeatedly stated – in its objective (paras 1, 30), its definitions (for example, of the substance of transactions (para. 14), the approach it requires (paras 51, 52, 61, 62) and its Application Notes. "Whatever the substance of a transaction it will normally have commercial logic for each of the parties to it" says FRS 5. If it appears to lack such logic, this may indicate that not all related parts of the transaction have been identified or that the commercial effect of some element of the transaction has been incorrectly assessed (para. 51).

Similarly, to assess commercial effects, for example, of an option, "It should be assumed that each of the parties will act in accordance with its economic interests" (para. 62).

But, these comments beg several questions: whose common sense, whose substance, whose commercial judgement, whose sense of smell?

Whose True and Fair?

The same goes for true and fair. The Panel has said it will not hesitate to take action against a company if it does not give a true and fair view. But what if the company argues it *has*, and its view is legitimate?

The issue could arise where there are no specific rules, where there are specific rules but the company has departed from them to give a true and fair view, or where the Panel thinks the company which has followed specific rules should depart from them to give a true and fair view. In each case the company could reply: our reporting *is* true and fair.

Subjectivity

What is going on is a clash of subjective interpretations – in good faith or otherwise – over what is substance, what is true and fair, what *is* creative accounting, in the particular circumstances of the case. Indeed the law could be seen as recognising the scope for different interpretations of such broad principles.

The law requires only that *a* true and fair view be provided. Does this not imply that a company could argue to have complied with the law even if it is also acknowledged that the ASB's or the Panel's view is different? The courts have already acknowledged that different opinions are legitimate. In the *Lloyd Cheyham* case (1987) it was said by the judge that an accountant

> of very considerable ability . . . underestimated the extent to which other professional practitioners could responsibly adopt different practices from that which he could adopt.

Grey Areas

The Panel acknowledges there are 'grey areas' and that these may cause difficulties:

> The grey areas are a real problem. We are dealing with what are necessarily very sophisticated rules, designed to meet the needs of a huge variety of industries and commercial concerns. There is bound to be room for honest debate and difference of opinion. (Glasgow, *Accountancy*, April 1993:36)

So, how can the Panel *require* a particular treatment if there is no clear mandate?

Pentos (PN28)

Pentos was questioned by the Panel about its 1993 treatment of reverse premiums received in respect of property leases. The Panel noted that:

> existing requirements in the law and accounting standards did not provide unequivocal guidance as to the correct accounting treatment of reverse premiums.

But it did not seek to fill the gap itself; it drew the matter to the attention of the ASB. UITF Abstract 12 was the result.

Edwin Glasgow has explained the rationale for this approach:

> During the course of its work the Panel encounters a number of grey areas in financial reporting – i.e. areas where there may be some genuine uncertainty or divergence of practice. Where the point at issue appears to the Panel to be a clear contravention of the Act or accounting standards it plainly falls within the Panel's remit and is pursued in that context. But where the ground is less certain it is a very important function of the Panel to draw such matters to the attention of Accounting Standards Board or, where appropriate, other regulators. Because it is highly desirable that uncertainties or ambiguities should be tackled as quickly as possible the ASB's Urgent Issues Task Force has a particularly important part to play, and the Panel is grateful for its support. (FRC, 1996:33)

Glasgow believes that the notion of grey areas can be played on. He is sceptical of some directors who resort to the 'it's a grey area' argument: "that's when I reach for my revolver. They know perfectly well what the rule is. It's just that they haven't succeeded in keeping within it."

Certainly a number of companies have argued 'grey areas' and that their treatment is fair and appropriate – though not all have succeeded.

Caradon (PN34)

Caradon showed its non-equity interests (7.25% Convertible Cumulative Redeemable Preference Shares of 15p) as £24.3 million on its 1994 balance sheet – their nominal value. The amount attributable to non-equity interests calculated in accordance with FRS 4, however, was £163.1 million. The company described the issue as a "grey area" and the way it had accounted for non-equity as reflecting "reality and common sense" (*FT*, 9 November 1995). Its auditors, Price Waterhouse, had not qualified the accounts. The Panel disagreed, and insisted that the shares should have reflected the cash received on issue rather than the nominal value which was "of little relevance" (*FT*, 9 November 1995). The directors 'corrected' this treatment in the company's 1995 interim results statement and promised to ensure that the analysis of shareholders' rights in the 1995 accounts would contain the information required by FRS 4.

Forte (PN7)

Forte, however, fared better. Donald Main, finance director (and subsequently ASB member), successfully countered a Panel inquiry on Forte's non-depreciation of assets. He argued:

> Our philosophy is that we invest heavily in our property on a regular basis to maintain and improve the buildings so they appreciate in value. There is no logic in depreciating them. (*FT*, 5 February 1992)

In Forte's accounts for the year to 31 January 1991, land and buildings held freehold on long leases were valued at £2.7 billion compared with £2.6 billion for the previous year. Donald

Main said the company spent about £91 million in 1990 improving buildings. The Panel accepted Forte's explanation. Allan Cook, technical director of the ASB, acknowledged: "This whole area is in dispute at the moment. We will not dodge the issue but we want to address it as a whole and not slate individual companies" (*FT*, 5 February 1992).

Black v. White Areas

Experience in the making of FRS 5 shows considerable scope for diverse opinions, even in the abstract, on what substance is. We saw in Chapter 10, for example, that some of the major accounting firms have been at odds with the ASB over what constitutes the substance of pension funds. In this case Ernst & Young analysed the nature of pension funds to conclude they constituted quasi-subsidiaries and should be on balance sheet. The ASB, however, analysed them and decided they were not quasi-subsidiaries and should be off the balance sheet.

This suggests not so much that there may be grey areas where no one is quite clear what the appropriate treatment is, but 'black v. white areas', where different parties are quite clear what the appropriate treatment is, but hold widely divergent views. We've seen evidence of this more generally in auditor comment on Panel decisions.

Early in the new regime, *Company Reporting* (December 1992; March 1993) suggested that disagreement with ASB standards was leading to a "growing tendency" for companies to use the true and fair override to opt out of accounting requirements: "These companies find the ASB's opinion of what represents a true and fair view to be at odds with their opinion." Several examples were given by the *Financial Times* in 1993:

- non-depreciation of investment properties, as specified in SSAP 19;
- offsetting government grants from non-depreciating fixed assets – notably infrastructure of the water companies;
- placing convertible capital bonds in the balance sheet in reserves rather than under long-term creditors;
- deducting goodwill from gross shareholders' funds to provide a net figure, rather than showing it separately;

- non-consolidation of investments by investment trusts and venture capital companies;
- non-consolidation of subsidiaries held for disposal;
- commodity brokers showing investments at market value, and passing any increases in value through the profit and loss account (*FT*, 6 January 1993).

Norman Mazure, chairman of Shield Group, put the issue in a nutshell. When faced with a Panel investigation of the company's non-compliance with SSAP 6 (PN6): "We believe the standard gave the wrong answer" (*FT*, 1 February 1992). This is an argument which has occasionally been put – and registered – by industry members of the ASB.

FRS 7, 'Fair Values in Acquisition Accounting' (ASB, 1994), "probably one of most controversial" (Kirk, 1995: 52) of the FRSs was only passed by a majority vote and Donald Main recorded a dissenting opinion which

> represents the general view of most accountants in industry. He believes that the ASB has gone too far in totally banning reorganisation provisions at the date of takeover. In his belief the purchase consideration would have been adjusted by the acquirer to take account of future costs/reorganisations and should therefore be permitted. (*ibid*)

More recently, there has been controversy over the question of what is the substance of a transaction, in the context of the Private Finance Initiative (PFI).

Private Finance Initiative

For a long time in 1997–98, the Treasury and the ASB were at loggerheads over the accounting treatment of PFIs. According to the ASB:

> in a typical PFI contract, a private sector 'operator' constructs a capital asset (examples are roads, bridges, hospitals, prisons, offices, computer systems and schools) and uses the asset to provide services to a public sector 'purchaser'. (ASB PN122, 10 September 1998)

The concern, according to Tweedie had been that the assets and liabilities under PFI contracts end up on nobody's balance sheet

(*The Times*, 10 September 1998). The ASB took the stance that, under FRS 5, the government should not pretend that PFI property assets are owned by the private suppliers; if the risks of ownership remain with the government they should be brought onto the balance sheets of government departments.

The essence of the dispute was whether elements of the services provided under PFI contracts should be separated out in the accounts. The ASB said they should, because they can bear profits or losses; the risk of owning property should be assessed even if they are mixed up in service payments.

The Treasury said they should not. It is, it said, buying in services, and since the liabilities are passed to the private sector, they should be off the balance sheet. Removing assets and the matching liabilities to pay for them would be advantageous to government accounting figures for the public sector borrowing requirement, which reflect cash, income and spending.

The Treasury presented its approach as perfectly legal. As the ASB's Foreword to Accounting Standards states (para. 21), the prescription of accounting requirements for the public sector is a "matter for the government". But the ASB added:

> it can be expected that the government's requirements in such cases will normally accord with the principles underlying the Board's pronouncements, except where in the particular circumstances of the public sector bodies concerned the government considers these principles to be inappropriate or considers others to be more appropriate.

Nonetheless, the Treasury disagreed with the ASB's view of the substance of PFIs – and was "confident that ours is the correct basis". It followed the tactic of enlisting expert opinion in support: "and so are a number of PFI experts outside the Treasury" (*Accountancy*, January 1998:14).

The Faculty and Institute of Actuaries sided with the Treasury describing the ASB's draft as "fundamentally flawed". It "betrays a complete misunderstanding of how PFI works" (*Accountancy*, April 1998:13) The CBI, while backing the ASB's bid to bring government accounting into line with the corporate sector, expressed concern about the ASB's analysis and offered its services to the ASB, which it saw as "lacking expertise" (*Accountancy*, April 1998:13). The door has been left open for a critique of the appropriateness of ASB – or Panel – expertise in judging matters of commercial substance.

The controversy underlined the possibility of there being more than one interpretation of 'substance' and directly raised the issue of 'whose substance counts?'. As Brian Singleton-Green observed:

> We do not know whether the ASB has got this one right. There are serious arguments on both sides of the case. (*Accountancy*, February 1998:13)

Has the Panel got it Right?

If there have been so many "serious arguments on both sides" on what substance means in the making of standards – has the ASB got it right? – there can clearly be "serious arguments on both sides" when it comes to *applying* them – has the Panel got it right? The Panel is conscious of the subjectivity issue. According to Glasgow, it will go ahead only on the basis of a "clear consensus" among Panel members.

COMMERCIAL SUBSTANCE

A particular can of worms could be opened by the ASB's emphasis on *commercial* substance. Disagreement over this might boil down to credibility.

Commercial Credibility

How credible would the Panel be on this issue vis-à-vis companies backed by big accountancy firms? Any specific Panel team will normally include an auditor and a representative of industry or finance (someone who can, as one regulator put it, say "I've been there and would definitely not do that" or indeed "even I wouldn't have done that!"). The range of expertise is important for the Panel's commercial credibility. "My Panel members were all working people" as Glasgow put it.

Nonetheless, one leading accountant criticised the Panel as "driven by lawyers who don't have an accounting background". He himself had

> fundamentally disagreed with a number of the Panel's decisions. I had assumed the Panel would act only on issues where the big firms' technical partners would agree with them. But on a number of occasions they have *all* disagreed.

If commercial substance becomes a significant issue, a likely scenario is the development of an industry in expert opinions on what the commercial substance of a particular transaction is.

At its meetings or hearings, the Panel encourages auditor participation and is "prepared to receive representations . . . from third parties where it appears to the Panel they may have relevant information to contribute" (Working Procedures, para. 10). But what if these opinions conflict with the Panel's? What if the Panel finds itself lined up against experts from the entire accounting establishment as expert witnesses for the other side?

Proving Commercial Substance

Commercial substance may seem clear enough on the surface but prove more open to argument when the surface is scratched. Consider British Airways' treatment of leases.

British Airways

BA leased a number of jumbo jets but they were not treated as finance leases, and so were not reported in the accounts. Instead, as was revealed in BA's privatisation documents, they were treated as 'extendible operating leases', with options to return. They were accordingly off balance sheet. In the words of Ian Griffiths: "This is rather odd. It is one thing to rent a photocopier; it is something else entirely to rent a Jumbo jet" (1995:125). Put another way: how can BA be an airline company without its jumbo jets on its balance sheet?

ACCA, in commenting on FRED 4 that there may well be "circumstances when it could be argued that operating leases should be placed on the balance sheet", gave as an example "when an airline holds its aircraft through certain long-term leasing leases" (Letter to ASB, 30 April 1993). FRS 5, too, refers to commercial commitments without strict legal obligations: for example, a party "may need the asset to use on an ongoing basis in its business" (p. 63). This could cover the BA situation: BA had a legal option to return jets but arguably a commercial necessity to remain in business as an airline company *with* aircraft. It cannot 'walk away' from its aircraft and still be an airline. Or can it?

Certainly, citing FRS 5, BA *has* brought the leasing arrangements of 24 aircraft on balance sheet in its accounts for the year ending 31 March 1995. The related lease commitments will be included under lease obligations. This could be seen as another victory for the new regime and for FRS 5, one of the 'below the waterline' victories the regime may have achieved, i.e. without the need to investigate and to cajole the company into compliance. But problems may still exist if the company, especially one as large as BA, had decided to resist.

First, according to the company:

> operating lease arrangements allow the Group to terminate the leases after a limited period, normally every five to seven years, without further material financial obligation.

In other words, BA could, under the terms of its leasing agreement, return aircraft without penalty or further liability. And, this apparently is exactly what BA did in 1994. Five jumbo jets were returned, not apparently because of Review Panel interest in BA's accounts (although we cannot know this), but allegedly because of BA's ever-increasing efficiency in the use of aircraft. Thus, the operating lease treatment of the aircraft could be seen as appropriate; the options were real ones. This leads to a second point.

BA could also argue that it, not the Panel, can better assess the 'commercial reality' of the situation. After all, the argument would go, BA did not get to where it is today – not only the 'world's favourite airline' but one of the most profitable – by not having a sophisticated commercial expertise. It should be given credit for increasing efficiency rather than criticised for accounting treatments that 'outsiders' would regard as inappropriate.

Of course, the Panel might itself respond with the question: how far are your profits themselves a product of off balance sheet financing? Citing FRS 5, BA also decided to consolidate its 49% associated undertakings in TAT European Airlines and Deutsche BA as quasi-subsidiaries of the company. As a result of these changes, profits were affected, albeit only slightly: a reduction of £3 million on first half profits after tax of £256 million (*Accountancy*, January 1995:86). According to BA, the annual negative effect will progressively diminish and become favourable around the year 2002.

Whether or not the impact in earlier years may have been much more significant can only be guessed at. The value of fleet assets and related borrowings were increased by about £870 million and £905 million respectively (BA Annual Report). Opening reserves were reduced by £52 million, of which around £45 million reflected the additional depreciation and interest that would have been charged under FRS 5 in the earlier years of the operating leases. All in all, the ratio of net debt to total capital increased by 10.5 points to 64% (*Accountancy*, January 1995).

LEGAL SUBSTANCE?

Companies might have another ploy to try. An unknown issue is how the courts will sustain enforcement of commercial substance. They may well do so, listening to an army of experts on each side. But companies might point to past cases in several closely related legal settings to argue that the concept of 'substance over form' in the context of transactions means *legal* substance, not the commercial substance set out by the ASB in FRS 5. Indeed, this has been the general judicial approach taken to this question. Were judges to adopt a similar attitude to FRS 5, the Panel might find one of its key weapons severely compromised.

In 'sale or loan' transactions, while all may agree that "it is the substance of the transaction that has to be looked at and not just the form" (Mr Justice Knox, *Re Curtain Dream*, 1990), in the *Re George Inglefield* case (1933), Lord Justice Romer observed, "to point out that it is a transaction of financing throws *no* light on the question *we* have to determine" (p. 27, emphasis added). The Law Society Company Law Committee said the same thing in relation to proposals that were incorporated into FRS 5 (ED 49, p. 12):

> The fact that in substance a transaction is one of financing does nothing to assist in its analysis and cannot of itself justify the accounting treatment of a sale as a loan.

Because factoring is a financing transaction and has the same effect as a loan against the security of the debt "does not mean that it is a loan and not a sale" (p. 10). The question is not whether the transaction was one of financing, but whether the financing was by means of a transaction of mortgage and charge or by means of a transaction of sale (*Re George Inglefield*, p. 27). So, to the Law Society Company Law Committee, the initial reaction of the ASC to treat a sale and repurchase agreement as a financing rather than a sale was "prejudiced" (p. 16) and a "fundamental weakness" (p. 12) in the application notes of ED 49.

While the ASC, the ASB and, by implication, the Review Panel find the substance following an analysis of the *commercial* effect of a transaction, lawyers find the substance after consideration of the *legal* rights and obligations of the parties to be derived from an examination of the true agreement between them. Whereas the ASB and Panel, in their analysis, concentrate on the ends of the transaction, lawyers acting for companies may emphasise the means (see generally, Tolley, 1988, pp. 225–227). One produces the economic substance; the other produces the legal substance. Companies could argue it is the latter that matters in court.

Artificial tax avoidance was tackled in the courts by looking through the form to the substance. The ASB and FRC have drawn parallels between the new regime in financial reporting and the 'new approach' in tax. But the new approach in tax looked through form to *legal* substance *not* commercial substance: "the true nature of the *legal* obligation and nothing else is 'the substance'" (Lord Wright, in *Ramsay*, 1981, emphasis added).

Polly Peck International (PPI)

This judicial approach to 'substance' has been confirmed in a recent case involving Polly Peck International, a company regularly featured in creative accounting books (see e.g. Smith, 1992; *Re Polly Peck*, 1996). Between 1987 and 1990, PPI arranged eight bond issues representing £400 million in all from various banks. The bonds were unsecured, unsubordinated fixed-rate bearer bonds issued by a wholly owned special purpose subsidiary of PPI, Polly Peck International Finance Ltd. PPIF was incorporated in the Cayman Islands and guaranteed by PPI. PPI was placed in administration in 1990 and in May 1995 a scheme of arrangement was approved. PPIF was placed in creditors' voluntary liquidation in March 1995.

The supervisors of the PPI scheme of arrangement asked the court whether the court might 'lift the corporate veil' so as to prevent PPIF from maintaining a claim against them separate from that of the bondholders. In other words, should the two claims, by PPI and PPIF, given their close connection, be treated as claims in respect of the same debt? The judge, Mr Justice Robert Walker, refused. He commented that "when the law is looking for the substance of a matter, it is normally looking for its *legal* substance, not its economic substance (if different)" (p. 444). He thus looked at the legal documentation to discover what the substance was. He also noted that the separate legal existence of group companies were particularly important – and should therefore be respected – when creditors became involved. In other words, in these circumstances, he would be reluctant to 'lift the corporate veil' – to look beyond the legal form – to identify the commercial substance.

It is possible that similar reasoning could be used in a financial reporting group accounts context. By arguing that the legal authority for a substance over form approach is for legal rather than commercial substance, the ASB's approach and the power of the Review Panel could be challenged.

Conclusion

Where there are no clear rules, or the area in question is grey, a company may be well placed to counter the Panel's view. This may be true even in areas that are not 'grey', but are governed by specific rules. The Panel has, on several occasions, rejected companies' use of the true and fair override to depart from specific rules and required adherence to them. Could companies, however, challenge the Panel on the basis of what is true and fair? Challenging the Panel's judgement of what is commercial substance or requiring it to show that a true and fair view has not been given may thus put the Panel on the defensive.

This chapter has looked at how companies might challenge the Panel on the basis of 'whose sense of smell?' But a different set of challenges could arise over the legitimacy of the Panel's enforcement of substance or true and fair. We'll look at these in Chapters 14 and 15.

14
Challenging Accounting Standards

When the Panel challenges companies' accounts on the basis that they do not report the substance of transactions, it is enforcing FRS 5, an accounting standard. The Panel's legal authority, however, is to examine accounts to see whether they comply with the requirements of the Companies Act 1985. Is compliance with accounting standards, or with all aspects of accounting standards, necessary under the law to comply with the requirements of the Companies Act?

The ASB has gone to considerable lengths to argue this is the case. It has done so in order to bring its standards under the aegis of the Panel and to ensure the threat of the court is available to enforce them. The Panel has been explicit and consistent on how it sees its role in relation to accounting standards:

> a main focus is on material departures from accounting standards where such a departure results in the accounts in question not giving a true and fair view as required by the Act. (Panel Press Notices)

The requirement to comply with accounting standards in order to give a true and fair view is one of the key weapons of the new regulatory regime. And in enforcing them, the Panel would no doubt argue, as did Mary Arden QC (as she then was), that:

> an accounting standard which the court holds must be complied with to meet the true and fair requirement become[s], in cases

> where it is applicable, a *source of law* in itself in the widest sense of that term. (ASB, Foreword to Accounting Standards 1993: Appendix, para. 15, emphasis added; see Appendix 1)

But, could the Panel's authority to enforce accounting standards be challenged? Could the legal status, authority and power of the ASB and of its standards be questioned? The claim that there is a symbiotic link between accounting standards and true and fair is no more than that: an assertion backed by counsel's opinion. Could companies reject the assertion and counter the opinion? By doing so, they could seek to undermine the Panel's authority to enforce standards, and so undermine the power of standards themselves.

THE STATUS OF ACCOUNTING STANDARDS

As we have seen, accounting standards were accorded statutory status for the first time in the Companies Act 1989. But, while they may be *referred* to in the Act, nowhere is there any explicit *statutory* requirement that they be *complied* with. What the statute *does* say is that companies must state that accounts have been prepared in accordance with applicable accounting standards and that, *if not*, particulars of any material departure from standards, and the reasons for it, shall be given (Companies Act, Sched. 4 para. 36A, emphasis added). It does not say that departures are *not* permitted and as Mrs Justice Arden put it "It does not follow from this that one cannot show a true and fair view without following accounting standards" (1997:676).

Source not Force?

Indeed, as the Law Commission, of which Mrs Justice Arden was until recently the chair, put it, accounting standards "do not have the force of law" (1998:15). In any case, the need to declare departures clearly implies that departures *are* envisaged. And that is all: the Dearing Committee proposal that parties departing from accounting standards should have the onus of proof that the financial statements did give a true and fair view was rejected.

There is thus *no* statutory rebuttable presumption in any legal proceedings that standards should be followed. In fact, Parliament deliberately chose *not* to give the Panel this "stronger hand" (FRC, 1991:6, 2.7) despite it being recommended by Dearing. Nor does it follow that accounts which do not comply with accounting standards will always be qualified by auditors. The record of the Panel investigations demonstrates this clearly. As for the ASB's Draft Statement of Principles and other documents, these have *no* direct legal status at all, except via reference to them in accounting standards.

In enforcing accounting standards, therefore, the Panel will ultimately have to rely on the claim that compliance with accounting standards is necessary to meet the true and fair requirement. But, is the ASB the 'custodian' of 'true and fair'? Do accounting standards have the authority to 'fill out' the meaning of true and fair? Can the ASB insist that reporting substance is 'true and fair'? An alternative view could be presented. While the aim of the ASB may well be to make accounting standards which spell out the meaning of 'true and fair' – and its role in so doing has been established – its actual powers have *not* been spelt out in statute. And while the rhetoric surrounding the ASB is full of its power and might, it could be argued that its *legal* authority to develop its own model of regulation is not beyond question.

Similarly, the legal status of accounting standards may have been enhanced by the amended Companies Act, but where is the *legal* authority for standards to fulfil the role required of them in Panel investigations? How far can the ASB go in making accounting standards? Does it, for example, have a 'blank sheet' or could it be argued that it has gone 'too far'?

BLANK SHEET?

It could, of course, be argued that the ASB does now have a great legal power. FRS 1, the ASB's very first standard, may be an example of this power in action. It requires companies to provide a cash flow statement although there is no requirement for this in the Companies Act. FRS 1 has been described as a "quantum leap in the ASB's financial reporting reform process" (Ernst & Young, 1997:1474 and 1525). The justification for FRS 1, according to the ASB, is the requirement to give a true and fair view: the cash flow statement forms

> an essential element of the information required for accounts to give a true and fair view of the state of affairs of [large] companies at the end of the financial year, and of the profit or loss for the year. Accordingly, non-compliance with the standard may be a matter to be taken into account by the Financial Reporting Review Panel or the court in any consideration of whether or not accounts comply with the Companies Act. (ASB, PN6, 26 September 1991)

It was non-compliance with FRS 1 which led the Panel to investigate Intercare's 1992 accounts (PN27). The Panel successfully persuaded the directors to comply with FRS 1 and produce a cash flow statement in its 1993 accounts. But, the ASB's claim is pure assertion and could be contested. As Ernst & Young point out, "the relevance of a statement of cash flows to the truth and fairness of the financial position or the profit or loss for the period has never been entirely clear" (1997:1477).

Of course, if the ASB has a 'blank sheet', then not only can it require a cash flow statement to be presented, it can go even further and make standards which contradict specific statutory provisions if it believes it necessary in order to give a true and fair view.

True and Fair Override

The Companies Act recognises that compliance with statutory provisions may not be *sufficient* or *consistent* with the requirement to give a true and fair view (Companies Act 1985, ss. 226(4)(5); 227(5)(6)). If the ASB *is* the custodian of true and fair, it can determine the consistency or otherwise of statutory provisions with the requirement to give a true and fair view. It could then seek to invoke a formula which is "capable of almost infinite application" (Alexander, 1993:70):

1. In circumstance X, the law says that Y is required.
2. In circumstance X, we think the law should say Z is required.

3. A true and fair view is required above all else.
4. A true and fair view is what we (accountants) say it is.
5. Accountants say that in circumstances X, a true and fair view requires Z.
6. In circumstances X, Z is required.

Both the ASC and the ASB have done exactly this, most significantly in SSAP 19.

SSAP 19

In SSAP 19, 'Accounting for Investment Properties', in 1981, the ASC invoked the true and fair override as a reason for requiring, "*as normal* practice" (Alexander, 1993:69, his emphasis) a departure from a particular requirement of company law. The EC Fourth Directive made depreciation a legal requirement and the UK government was obliged to implement this provision, which it did in the Companies Act 1981. The property industry had lobbied hard against such a requirement on the grounds that it was inappropriate to depreciate investment properties "as it is the current value of such properties which is of prime importance as a measure of performance" (Ernst & Young, 1990: 457).

According to Ernst & Young (1990:457):

> A compromise was eventually reached based on the proposition that to depreciate investment properties would lead to the financial statements not giving a true and fair view, and it was therefore necessary to invoke the 'true and fair override'. Whilst this proposition may well be debatable, it was politically expedient at the time since it provided a means of reconciling the views of all those concerned in the controversy, thus enabling SSAP 19 to be published in November 1981.

SSAP 19 thus requires all investment properties to be included in the balance sheet at open market value and to be valued regularly. The ASC acknowledged "without argument" that its provisions on depreciation of fixed assets conflicted with (what is now) the Companies Act 1985, Schedule 4, paragraph 18. This problem was addressed in paragraph 19 of the SSAP:

> The application of this Standard will usually be a departure, for the overriding purpose of giving a true and fair view, from

> the otherwise specific requirements of the law to provide a depreciation on any fixed asset which has a limited useful economic life. In this circumstance there will need to be given in the notes to the accounts 'particulars of the departure, the reasons for it, and its effect'.

A similar approach was adopted in ASC proposals to tackle the key creative accounting and off balance sheet vehicle: the 'quasi-subsidiary'. The history of this proposal suggests that counter-arguments can be constructed to challenge the ASB's authority when making standards in this way.

The Quasi-subsidiary

In ED 49, which preceded FRED 4 and FRS 5, the ASC explicitly referred to the true and fair override mechanism to justify its proposal that quasi-subsidiaries should be consolidated in group accounts:

> The nature of quasi-subsidiaries is such that their existence will often of itself constitute such special circumstances requiring them to be treated in the group accounts of the group that controls them in the same way as legally defined subsidiaries in order to give a true and fair view.

The effect of this would have been to require the 'automatic' consolidation of most quasi-subsidiaries, via the true and fair override. Consolidation would be the 'normal treatment'.

But, does the ASB have the authority to use the override mechanism in this way? Could the accounting standards which are based on it be challenged? SSAP 19 and the quasi-subsidiary proposal are not the only examples. In FRS 10 ('Goodwill and Intangible Assets'), the ASB has again invoked the override to allow companies to avoid amortising goodwill that has an indefinite life. (FRS 10, para. 18) And FRED 17, 'Measurement of Tangible Fixed Assets' (ASB, October 1997), also refers to the override in its proposed standard which will supersede SSAP 19. In fact, there are several grounds for challenging the authority of the ASB not only to use the override mechanism but to make *any* rule in an accounting standard that is *not* in compliance with statutory requirements.

European Law

Since the true and fair view concept is contained in the Fourth and Seventh Directives, the question of legal authority is no longer a matter simply of what is provided in the Companies Act. True and fair is now part of European company law and it could be argued that it should be interpreted in accordance with those Directives and the jurisprudence of the European Court of Justice.

It is a basic principle of European law that where domestic law conflicts with European law it is the latter which has 'primacy' or 'supremacy'. The ASB Foreword to Accounting Standards declares that FRSs are drafted in the context not only of UK legislation but also EC Directives "with the aim of ensuring consistency between accounting standards and the law" (para. 34).

At European level, use of the true and fair override in the standard-setting process has been frowned upon. One of the key accounting regulators, a senior official in DGXV of the European Commission, is Karel Van Hulle, an accounting law expert. He has written and spoken extensively on the implementation of the Fourth and Seventh Directives. He has pointed out that it was due to concerns about corporate *abuse* of the override – directors departing from unwanted provisions, and using the override as "a justification for bad forms of creative accounting" (Van Hulle, 1993:101; 1997:713, referring to Niessen, 1990) – that both the Fourth and Seventh Directives contained restrictions on when the override could be invoked.

Exceptional Circumstances

To prevent abuse, both Directives stated that 'derogations' – i.e. departures – can only be made from *specific* provisions and *only* in *exceptional* cases (Art. 16.5; Van Hulle's emphasis); disclosure in the notes is required of the derogation, its justification and its effects. These provisions have been transposed into UK law in the Companies Act. Since the override is only available in 'exceptional cases', it is arguable that the ASB can*not* require, as normal treatment, departures from the Act.

International Harmonization

Article 2(5) (sentence 2) of the Fourth Directive does give a national option to Member States to define the exceptional cases in which a departure might be possible and to lay down the relevant special rules. Does this provide the licence the ASB needs to make any rule? Not as far as the Contact Committee on the Accounting Directives is concerned.

The Contact Committee was set up by the Fourth Directive (Article 52), is presided over by the European Commission and is composed of Member States' and Commission representatives; it is an authoritative source of interpretation. An important function of the Contact Committee is to facilitate a harmonised application of the Fourth and Seventh Directives. The Committee has stated that the true and fair override "must be applied in relation to a given company and not in relation to all companies or a category of companies" (Commission of the European Communities, 1990). The reason for this, according to Van Hulle, is that the Directive is an instrument of international harmonization and it is difficult to reconcile harmonization with too much individual freedom. Van Hulle states that Member States may not adopt rules which derogate from the provisions of the Directive by invoking the true and fair override.

> If each Member State could set aside one or more agreed provisions of a Community Accounting Directive because it or they conflict with that Member State's perception of true and fair, we can forget harmonization. (Van Hulle, 1993:102)

Van Hulle's views and the opinion of the Contact Committee have been echoed in an Interpretative Communication adopted by the European Commission in early 1998 (98/C 16/04). In this, the Commission "comments on topics where authoritative clarification appears to be required" (para. 2). The Communication

> aims to give guidance to bodies responsible for setting accounting standards in the Member States, to accounting professionals and to investors and other users of company accounts. (Cameron McKenna, European Newsletter, March 1998:20)

It states that Member States may not use the true and fair override to

> introduce an accounting rule of a general nature which is contrary to provisions of the Directive, nor can they use [it] to create additional options allowing for accounting treatments which are not in conformity with the Directive (para. 6). (Accountancy, March 1998:11)

European legal authority could thus be cited to reject the notion of a power on the part of the ASB to issue a standard that routinely requires a departure from clear statutory or European rules.

LAW FIRST?

The implications for companies wishing to challenge the Panel are readily apparent. Accounting standards may complement, but not contradict, statutory provisions. There is no freedom on the part of the ASB because, in Van Hulle's words, "*The law must be complied with*" (1993:102, our emphasis). On this analysis, the ASB does *not* have a blank sheet in areas covered by the statute; so companies subject to a Panel investigation can always pose a challenge: is the accounting standard upon which the Panel relies in conformity with the legal requirements? Law *constrains* what the accounting regulators can do and accounting standards do not replace the need to comply with the law: it is the law which has to be applied. To support this challenge to the Panel, companies could point to recent ASC and ASB proposals as evidence of their acknowledgement of this.

FRS 2

The ASB's careful spelling out of its claims that standards have legal status and its solicitation of counsel's opinion to support it might be seen as a defensive strategy against repeated claims, for example by the Law Society Company Law Committee, on the limits of accounting standards. In ED 50, for example, the ASC sought to provide guidance on the Companies Act 1989. Immediately, its legal authority to do so was challenged. The

Committee pointed out that practising accountants will be called upon to apply the statutory requirements as well as the accounting principles contained in a standard, so concern about the ASC's interpretation of the law was more than "pedantry" (Law Society, 1990, ED 50, p. 6). According to Arthur Andersen, there was a

> need for much greater integration between the 1989 Act and the eventual SSAP . . . The approach in ED 50 to the relationship between the ED and the Act . . . may have been justified in the early days of the ASC when the law was very much less detailed than it now is and SSAPs were setting out practices in areas largely not dealt with by the law. Now that legislation is very much more detailed and covers many more areas it is necessary to recast the format of SSAPs. (Arthur Andersen, Letter to the ASC, ED 50, 30 November 1990)

ED 50 became FRS 2 under the new regime, with enhanced legal status for the ASB and its standards. But, the ASB did not challenge the idea of statutory limits.

By the time FRS 2 was published, the ASB had indeed adopted the definitions and language of the statute. FRS 2 states that its definitions should be interpreted by reference to the statute (para. 1). The Statement of Standard Accounting Practice it contains "should be interpreted by reference to the full provisions of the Act notwithstanding that the statement summarises certain provisions of the Act." In this sense, FRS 2 was less a *source* of law than *subject* or even subordinate to it.

This in turn meant that the limitations of the statute also survived. The ASC and ASB identified and sought to remedy some obvious loopholes in the statutory provisions, such as the use of the various statutory exemptions to avoid consolidation. But these proposals did not succeed. For example, the proposal in ED 50 that in some cases a parent undertaking using a statutory exemption from preparing consolidated financial statements should still consolidate as a way of making necessary additional disclosures attracted adverse comment; it was dropped. The claim – which the ASB conceded – was that standards could not remove statutory exemptions.

Directors' Stock Options

The ASB similarly dropped a proposed UITF Abstract in 1994 when it discovered it lacked strong legal backing. At that time the Companies Act contained a variety of provisions relating to directors' emoluments but it did not explicitly require the disclosure of the aggregated number of stock options by price or the option's prices applicable to each director. The ASB wished to address companies' reluctance to disclose directors' perks and was "on the verge" of issuing an Abstract. The UITF had reached a consensus (*Management Accounting*, July/August 1994:8).

But the difficulty of finding a reliable valuation method before the options were exercised and which allowed inter-company comparisons threatened the legal authority for imposing the requirement: "The UITF has received legal advice that the disclosures suggested . . . cannot be construed as being necessary to meet the legal requirements" (*ibid*); "the relevant statutory provisions do not provide the basis for a mandatory UITF statement" (*Management Accounting*, November 1994:2). So, "to protect the stature of its previous Abstracts" and to avoid "serious trouble for the Financial Reporting Review Panel" (*Accountancy*, June 1994:25), the UITF was forced to publish its first *non-mandatory* statement. Subsequently, the matter was dealt with by an amendment to the Companies Act (The Company Accounts (Disclosure of Directors' Emoluments) Regulations 1997 (SI 1997/570)).

Yet, the ASB is persisting with the SSAP 19 approach in FRED 17. It will be interesting to see how it responds to the European Commission which is understood to have written to the ASB in the wake of FRED 17 indicating that the ASB's use of the override is not acceptable (*Accountancy*, March 1998:11). It may decide to avoid any suggestion of confrontation and await standard setting at an international level. According to *Accountancy* though, "there is no indication that the ASB intends to change direction." This does not mean, however, that companies cannot challenge Panel enforcement of such standards. Again, the arguments used against ASC and ASB proposals can be cited as a precedent.

Unlawful Behaviour?

In ED 49 (a draft of FRS 5) the ASC used the override in its proposal on the quasi-subsidiary. This was the subject of a similar critique by lawyers. In comments on ED 49, the Law Society Company Law Committee asked the ASC to

> explain the relationship between practical application of the conceptual approach and of the law, both generally but particularly in relation to the override. We are at present unclear as to what that explanation might be and, without it, practising accountants could be led into a trap. (1990, ED 49, pp. 13–14)

The trap was to require accountants and company directors, on the authority of the ASB and its accounting standards, to act 'unlawfully', with all the implications that implied – both civil liability, in an era of growing concern about professional negligence litigation, and criminal liability. As *Accountancy* observed, following the European Commission interpretation of the true and fair override and the apparent determination of the ASB to proceed with FRED 17,

> All this leaves UK auditors looking vulnerable. Observers point out that, if a property investment company, for example, goes under, creditors could argue that had it depreciated its assets, the profits it reported would have been smaller, it wouldn't have paid out such high dividends and it could well be still trading. And it is the deep-pocketed auditors who signed off the accounts. (March 1998:11)

The ASC and ASB were put under similar pressure in relation to FRS 5 and their quasi-subsidiary proposals.

FRS 5

Anticipating the view later expressed by regulators, lawyers and accountants at European level, the Law Society Company Law Committee, in relation to the proposal in ED 49, also argued that the true and fair override can only be operated in legally specific circumstances:

> Where the application of ED 49 leads to a recharacterisation of a transaction which conflicts with the legal analysis . . . the

> accounting treatment is likely to result in the departure from the statutory requirements. This is lawful only if there are special circumstances which would allow the use of the override . . . where the circumstances are not 'special' then use of the override is impermissible and the transaction may not be recharacterised. (Law Society, ED 49, p. 14. See also Law Society, 1990, ED 55)

The Committee accordingly rejected the ASC proposal that the override could be applied automatically, because of the mere existence of a quasi-subsidiary or the identification of 'special circumstances' in an FRS:

> it is always necessary to consider whether the circumstances are 'special' and, if so, whether it is necessary to depart from the statutory requirements in order to give a true and fair view . . . such a process must be undergone wherever there is a conflict between the legal and accounting analysis of a transaction. (Law Society, 1990, ED 49, p. 4)

In the end, the ASB, in FRS 5, *dropped* the suggestion that the 'override in special circumstances' provision should be relied upon to justify consolidating a quasi-subsidiary. Instead it referred to the statutory requirement to provide additional information:

> Companies legislation also requires that where compliance with its provisions would not be sufficient to give a true and fair view, the necessary additional information shall be given in the accounts or in a note to them. Inclusion of a quasi-subsidiary in group financial statements is necessary in order to give a true and fair view of the group as legally defined. (FRS 5, para. 100)

But herein lies a potential escape route for companies willing to disclose in the notes (those reluctant to disclose anywhere in the financial statements will have to seek another escape route). A loophole might be found in 'note compliance'. We look at this in Chapter 15.

LAW LAST?

As we have seen, then, the 'European dimension' of financial reporting can be cited to attack Panel enforcement of particular accounting standards. A further European argument can be invoked to resist any inclusion of a quasi-subsidiary under FRS 5.

This argument was hinted at by European officials who described the provisions of the Seventh Directive as "maximalist" provisions. In other words, the argument is that not only is the ASB unable to contradict specific legal provisions, it is also unable to go beyond them, which is what FRS 5 tries to do in relation to consolidation of quasi-subsidiaries. This argument has been given strong support recently, in the same European Commission Interpretative Communication we referred to earlier. This, as we noted above, informs Member States that they may not introduce accounting rules which are contrary to the provisions of the directives. However, it goes on to state: "nor can they . . . create additional options allowing for accounting treatments which are not in conformity with the directive" (*Accountancy*, March 1998:11).

This – and more – is what the ASB in FRS 5 does: it creates an additional requirement which is not included in the directive.

THE MIGHT OF LAW REBOUNDS?

The ASB has acknowledged that it is constrained by specific legal provisions whether or not it believes they are appropriate for giving a true and fair view. The ASB would like to develop standards by "considering how its principles of accounting apply to the possible accounting options available" for a particular accounting topic. But

> in deciding what is the most appropriate treatment the Board must also consider the environment in which its standards are to be applied. The legislation with which reporting entities must comply forms an important part of that environment. Accordingly, FRSs are drafted in the context of current legislation and European Community Directives with the aim of ensuring consistency between accounting standards and the law. (ASB, Foreword to Accounting Standards, para. 34)

Paradoxically, therefore, now that the 'might of law' has been brought more clearly into play in the standard-setting process, it might be argued to actually limit the power of the ASB to make the standards it would like to make and which purport to give guidance on how to comply with the true and fair view requirement. Such a legal limit may impact on Panel enforcement too.

In the Other Corner

The ASB and the Panel could, of course, reject these arguments. On the status of accounting standards, the ASB or Panel could reply that they reflect and contribute to GAAP, and GAAP is very relevant in law. They could point to the consultation processes behind standards to support this. Mary Arden QC attached considerable significance to this in her opinion. Whatever grumblings and disagreements there may be, it could credibly be argued that the ASB has support for its standards – and it is careful to maintain it.

On the European front, Mrs Justice Arden's views could once again be used in support. She has recently argued that the Directives permit separate development of the true and fair requirement in each Member State (Arden, 1997). She points to the preamble to the Fourth Directive: "what is mandatory is the layout and minimum content. The preamble does not provide for both mandatory layout and mandatory content" (p. 679).

Citing the UK's requirement of "very extensive disclosure on transactions involving directors", she adds that Member States have power to impose additional disclosure. She also finds it "inescapable" that different accounting solutions are appropriate to different environments. And not all the accounting treatments specified in the accounting directive "result in what would be regarded throughout the European Union as a true and fair view". She concludes:

> For all these reasons . . . the accounting directives cannot preclude the separate and lively development of accounting principles in the United Kingdom within the guidelines provided by those directives. (p. 679)

There may be an equally lively debate ahead on which view wins out.

15
True and Fair: Override or Overridden?

Creative compliance – with statutory exemptions, regulatory gaps, detailed definitions and the like – threatens control precisely because it is based on specific legal and accounting rules. Rules, as we saw in Chapter 10, are strong 'material' for creative compliance.

The Panel, however, could point to the *overriding* statutory requirement to give a true and fair view. It might point to the statutory requirement on directors to give additional information or even to depart from specific provisions where literal compliance was insufficient, or inconsistent with the requirement, to give a true and fair view. To Tweedie the true and fair override is key to the control of creative accounting.

We saw in Chapter 13 one way companies could respond to the Panel's view of true and fair in a battle of subjective judgements. But where the company has creatively complied with specific rules, it has a number of additional arguments it could deploy to counter the Panel. What is the authority of the *Panel* to invoke the true and fair override? How could companies argue against the Panel's claim: "you've got to depart in order to comply with true and fair"?

TRUE AND FAIR: COMPLIANCE WITH RULES?

Companies could argue that strict and literal adherence to clear prescriptive rules is equivalent to giving a true and fair view.

Support for such a view can be found at both national and European levels. Panel enforcement *practice* has given a clear message that clear rules should be followed. This might come back to haunt it.

Ransomes (PN41) was investigated over its treatment of equity/non-equity under FRS 4. Paul Hollingsworth, the company's finance director, claimed, "we were raising some interesting issues" about the appropriate treatment. However, "they were concerned with the letter of the standard" (quoted in *Accountancy*, December 1996:41).

Indeed the Panel may have emphasised the need for compliance with clear rules even at the *expense* of giving a true and fair view. Two examples illustrate this point very clearly. The first is a case we presented in Chapter 4 as an example of Panel 'benign big gun' victory, Guardian Royal Exchange. The second is GPG.

Guardian Royal Exchange (PN49)

In 1996, GRE's UK subsidiaries were subject to a new rule. The Insurance Companies (Reserves) Act 1995 required them to maintain an 'equalisation reserve' (as had German law required GRE's German subsidiaries for many years). These are amounts set aside in 'normal years' "to meet some large unknown and unknowable loss that may or may not be incurred at some point in the future" (Brian Singleton-Green, *Accountancy*, February 1998:3). The 1995 Act also amended the Companies Act Schedule 9A so that equalisation reserves are treated as charges against the current year's profits and as liabilities of the individual insurance companies concerned. Quite clearly, then, the subsidiary companies were bound by a new rule when preparing their annual accounts, and they complied. But, what about the group accounts?

GRE's directors decided to exclude the subsidiaries' equalisation reserves. According to GRE's accounting policy:

> Equalisation reserves are over and above the provisions required to meet the anticipated ultimate cost of settlement of outstanding claims at the balance sheet date, and, as such, are not liabilities at that date. These reserves are excluded from the group accounts

> in order to ensure consistency of treatment [with GRE's subsidiaries in other countries where the creation of equalisation reserves was not a legal requirement].

The notes to the accounts set out the effects of exclusion: an increase in profit before tax, distributable shareholders' funds and earnings per share of £33 million, £75 million and 2.76p, respectively.

GRE's auditors agreed with this analysis, as did other analysts. KPMG consultant Roger Whewell pointed to FRS 5's definition of a liability as an entity's obligation to transfer economic benefits as a result of past transactions or events:

> The statutory requirement to account for a reserve as if it was a provision therefore raises the fundamental question of whether the accounts of insurance companies that are materially affected by equalisation reserves can give a 'true and fair' view. (*Accountancy*, February 1998:82)

Brian Singleton-Green, in the same issue of *Accountancy*, argued that the new legal requirement put insurance companies in a "ludicrous position . . . *No accounts that do this . . . can possibly give a true and fair view*" (p. 3; our emphasis).

Whewell concluded that GRE's approach in its group accounts was "entirely logical in terms of accounting concepts". The Panel, however, disagreed. It demanded that GRE include the equalisation reserves.

Every other UK listed insurance group had done this in their group accounts, albeit reluctantly, following the issue of a bulletin (1996/4) by the Auditing Practices Board. The Board had sought legal advice which was

> to the effect that the statutory regime did not permit an argument that the treatment of equalisation reserves as if they were provisions would be inconsistent with showing a true and fair view. The advice specifically confirmed that equalisation reserves could not be excluded from insurance companies' or groups' accounts in order to seek 'to ensure that those statements conform with generally accepted accounting principles or practice'. (Whewell, p. 82)

The Panel took the same line. It pointed out that the Companies Act requires that group accounts be prepared as if the subsidiaries in the consolidation were a single company (Sched. 4A, para. 1). And it rejected the directors' argument that adjustments could and should be made "as appropriate in accordance with GAAP" (para. 2(1)). It did so in these terms:

> the legal requirement for the inclusion as a charge and a liability in the consolidation of the subsidiaries' equalisation reserves makes the requirement *ipso facto* an element of UK GAAP both for the purposes of individual UK companies and for the consolidated accounts of a UK parent company. (PN49)

According to Whewell, the APB's interpretation, which the Panel endorsed:

> will mean that UK insurance groups' group accounts . . . will simply give a *legalistic true and fair view,* rather than the 'traditional' UK true and fair view.

The Argyll Syndrome?

The Panel won, in the sense that GRE, while strongly defending its stance, was not prepared to go to court over it. But the victory could prove a hostage to fortune in the future. Others might creatively comply with rules, and point to this case to argue that they cannot be overridden by the true and fair requirement. The Argyll syndrome could be repeated.

GPG (PN12)

GPG prepared its accounts for the year ended 30 September 1991 in accordance with the *proposed* accounting requirements outlined in an ASB exposure draft (FRED 1, The Structure of Financial Statements). The company had treated a £5.8 million profit, mainly generated by disposal of a subsidiary, as an exceptional item rather than as an extraordinary item. As a result the accounts failed to comply with two *existing* SSAPs (3 and 6).

Although the effect was to more than double both profits and earnings per share, it is highly arguable that the accounts did present a true and fair view since an accounting standard incorporating the most significant proposals of FRED 1 was subsequently issued. As Singleton-Green, writing in *Accountancy*, noted:

> This would have made a fascinating case. Again the company did not breach any of the detailed requirements of the Companies Act. The Review Panel would have had to try to persuade the court that complying with FRED 1 failed to give a true and fair view, and it would have been presenting this argument at the same time that companies generally were being compelled to comply with FRS 3 (a not fundamentally revised version of FRED 1) in order to give a true and fair view. (December 1992:117)

It was for this reason that the Panel concluded that it would take no action: "In normal circumstances . . . the Panel would be likely to seek revision of the accounts in question." Yet, according to the Panel, substitution of the proposed requirements of an exposure draft for those of an existing standard was "not acceptable"; there is a "requirement to comply with current accounting standards". But what about 'true and fair'?

Is this another hostage to fortune? Could not other companies cite the GPG investigation as a precedent for literal compliance? If GPG's claim of true and fair was rejected in the face of "current accounting standards" could not the Panel's claim be countered on the same basis? "Change the rules first" could be the response: "it's not the Panel's job to make new rules."

Separation of Powers

Companies could argue that there is a "separation of powers" in the new regulatory regime. It is the ASB (and Parliament) who makes the rules; the Panel's role is merely to enforce them. Since accounting standards gain their legal authority via the claim that compliance with them is normally necessary to give a true and fair view, companies could argue that they have complied with true and fair by following, to the letter, accounting standards.

The separation of powers idea has been specifically recognised by the new regime. According to Glasgow, it is "very important that a separation of powers between the standard setting and the standard-enforcing bodies is seen within the Financial Reporting Council" (quoted in *Accountancy*, April 1993:35). The current Panel Chairman, Peter Goldsmith QC, emphasised this point:

> The Panel is quite separate from, and independent of, the Accounting Standards Board and it has a quite different role. Its task is not to make or alter the rules, but rather to secure their enforcement as they stand . . . It is important to reiterate that the Panel's function is to secure the enforcement of the existing rules, not to make new ones. (FRC, 1998:61, 63, emphasis added)

We saw in the *Pentos* case how the Panel referred the issue of reverse premiums to the ASB and how the UITF came up with an Abstract within six months. Sir David Tweedie cited UITF 13 on ESOP trusts as a "classic example of the role of the UITF in removing diversity of practice and interpreting an existing standard where it was required" (FRC, 1996:25). Companies could argue that this is the appropriate procedure for the Panel to follow even if compliance with rules in accounting standards does not, in the opinion of the Panel, give a true and fair view. The Panel's decision to take no further action in the first Associated Nursing Services (PN11) and Williamson Tea Holdings (PN10) cases was seen by Andrew Jack of the *Financial Times* to suggest that:

> the practices currently being adopted are acceptable within existing accounting standards. Any changes to these standards need to be introduced by its sister body, the Accounting Standards Board. (*FT*, 11 August 1992)

European Level

Companies could present additional arguments, which have been cited at European level, that compliance with concrete accounting rules is equivalent to giving a true and fair view. According to Dieter Ordelheide, the

> most important source for understanding the content of the European true and fair principle are the more concrete accounting principles . . . (hereafter accounting rules) . . . An accounting method which complies with them is – irrespective of

> exceptional cases – in accordance with the general norm. (Ordelheide, 1993:81)

This has been presented as mere common sense:

> it is evident that this must be the case. The establishment of rules through a regulator makes sense only if the regulator does not establish a rule which allows the other rules to be overruled easily at the same time. No legislator would be willing to accept such an up-front capitulation. (Ordelheide, 1993:81)

The legislative history of the Fourth Directive endorses this view:

> The Council and the Commission conclude that the application of the provisions of the Directive will normally suffice to give the true and fair view desired.

This statement was the second out of 22 so-called Council Declarations which were entered in the Minutes of the Council Meeting at 25 July 1978 at which the Directive was adopted (attached to Doc. R/1961/78/(ES 93) v. 18 July 1978). According to Van Hulle, such Council declarations are very common in all areas of Community law and are often used by Member States to clarify the application of a provision of a Directive in a particular case.

Germany

In Germany, this statement, together with comments by other authoritative sources (such as Herbert Biener, who was a civil servant in the Ministry of Justice responsible for the transposition of the Directive in 1979), allows for interpreting the true and fair view of the Fourth Directive in accordance with the specific provisions of the Directive (Ordelheide, 1996). Our research in Germany suggested too that accounting there operates in practice as though the true and fair override did not exist. One accountant described German practice as follows:

> If it falls outside the definitions and the true and fair view is distorted as a result, we *should* in Germany revert to substance over form and account for economic reality. But whereas the UK

must override the specifics of law, the view in Germany is that law and GAAP lead to true and fair; there is therefore no specific override.

UK

A UK company therefore could argue that by complying with the 'specifics of law' and accounting standards a true and fair view has resulted. This may not conform with the 'British' concept of the true and fair which was 'exported' into Europe via the Fourth and Seventh Directives, but it does equate with the European law concept of true and fair which is "now filled with a legalistic system instead of a professional one" (Ordelheide, 1993:82). In other words, specific rules rather than professional judgement – or even the judgement of the Review Panel – are what constitute true and fair. The Panel cannot override them, even citing the true and fair override.

It may be then that adherence to specific 'requirements' in the Companies Act and in SSAPs and FRSs, *which have been endorsed by the ASB*, could be used as an argument to try to constrain the Panel if it sought to use the true and fair override too assertively. If there is disquiet over compliance with these requirements – especially creative compliance – the appropriate response is to demand that the ASB (or UITF) rewrite the rules, and not to allow the Panel to 'usurp' them. The argument of directors would be: we adhered to your rules; you must adhere to them too until you decide to change them for future transactions. Trafalgar House used exactly this argument with the Panel and, although it ultimately agreed to amend future accounts, it stuck firmly to the view that it was under no obligation to comply with a UITF Abstract not in force at the time of its accounts.

When is an Extension a New Rule? RMC

In the RMC case (PN51), the Panel used the true and fair requirement not to override specific rules but to deal with a regulatory vacuum. There was no rule to require the company to disclose fines, but the Panel thought they ought to be disclosed. Singleton-Green drew from this a lesson for directors: "corporate governance criteria now have to be taken into account in deciding whether an item is material to the true and fair view." But he had also noted that:

> the true and fair view requirement is fairly specific. It is not intended to cover everything that the users of accounts might wish to know about. It is restricted to the group's state of affairs at the end of the financial year, and the profit and loss for the financial year . . . the item not disclosed by RMC . . . does not look to us to be material to a true and fair view of its profit for the year. (*Accountancy*, June 1998:3)

The Panel's action was, he said, a "major extension to the true and fair view requirement". So a different lesson could have been drawn. The right of the Panel to engage in a "major extension" could have been questioned.

NOT(E) COMPLIANCE

A second strategy might be to question the *nature* of the true and fair override. Must a true and fair view be given in the numbers or can it be given in the notes?

Directors may acknowledge that following specific provisions has not led to a true and fair balance sheet or profit and loss account. In other words, the numbers in the accounts are defective. The Companies Act requires that individual company and group balance sheet and profit and loss accounts shall give a true and fair view.

But, in response to a Panel request for them to revise the numbers there could be legal grounds for directors to argue, first, that overall a true and fair view has been given and, second, that, as a result, they cannot lawfully depart from specific requirements and change the numbers.

Both propositions are based on the claim that a true and fair view has been given via the *notes* to the accounts. Let us first see why disclosure in this way could be attractive to companies. The 1980s' accounts of Rosehaugh, a property development company, illustrate this very well.

Rosehaugh

According to *Accountancy*, "Calculating the total borrowings of Rosehaugh . . . is complicated because of the interests held in 16 related companies" (February, 1990:32). In the notes to the group accounts, details of these companies were supplied in over seven pages of notes. But:

> while Rosehaugh provides a lot of information about its related companies, it requires much digging to appreciate the scale of the off balance sheet finance. (*Accountancy*, February 1990:32)

One of the problems with Rosehaugh's notes therefore, in this and in subsequent accounts, was that you had to be a "professor of accounting to get a proper picture" (Christopher Hird, House of Cards, Radio 4, 1991) of the financial position. However, in providing additional information in the notes it could argue that it had fulfilled the statutory requirement to give a true and fair view. Indeed, this was a view taken by a professor of accounting. According to Professor Ken Peasnell:

> I think they've tried to discharge their obligation to give a true and fair view by providing large amounts of additional information. Note 12, for example, is the longest note I've ever seen in a set of accounts. There is a summary of the balance sheet and income statements of the companies in which they have a related interest, and so there is lots of information; there's lots of additional descriptive information.

'Non-disclosing disclosure'

This could, however, be seen as 'non-disclosing disclosure'. Accountants interviewed in McBarnet's related research on tax avoidance talked of the 'extended disclosure' approach as a technique for obscuring 'sensitive' information, 'tucking it away' in masses of detailed small print. In note disclosure in general the information is there, and can be pointed at to demonstrate compliance with the requirements of law. But it is 'there' in a way that is not as obvious as the hard figures above it, and requires work to unravel its significance.

Tweedie and Kellas criticised the whole idea of disclosure in notes rather than numbers over a decade ago, describing it as "nonsensical":

> simply to give additional information which does not amplify the information shown in the accounts but in effect contradicts it . . . There is a world of difference between a true and fair view and the means to a true and fair view. (1987:92)

And the new regime has taken a similar view. So when, in 1994 the ASB tackled acquisition accounting and the proposition was put to it that the inadequacies of the system could be met by better disclosure, the ASB rejected it: "In the ASB's view deficient accounting cannot be put right by disclosure alone" (*Management Accounting*, November 1994:3). This is confirmed in the ASB's Draft Statement of Principles (para 6.13): "disclosure . . . does not correct or justify a misrepresentation . . . in the primary financial statements".

The Panel too has been tackling what it sees as defective 'numbers', at least where companies have departed from specific statutory requirements, for example British Gas (PN14), Intercare (PN27) and BET (PN29). As Sydney Treadgold, former Review Panel Secretary, put it in the context of the Warnford Investments case, "It is not enough just to have a qualified audit report or to disclose in the notes. You have to comply with the provisions of the Companies Act" (*FT*, 3 April 1993).

So how could companies resist if the numbers do not give a true and fair view? The answer is that they could *concede* the point, but argue that the appropriate remedy is to provide additional information in the notes. Indeed, they could claim it would be *unlawful* to depart from specific provisions.

First, the company could point to the Companies Act (ss. 226(4), 227(5)): where compliance with statutory provisions "would not be sufficient to give a true and fair view, the necessary additional information shall be given in the accounts *or in a note to them*" (emphasis added). In Chapter 14, we noted the ASB's reliance on this provision to justify requiring consolidation of quasi-subsidiaries in FRS 5. The ASB added: "inclusion of a quasi-subsidiary in group *financial statements* is necessary in order to give a true and fair view" (FRS 5, para. 100; our emphasis). But that is not what the statutory provision says. It requires the necessary additional information to be given in the accounts *or in a note to them.*

Creative compliance might lead to *numbers* which are not true and fair; the company would provide corrective information in the *notes* – Rosehaugh repeated. If the Panel still insisted on a change in the numbers – and departure from specific provisions – directors might have a second line of resistance.

The True and Fair Two-Step

The argument would be that the true and fair override is available *only* if the provision of additional information still fails to produce a true and fair view. In other words, the override is the second of a two-step process. To depart from specific provisions when a true and fair view could be given via additional information is unlawful.

In the 1980s, this was certainly the view of lawyers such as Ralph Aldwinckle. In 1989 though, the Companies Act was amended with a view both to clarifying when the override mechanism could be invoked and to making it more readily available (DTI, 1988, para. 12). The aim was to support accountants such as Tweedie who wanted even then to 'get the numbers right'. According to the DTI, this was possible under European law:

> there is no implication in Article 16 [of the Seventh Directive] that paragraph 5 [the override] can only be applied where paragraph 4 [additional information] would not be sufficient. (DTI Press Notice, 'Changes in the Definition of Subsidiary Announced' 16 August 1988, para. 12)

The amended Companies Act now states (Companies Act 1985, ss. 226(5); 227(6)), quite simply, that if in special circumstances compliance with any statutory provision is

> inconsistent with the requirement to give a true and fair view, the directors shall depart from that provision to the extent necessary to give a true and fair view.

Unlike the older version of the Act, no reference is made in these subsections to the provision of additional information.

The DTI felt the new wording would

> make it clear that in appropriate cases [the override] can be applied even though additional disclosure under section (4) might arguably be sufficient. (DTI Consultative letter, 16 August 1988)

On this basis, the Panel could demand that a company like Rosehaugh must change its numbers.

Or could it? Could a company still argue that a true and fair view can be given via additional information in the notes, for example, *without* consolidation of a quasi-subsidiary? How would Rosehaugh argue in the 1990s if there had been compliance with specific provisions felt by the Panel to be 'inconsistent' with the requirement to give a true and fair view? Is the authority given by the true and fair override as strong as intended by the DTI or desired by the regulators? Do the amended provisions of the Companies Act provide an answer to corporate resistance on the lines of: 'where does it say the notes are not sufficient and where does it say you can make me change my numbers'?

True and Fair Overridden?

A company might cite arguments put by both European and UK lawyers in support of disclosure in the notes rather than override in the numbers.

European Law

Under European law, there is a strong argument that there is *still* a two-step process which must be followed. Karel Van Hulle (1993) has argued that a two-stage process is envisaged in the text of the Fourth Directive and was certainly what those who drafted it expected. The Contact Committee on the Accounting Directives came to the same conclusion: application of a specific provision of the Directive can be waived *only* if the additional information is in itself not sufficient to give a true and fair view (Commission of the European Communities, 1990, cited in Van Hulle, 1993:102, emphasis added).

The recent European Commission Interpretative Communication, adopted in 1998 (98/C 16/04), confirms this view. Although the views expressed in the communication "do not necessarily represent the views of the Member States and should not, in themselves, impose any obligation on them" (para. 2), the European Commission states quite categorically, in relation to Article 2(3) to (5) of the Fourth Directive (the true and fair view) that:

> only where additional information is *not* sufficient to give a true and fair view can any provision of the Directive be departed from. Such a situation will only occur in exceptional cases. (para 5, emphasis added)

Germany

Germany adopted this 'additional information' approach in its transposition of the Fourth Directive. German law – para. 264(2) sentence 2 HGB to be precise – states that where, in those exceptional cases, departure from provisions is necessary in order to give a true and fair view, it shall be by way of additional information in the notes only. As Ordelheide, a German accounting expert, observes:

> Departure from the provisions of the law has not been allowed for . . . For adequate information of capital markets it makes no serious difference whether the information that gives a true and fair view in those exceptional cases is given in the notes or in the balance sheet and profit and loss account themselves . . . the application of the true and fair principle [is restricted] to the notes in case it contradicts with the provisions for the recognition and valuation of balance sheet items. (1990:13)

Ordelheide has cast his eye over UK law too and argued that the Companies Act:

> which requires that each individual part of the annual accounts has to comply with the true and fair view principle, exceeds the (true and fair) requirement of Art. 2 of the Fourth Directive. (1993:85)

By implication, therefore, European law will be complied with if, overall, a true and fair view has been given 'à la Rosehaugh':

via the notes rather than the numbers. European law can also be cited to argue that it is the overall picture which matters, not just the numbers in the balance sheet and profit and loss accounts. This interpretation has been given a boost recently by a UK legal authority.

British Courts of Law

In an article in *The European Accounting Review,* Mrs Justice Arden considered the true and fair view from the viewpoint of the British courts of law (Arden, 1997). Recognising that the ultimate legal authority is the European Court of Justice, Arden pointed out that the accounts comprise the balance sheet, the profit and loss account *and* the notes on the accounts: "These documents shall constitute a composite whole" (p. 675). And it is the accounts, as defined here, which "shall give a true and fair view".

Companies, such as Rosehaugh, could cite Arden and argue that their accounts, including the notes, present overall a true and fair view. As such, there is no need to depart from specific requirements in order to give a true and fair view.

In short, companies may employ a note disclosure strategy which protects their balance sheets and profit and loss accounts and have a legal response readily available which challenges the legal basis of invoking the override.

Law in Action

Enforcement powers could then be challenged on the grounds of enforceability. There is a whole range of ways in which the Panel might potentially be challenged, and it might potentially respond.

But how would these arguments fare in court? And what impact might they have in practice more generally? In Part II we looked at the enforcement process, in Parts III and IV we have looked at 'law' – legal arguments. Now we'll look at the role of those legal arguments *in* the enforcement process and beyond. We'll look at 'law in action'.

PART V
LAW IN ACTION

16

Law in the Courts: Or Why Lawyers Can't Give a Straight Answer

What would happen if any of these issues were to go to court? Who would win?

Statute and standards can be drawn on, as we have seen, to argue that specific practices are 'perfectly legal'. The same regulations can be drawn on to argue they are not. Which interpretation is correct? Are the arguments we have reviewed in Parts III and IV strong or weak?

These are chicken and egg questions, because there can be no certain assessment of a case as strong or weak *until* it has won or lost in court. Which argument is 'correct' means merely which would be endorsed by the courts, and there can be no certainty on that before it happens.

Second Guessing

The market for counsel's opinion is the result of this. Going to a barrister for an opinion can have several functions. Sometimes it is just to seek "a protective opinion" as one solicitor put it. It is 'insurance' in the event of problems arising in the future. We'll see more of this in Chapter 17. Barristers may, of course, hold different views on the law and how it applies in your case. If 'insurance' is the goal, the 'right' opinion – one that supports your treatment – is important.

That's why opinion shopping is common practice, though getting endorsement by the *right* lawyer is seen to be significant too. There tends to be a race to get top counsel on side if a dispute is on the horizon. "Our big mistake was not getting to leading silk first" as one corporate counsel put it. Brand name factors operate in law as in any other business.

Another function of seeking counsel's opinion, however, is to get real advice on how the courts would respond to an argument. As one solicitor put it:

> We don't go to counsel for technical advice. *We're* the specialists. We go to counsel because he'll [sic] tell you how a court will react.

One of counsel's roles, in short, is to second-guess the judges.

Unpredictability

But second-guessing is still guessing. Even if a company's legal advisers are really confident they are right, that the other side is on weak ground, "taking a flier", as another corporate counsel put it, they can't be sure they won't lose. And even if *they* think *they* themselves are "taking a flier", "being bullish", "on flimsy ground", they might win.

Indeed for some lawyers, this is the thrill – or the sport – of litigation:

> I have seldom felt more pleased with myself than when I persuaded three out of five law lords to come to a conclusion I was convinced was wrong. (Cross, 1973).

Advocacy might play a part, and so might the workings of the judges' own minds.

WHY ARE JUDGES UNPREDICTABLE?

Why are judges unpredictable? For a dispute to reach the courts, both sides must believe they can make a case, however 'flimsy' or 'bullish'. And 'fliers' may be worth taking precisely because one can never be quite sure how judges will respond.

Even if similar disputes have been brought before the courts and the judges have consistently found against cases apparently similar to your own, it is always possible judges will accept the circumstances of your case justify a different treatment. Nor can there ever be any absolute certainty that *this time* the judges won't feel it's time to take a different approach.

Law in the courts is dynamic. It does change – through subtle distinctions, or less subtly through judges overtly adopting an avowedly 'new approach'.

In the Nature of the Beast

That this variation and dynamism is possible within one body of law is partly because law in itself is complex and elusive, open to different interpretations: its application to specific facts, even more so. There may be contradictory pulls in law, each justifying reasonable but different outcomes – principles *and* rules to draw on, different cases with which to draw analogies and from which to draw different conclusions. Every rule can have its exception.

Opinion shopping among barristers underlines the scope for variable interpretation. Judges can take different approaches to interpreting the law or facts of a case in just the same way as the bar from which they are drawn. There may even be dissent between judges sitting together to decide a case, with one or more judges registering dissenting opinions.

Judges

Then there are different judicial personalities, or political persuasions. Or particular judges might have particular bees in their bonnets. A crusading judge could have a significant impact in an area like creative accounting, as Lord Templeman had in tax avoidance. A judge who saw creative accounting as making an ass of the law, might cut right through the 'perfectly legal' argument even without the benefit of new regulations. Others might consider this an over-extension of judicial authority.

JUDICIAL APPROACHES

This is in fact an old battle in law more generally. There are different views on how law should be interpreted – literally or purposively. Which approach judges take could be significant for one key issue in the control of creative accounting. It could have a significant effect on whether literal compliance with specific rules is accepted as enough to make a practice 'perfectly legal' or not – whether creative accounting based on creative compliance will succeed in the courts or fail.

Going by past records, judges could take either line.

Literalism

A recent example of literalism in the context of acknowledged creative compliance, was the *Radio Authority* case (1995). This case was on broadcasting regulation, but it had close parallels to issues in financial reporting. The creative compliance 'vehicle' was a deadlocked joint venture company and the issue was one of 'control'.

The judge in this case, Mr Justice Schiemann, saw the vehicle clearly for what it was: an attempt to escape statutory restrictions in this case on the holding of broadcasting licences. The maximum number lawfully allowed to be held by one person was six. EMAP planned to take over Radio City, but if it did so, it would hold eight licences. A deadlocked joint venture – given the name 'Newco' by the judge – solved the problem. It was 50% owned by EMAP and 50% by Schroders, the merchant bank.

As the judge observed, it was common ground that the purpose was to avoid ownership rules contained in Broadcasting Act regulations. Matters were arranged so that:

- EMAP would not have a controlling interest in Newco;
- Newco was 'deadlocked': EMAP would not have the power under the articles of association or other document regulating Newco to secure that the affairs of Newco were conducted in accordance with EMAP's wishes;
- in the management of Newco, EMAP and Schroder's formally had equal rights; and

- EMAP had no legally enforceable right to control Newco or the way Schroders exercised its powers in relation to Newco.

The court was aware that it would not be in the commercial interests of Schroders to oppose the wishes of EMAP. EMAP and Schroders also had 'call' and 'put' options: Schroders could at any time put its shares to EMAP but not to any other party: EMAP could at any time call Schroders' shares.

Despite the 'substance' of these arrangements, the court *refused* to overturn the decision of the regulator involved, the Radio Authority, that it would not treat the takeover and the proposed ownership arrangements as rendering EMAP the holder of too many radio licences. The judge was keen to "limit the scope of the judgement to what it is necessary to decide" (pp. 345–346); it was also a case of 'judicial review', the test being whether the Radio Authority's decision was a 'legally sustainable conclusion' and not whether the court would have come to the same conclusion. But creative compliance won the day. What reasons did the judge give?

The Broadcasting Act, like the Companies Act, had a test of 'control'. In this, according to the judge:

> Parliament has proceeded, not with a broad brush, but by using very detailed provisions covering nominees and various specific shareholdings and various specific methods of securing control. (p. 346)

Referring to the device used, he said Parliament:

> could have struck down this type of arrangement. It failed to do so, either by providing that the Authority is to adopt a broad brush approach or by including the present arrangement in the detailed enumeration of all sorts of possible arrangements which were to be struck down. (p. 349)

A similar, literalist, approach might be taken in a financial reporting case.

Directors or their advisers might argue a deadlocked joint venture, for example, falls beyond the definitions (specific and broader) of a subsidiary in the Companies Act, and indeed, properly structured (at least according to Ernst & Young) falls outside even FRS 5's criteria. Since Parliament and the ASB have defined a subsidiary and even a quasi-subsidiary, it might be argued, and have defined them in ways which do not include this structure, it must be legitimate. A judge taking a literalist approach might agree. David Tweedie expressed concern about the impact of a legalistic judge on an FRS 5 case.

Looking Through the Literal

However, the courts are not always literalist or narrow in their approach. There are plenty of examples of the courts taking quite a different line, refusing to be bound by literal interpretations or legal form, especially if it has been artificially manipulated.

Judges gave short shrift to the 'drug shop' that complied with the law to "be closed at 10 p.m." by closing at 10 but reopening a few minutes later. Literally complying or not, the shop lost its case. As the judge observed "no one but a lawyer would ever have thought of imputing such a meaning" to the law (Cross, 1976:60).

Purpose

Judges might look to the *purpose* of a regulation to judge the *meaning* of particular words in it. Indeed, the purposive approach has been given a potential boost in recent years by the decision in *Pepper* v. *Hart* (1993). Since this case the judges have expressly permitted themselves to look to parliamentary debate and related material, to gauge legislative intent.

Substance

Long before the new accounting regime and FRS 5, judges have been willing to determine the substance of transactions and, in the words of Lord Handworth MR, to "tear away the mask or cloak" (*Re George Inglefield*, 1993) to do so; that is, to depart from the 'literal' effect – the mere words – of legal documents. Judges say they are aware that legal documents may be "shams" (Mr Justice Knox, *Re Curtain Dream*, 1990), that the existence of a company may be a "mere cloak" for an attempt to avoid legal obligations (*Gilford Motor Company*, 1933) and that it may be necessary, on occasion, to "lift or pierce the corporate veil" of limited liability (Ottolenghi, 1990).

When it comes to looking at the commercial function of documents or giving commercial effect to a transaction, a key part of FRS 5, judges may agree with Judge Anthony Diamond QC, in the *Kredietbank Antwerp* case (1997) that "the approach should be functional rather than literal or rigid".

There is no legal constraint on such judicial approaches. Nor do they require express statutory authority – though in the area of financial reporting, the Companies Act's overriding requirement that companies give a true and fair view of their financial situation and FRS 5's requirement that companies report the substance of their transactions could be invoked as express authority.

Collateral Advantage

There are also hints that new distinctions and new lines of interpretation could be constructed – with an eye to anti-avoidance.

Mrs Justice Arden has recently argued that the true and fair requirement should be used to "prevent an abuse of the rules" (1997:677). She specifically gave the example of off balance sheet finance where "parties may enter transactions with the object of getting a collateral advantage from the accounting point of view". While, she said "it cannot be said that the parties' transactions are a sham", nonetheless:

> in certain circumstances it is possible to take the view that they should be deprived of the collateral advantage that they seek to gain from the point of view of the *disclosure* in the accounts and that the off-balance sheet vehicle should be treated as on-balance sheet for accounting purposes. (1998:678, emphasis added)

Other judges might agree with this and with Arden's earlier opinion that accounting standards should be treated as 'sources of law' in defining what was required for a true and fair view. If this approach is taken in court, the orphan subsidiary, for example, would be caught in accordance with FRS 5. So too, would other transactions or vehicles which had the object of gaining such advantage in defiance of the overriding requirement to report substance.

WHO WOULD WIN?

Many of the current senior Chancery judges are seen by the regulators as likely to take a 'sensible' line, looking beyond literal compliance to purpose and principles. Several have considerable commercial experience and the hope is that they would be commercially minded in their approach. Not, however, that that means the Panel would necessarily win.

- **Multi-layered** – The Panel has taken quite a literalist stance itself as we have seen, for example, in the GRE case. And in practice both Panel and company are likely to go for multi-layered cases, covering themselves on all sides by arguing a case on the letter of the law, on principles and on the regulator's intent.
- **Substance** – What's more, even if the judges agree with the need to comply on substance, what they will decide the substance is in any particular case remains to be seen. We've seen just how much 'reasonable disagreement' over what constitutes substance has been expressed outside the courts. How is anyone to gauge which 'reasonable' view the judges will support?
- **Purpose** – Likewise, would judicial attention to purpose ensure a decision to override compliance with specific rules, or exactly the opposite? Both parties could argue on the intent of the legislation but argue contradictory cases. The Panel could undoubtedly point to clear statements in Parliament on the Companies Act 1989, and clear policy on FRS 5, that the intent was to defeat off balance sheet finance and discourage creative compliance. Even the European Commission's proposals for the Seventh Directive could be pointed at to show concern to avoid opportunities for avoidance. On the other hand, as this reminds us, company law is European law, and the overall objective of European law could also be invoked to press a different point.

  A purposive interpretation in this context could lead to

rigid adherence to specific rules as the criterion of compliance. The purpose of European law, it could be argued (and has been, as we've seen), is to harmonise. Too ready a resort to true and fair or substance to override rules could be presented as leading to too much variation to meet the purpose of the law.

- **Principles** – Even the acknowledgement of the existence of principles does not itself rule out literalist interpretation. Judges might take a narrow view of the reach of principles, for example. They might go along with a narrow interpretation of when the true and fair override comes into play. They could interpret compliance with specific examples of what a principle means, as compliance with principles.

Cases from Scratch

In any case there are many factors going into a judicial decision. In a sense the situation in financial reporting is particularly unclear because it is virgin territory: there is no record of cases yet to examine for what line the judges have been taking. Although analogies will be drawn from other areas, the courts will, in a sense, be starting from scratch. However, in many ways, every case is a case from scratch. Each particular constellation of interpretations of facts and law, of lawyers, of judges, can be seen as unique.

It All Depends

So it's not surprising lawyers can't give a straight answer. When it comes to forecasting who would win or lose in court on the arguments we've discussed, well, it all depends.

CASES WITHOUT COURTS

How the courts would approach a case may, however, be less important than it seems, or at least important in a different way. Law in action – the practical impact of legal arguments – can be just as significant outside the courts as in them. The shadow of enforceability hangs over the whole enforcement process. In Chapter 17 we look at the importance of cases without courts, and subtler ways of winning and losing.

17
Winning Ways: From Technical to Tactical

A case may win on law – and the party pressing it win the enforceability battle – without ever going to court. What's more, there are more roles for legal arguments than *technical* wins. They may also play a *tactical* role in how the enforcement process is managed.

TECHNICAL WIN – NO CONTEST

The courts may never come into play because *enforcement* may never come into play. For the Panel to seek corrective action even out of court it must be able to claim the company has breached statute or standard. Whether it does that or not, whether it even probes a particular accounting treatment, will depend on how 'bullish' an attitude it takes in applying the law.

If judges might take a broad or narrow approach to interpreting the law, so might the Panel. Indeed the Panel might take a narrow view where the judges' would have been broader, and vice versa.

Long Arm of the Law?

Whether the Panel takes a broad or narrow view of the reach of law will affect whether it accepts, for example, claimed loopholes as lawful or is prepared to challenge them. It will affect where the Panel draws the line between acceptable and unacceptable accounting. This in turn will affect whether it *polices* or tacitly *permits* particular practices. The narrower the approach to law, the more likely first cousins of old style creative accounting practices will be allowed to continue without challenge.

We've seen how companies might assume the law has a long reach and curtail their practices without ever putting the law to the test – the Oz effect. But the opposite might also happen. The *Panel* may take a narrow view and constrain the reach of its own enforcement.

The Parts Other Laws don't Reach?

To the layperson FRS 5 and the 'true and fair' provision might seem to 'reach the parts other regulations don't reach'. We've seen how companies might argue against that. But they may never have to. The Panel may itself assume there are strict limits to the reach of even these regulatory weapons.

A Narrower View

Edwin Glasgow expressed a very clear view that there are limits on the Panel's reach, if a practice can be demonstrated to fit clearly within the letter of the law: "some people drive a coach and horses through the spirit. There are practices I happen to think are offensive but they are perfectly legal".

FRS 5, says Glasgow, cannot be used against statutory provisions. What's more, it "shouldn't be used to put right defects in other FRSs if the practice is clearly allowed by the rules". True and fair is "too blunt an instrument". It should only be used in a "really clear case of abuse of principle". It cannot be used to counter something "which Parliament, rightly or wrongly, wrote in". Goldsmith's statement on the Panel's role as enforcing law as it stands, not making it (FRC 1998:61), could be seen in the same light.

Panel rhetoric is that:

> Where we are firmly of the view that accounts are not true and fair, we will not be deterred from taking action by the fact that

> there is room for forensic argument as to technical compliance with the particular SSAP. (FRC, 1992:24)

In practice, however, the Panel may take a narrower view of its powers, and concede to technical compliance. Glasgow indeed expressed the view that the Panel was, if anything, "too quick to accept the excuse that a practice was technically all right".

Policy and practice can, of course, vary. But the enforcement record to date could largely be seen as evidence of this view in operation, though the RMC case, for example, might be seen as rather more 'bullish'.

A New Gloss on Self-regulation

To the extent that the Panel acts on these views, two conclusions can be drawn. Either there is an unusually clear consensus on the limits of weapons to control creative accounting, or the Panel is *not* taking the widest possible interpretation of its legal powers. It may in effect be constraining itself either out of belief in the limits to its powers or in preference to being constrained by the court, or held liable if it ventures into risky areas and is found to be wrong.

This could be seen as a new gloss on the concept of self-regulation – not an industry or profession regulating itself, but regulators imposing limits on their own potential powers. This is a difficult and sensitive area for regulators and we will return to it in Part VI. But it does raise the question of where the Panel draws the line on what is 'perfectly legal' and what is not, and how far those who search out loopholes can expect a technical win with no contest.

TECHNICAL WIN – AFTER CONTEST

What of companies that are investigated? An effective legal defence argued by the company may win without ever going to court. The 'perfectly legal' argument after all may be put forward in perfect good faith, and the Panel may accept it as correct.

The Panel is Persuaded

Edwin Glasgow QC has commented, for example, that in many cases where the Panel has investigated departures from rules, people

> have persuaded us that . . . although the technical letter of the standard hasn't been complied with, the result is fair and the disclosure is adequate, and the treatment overall is acceptable. (Quoted in *Accountancy*, December 1996:41)

This was made public in some of the early cases – Forte (PN7), Associated Nursing Services (the first time, PN11), and Ptarmigan.

Ptarmigan Holdings (PN25)

Ptarmigan Holdings changed its policy for goodwill arising on consolidation. It used to write it off immediately to reserves in respect of all acquisitions. The policy was changed to one which capitalised goodwill on acquisition and amortised it over its estimated useful economic life. The company satisfied the Panel that there were special reasons for departing from the requirement that accounting policies should be applied consistently from one financial year to the next. The only action required was a fuller explanation in future accounts and in the listing particulars.

Most cases resulting in an outcome of "no cause of action" are, of course, never publicised.

The Panel Concedes

The 'perfectly legal' argument can also be a cynical tactic. Even if it is – and even if it is recognised as such – the Panel may, as we have seen, reluctantly concede it is within the law.

Sidelining the Issue

Legal arguments may help companies 'win' in another way. They may convince the Panel the area is sufficiently grey that they should refer the issue to the UITF for a ruling on *future* practice rather than take action against the company itself. This is what the Panel did in the Pentos case (PN28).

In the case of Forte's non-depreciation of fixed assets questioned by the Panel, but accepted, Allan Cook, technical director of the ASB, commented: "This whole area is in dispute at the moment. We will not dodge the issue but we want to address it as a whole and not slate individual companies" (*FT*, 5 February 1992).

Below the Regulatory Waterline

There is a good deal of talk about what goes on 'below the waterline', meaning corporate practice. But there is also 'below the waterline' *regulatory* practice.

The policy of confidentiality for companies investigated but cleared means the public record of investigations is currently confined almost exclusively to cases where the Panel has successfully required corrective action. There is no systematic publicity on the battles the Panel has chosen not to fight. The message is rather one-sided. We don't hear about the 'Panel-beaters'.

FROM TECHNICAL TO TACTICAL

A legal case in support of an accounting treatment may also be used by companies to *manage* the enforcement process. Legal cases are not merely esoteric technicalities for lawyers to argue out in court. On the contrary, legal arguments have *tactical* significance in the enforcement process as a whole.

Few cases ever go to court – in any area of law. Until an authoritative decision is reached in court, legal arguments are never more than untested claims. And *unless* they go to court that is the only status they ever have. But in one sense, what the law 'is', what the courts would decide, may not matter. Much of the time, the reality of the enforcement process is less about what judges decide, and more about strategies in the shadow of what judges *might* decide.

Bluff

In that sense relying on legal arguments *out* of court is like a game of bluff. No one can really be sure who holds the winning legal cards until they are played in court. But holding legal cards – regardless of whether they would win or lose in court – can still be vital in a number of ways. Being able to make a legal case for your actions matters out of court as well as in it.

Indeed, when it comes to winning and losing, *tactical* uses of technical arguments *outside* the courts may be just as significant as who would carry the day if the case ever went before the judges. A legal case can play a part both in pre-empting enforcement altogether, and in tempering its outcomes.

Pre-empting Enforcement

Legal arguments may help a company 'win' by pre-empting whistle blowing, so pre-empting detection and in turn pre-empting enforcement of the law.

The first potential whistleblower is the auditor. If auditors can be won over, accounts will not be qualified and one source of whistle blowing will be silenced. The reality of auditor independence has been questioned in recent years, as we have seen. But *even* if auditors are inclined to give directors the benefit of the doubt, they will want to know there is a case for doing so. Companies are always "looking for techniques to try on us", as one senior auditor put it. Auditors are on the line in Panel investigations. Indeed auditors have found themselves in the very uncomfortable position of having to take the rap if they are to have any chance of keeping the audit: the ultimate defence for directors is "the auditor said it was OK".

Research by Fearnley and colleagues suggests, indeed, that adverse findings by the Panel have a much greater impact on the audit firm than the client (*Accountancy*, August 1998:18). Given this, auditors are more likely to endorse practices if they are covered themselves by arguments that can be pointed to in the event of issues of auditor liability, perhaps to third parties, or disciplinary procedures, arising in the future.

Directors are required to blow the whistle *on themselves* if they depart from specific requirements in order to give a true and fair view but, where companies do not agree a particular practice is a departure from the Act, they do not report it (Chapter 3). If challenged they would contest, on legal grounds, any legal obligation to blow the whistle. What's more, there is no requirement to draw attention to practices that can be claimed to comply with specific requirements, even if *others* think they do *not* result in a true and fair view. Practices that can be claimed to comply with rules may therefore avoid detection by avoiding the obligation on directors to blow the whistle on themselves.

TEMPERING OUTCOMES

Where the Panel makes it clear it is not persuaded by a company's argument, the company might decide its best strategy is *not* to challenge the Panel in court, with all the risks that implies, but to optimise the settlement out of court. This means deflecting the potential sanctions of revision, costs and adverse publicity. For some indeed, that might mean securing an outcome where the benefits of a season of creative accounting have been reaped at relatively low costs.

In short the optimum strategy might be not to fight to the death for a zero sum outcome in the court, but to secure 'benign' enforcement from the Panel out of it. There are two ways to do this, and legal arguments are vital to both. The first is to persuade the Panel that the directors have acted in good faith.

Encouraging Softly, Softly Enforcement: Good Faith

A softly softly approach by the Panel may help ensure a company concedes to it. But having a legal argument to support its decision may also help a company ensure the Panel does take a softly, softly approach. Even if a company decides early in an investigation to concede to the Panel's view, it may still be important to the outcome to convince the Panel that the disputed treatment was selected in good faith. Regulators tend to take a harder line with those it sees as morally culpable (Hawkins, 1984). Evidence of good faith could therefore be expected to act as a mitigating factor, and help encourage a softly, softly approach.

Recall British Gas's 'double-counting' of three months' profits in its 1991 accounts through a change of year end, boosting profits by £1 billion. This was seen by the Panel as failing to meet the requirements of the Companies Act. However, it required no more of the company than that it alter this in its comparative figures in the following year's accounts. The Panel declared in the Press Notice that it accepted "the directors' assurance that there was no intention to mislead and that the company had acted in good faith".

By contrast, three of the seven revisions have involved two companies – Butte Mining (twice) and Associated Nursing Services (required to revise two years' sets of accounts) – whose 'moral credentials' – could be said to be suspect. Both were recidivists, in the sense that the Panel had investigated them more than once (although ANS was cleared the first time), while four directors of Butte Mining were being investigated and prosecuted by the Serious Fraud Office. Eventually, in 1998, three directors were jailed.

The Panel is not always convinced by protests of good faith. Lists of legal arguments, references to legal and accounting advice, grey areas, honest error may be taken with a pinch of salt. The Panel is only too aware of the 'good faith but not in good faith' problem. 'Mistakes' can be strategic. As Glasgow put it:

> We're not complete fools and it often becomes abundantly and amusingly apparent why a particular 'mistake' has been made. (*FT*, 28 September 1993)

But there is always an element of uncertainty: were the directors acting in good faith or not? What would the courts think? Would riding roughshod over these arguments lead to judicial review?

In any case companies can deploy other tactics to try to secure a 'benign' settlement.

Bargaining

For the Panel as well as the company, as we saw in Chapter 6, there are major advantages in settling out of court. This can create scope for negotiation. To come to the negotiating table the necessary bargaining chips are legal arguments.

Deflecting Sanctions

The objective of negotiation (in the absence of simple withdrawal by the Panel) will be to deflect the Panel's toughest sanctions – revision, costs and adverse publicity. Limiting the level of corrective action required, and co-operating on the public presentation of a case may be in part a product of 'benign' enforcement policy. But it is also clear that they are the product of negotiation. The Panel has been quite explicit in discussions with companies that it will not insist on formal revision *if* the directors are willing to make the necessary changes 'voluntarily'. Co-operation on publicity can also go beyond co-ordinating Panel and company press releases to bargaining over the content and timing of the Panel's own press notice, with companies making clear, for example, that securing a 'voluntary' change of policy would be 'assisted' if the Panel were to modify the way it presents the case in public.

Likewise, though delay is seen by the Panel as a problem, it is also the case that the Panel has shown itself willing to defer – briefly – a press release to suit corporate strategy for handling its public relations. All of this can be seen as bargaining in the shadow of the company's legal arguments.

The target of legal arguments may be wider than the Panel. It may be a matter of managing shareholder reaction, or judicial attitudes to the payment of costs if a case should go to court.

A Wider Audience: Damage Limitation

Winning and losing may be measured by companies in terms of how adverse the *commercial* consequences are. Legal argument can play a part here too. Damage limitation – on reputation, share price, shareholder confidence and so on – may be fostered by PR on the director's belief, with expert support, that the practice in question is lawful. Comment in the press against the Panel's legal position – or the law – can be a useful support too. Any threat to GRE's image over its brush with the Panel may well have been countered by the article in *Accountancy* by KPMG consultant, Roger Whewell, on the issues involved, and by the accompanying editorial, which saw the situation GRE had been placed in as "ludicrous" and not true and fair (Chapter 15) (*Accountancy*, February 1998). The legal stance taken by GRE was thus fully endorsed to a significant public at the same time as the Panel's press release.

The effect of the Panel's weapon of adverse publicity may be tempered by a refusal by directors to concede on legal grounds, and indeed by a willingness to counter attack. The important audience for directors may be not so much the Panel, as shareholders, analysts, the press. So, one company investigated by the Panel, and putting up a strong defence, could note that:

> the analysts probably think we're right, the institutional shareholders probably think we're right, the small shareholders don't care. It wasn't even mentioned at our AGM.

Not that this can always be assumed, of course. Trafalgar House's legal and accounting opinions did not stop its shareholders reacting with anger.

Costs

Directors have looked to legal arguments as a means of insuring against, and indeed pre-empting, being held personally liable in the event of compulsory revision by the courts. One corporate counsel described the discussion, at a full board meeting, of the potential risks involved in adopting a specific – controversial – accounting treatment, for which the Board believed it had a strong legal case.

The Companies Act states that the court, in making its order regarding costs (regarding both the court case and the preparation of revised accounts),

> shall have regard to whether the approving director knew or ought to have known that the accounts were defective and may exclude a director from the order or order the payment of different amounts by different directors. (s. 245B(5))

Judges, thought the board, would be unlikely to impose personal liability on directors who had clearly taken legal advice and had a legal case to support their decision.

Liability or Fraud Insurance

This way of thinking – planning ahead and covering against contingencies in the future – underlies most significant corporate decisions. Few directors, in financial reporting or any other area, want to be vulnerable to civil suits – or even criminal prosecutions – or to the criticism by press, shareholders or anyone else that they have been engaging in shady activity.

Ensuring there is a legal case to support decisions, however apparently strong or weak, provides that cover. Legal advice can be seen as fraud or liability insurance.

TACTICAL SUCCESS

The 'perfectly legal' argument, let it be repeated, may be put forward by directors in perfect good faith. It may also be a more cynical tactic, or a matter of practical risk management in an uncertain legal environment. Whatever the motivation, the 'correctness' of the legal argument must always be to a greater or lesser extent uncertain in the absence of a court decision. That goes for both sides. Edwin Glasgow told us the Panel would not take on a case it did not believe would win in the courts, and he expresses confidence that it would have won in any of the cases to date. But the Panel cannot know for sure what the outcome of a court case would be. After all, corporate counsel told us exactly the same thing.

In the meantime, however, the Panel can, and has, put pressure on companies to go along with its views, been seen as additional pressure on auditors to keep companies in line, acted as a catalyst for shareholders' hanging cases, all without going to court. We have seen the case for arguing the out of court success of the Panel in Chapter 4.

Companies too, however, may accomplish degrees of success on the back of untested legal arguments. Bluff, it might ultimately be, but bluff can be experienced as a very successful tactic by both sides.

For practical purposes the uncertain legal status of a case may not matter. Having legal grounds for an accounting decision will be important even if it *cannot* be known whether these grounds would win in court or not. Likewise for Panel intervention. For either side the case may still prove strong or weak *tactically*. If it serves its purpose it is strong for practical purposes. It is tactically effective whether it would have succeeded in court or not.

And whether it would have succeeded in court or not, we may never know. Indeed one measure of tactical success – for both sides – is optimising the outcome without resort to the courts, without the collateral damage of litigation, and without risking an uncertain judgement.

18
A Wider Lens

So far our focus has been on specific combats between Panel and companies. But the new regime also aims to exercise control by means other than the Panel and the courts. For a full picture a wider view is required. Indeed, even Panel enforcement needs to be set in the context of broader factors that can influence its operation. This chapter looks at enforcement – and enforceability – through a wider lens.

BEYOND THE PANEL

Though the Panel is the formal institutional agency for legal enforcement, in practice other mechanisms are employed directly by the ASB to enforce law and standards, and other resources are drawn on. The ASB has three potential mechanisms for enforcement without – or before – the Panel: the press, auditors and the UITF. The DTI can also play a significant role.

The Press

The press is an important whistle blower for the Panel, as we saw in Chapter 3, and adverse publicity is an important sanction for directors producing what the Panel sees as defective accounts. The ASB works hard to keep the press on side, and it uses the press *directly itself* to enforce its standards.

The ASB uses the press to put moral pressure on companies even where a company knows it can defend itself technically on what the ASB see as a legalistic interpretation of the issue. If the press implies the company is on the wrong side *morally*, Tweedie argues, a legal win might still do it little good, and the fear of that might pre-empt a company trying it on.

When companies engaged in what the ASB saw as an unacceptable practice over goodwill – buying another company for let's say £500 million, categorising £300 million as goodwill, leaving a purchase price of the rest of £200 million, subsequently selling at £220 million, in substance a disastrous loss, but recording it as £20 million profit – the ASB took on the companies directly via the press. It drew attention to the practice, and "named names". To Tweedie, the companies had "stuck their necks out and got them chopped off".

Auditors

Auditors are the first line of control vis-à-vis corporate creative accounting, and the ASB has tried to get them on side and to strengthen their position. Auditors were written to early on by the new regime, informing them of the increased exposure of directors, under the Companies Act 1989, to liability in relation to company accounts. The hope was that, with the Panel behind them, and the courts behind the Panel, auditors would be more robust in withstanding pressure from directors and more willing – and able – to support the new accounting standards; that they would be able to withstand, as one regulator put it:

> the chairman who says 'I didn't ask you if it was right or not. I asked you if you want to audit it or not.' Now the auditor can say, 'it's not a question of *our* view. If we gave you a clean bill of health, we'd both end up before the Panel. I can tell you that from experience. And we'll make it plain it wasn't on our advice.'

And there is some sense that this has happened. As one technical partner put it, "we tend to use the Panel as a stick to wave at companies". On the other hand the same partner observed a tendency for auditors to advise "*less* disclosure than they used to". Current research by Beattie and colleagues should shed more light on the subtleties of the auditor's role in the new regime (Beattie *et al.*, 1997).

What is clear, however, is that part of the ASB's policy is to try to use auditors to prevent creative accounting. One means of doing this is to issue auditors with pre-emptive warnings on specific issues even in the absence of a standard.

When a practice of which the ASB disapproves comes to its attention, a practice with no specific rule against it, the ASB will prime auditors with the information that the practice will not be tolerated. Doing this makes the ASB's view clear, so, it hopes, discouraging auditors from going along with the practice and setting a precedent for others. It removes from auditors the justification that they did not know the ASB would disapprove. It could also strengthen the auditor's hand in resisting corporate pressure. The ASB's argument is 'you're not going to win so do you want to lose in public or toe the line now?'

This could be seen as enforcement 'below the waterline' via ASB management of auditors rather than intervention by the Panel afterwards.

Managing GAAP

Auditor support has been important in other ways. Early in the new regime, for example, there was concern over the legal status of UITF abstracts. Could they be *enforced*? The treatment of UITF abstracts as standards – endorsed by Arden's opinion – was, in a real sense, 'bluff'. The UITF had no status as a standard-setting body. But the ASB constructed 'consensus' by persuading the big firms to agree that they would follow UITF abstracts in audit. Representatives of the firms, plus on-side industrialists and public interest spokesmen then supported this, so a generally accepted accounting practice was created.

The ASB can be seen as seeking to control what is taken as GAAP not only formally, by issuing authoritative standards, but informally, by managing practice.

The UITF

UITF action – and the threat of it – is another weapon for control which the ASB can use directly. The availability of a body which can (in theory at least; in practice it could get swamped) produce instant pseudo-standards, lends weight to dark threats by the ASB that there's no point in taking a particular line because it will be stopped.

Everybody's Doing It

Threat of the UITF is used particularly to counter 'combined attacks' where a whole sector acts in concert to produce in effect *their* GAAP. The Panel might not feel equipped or funded to "take on a dozen banks" as Tweedie put it, but the UITF can, by treating the issue as a generic problem to be handled by a new UITF abstract.

The UITF is a weapon for counter-attacking a legal case that the practice is true and fair, *because* it is generally accepted practice, because *everybody's* doing it. The UITF is a mechanism by which the regulators can seek to stay in control of GAAP and therefore of the legal battle over what is true and fair.

A Drift to Rules

Two issues should be borne in mind here, however. First, the UITF could become a threat to the principles-not-rules approach which the new regime says it wants. The UITF by its nature tends to deal with quite specific issues as they arise. The danger is that the regime will end up with a rule for everything, and rules, as we know, can be used counter purposively. The ASB – or Panel – may insist the principle is what matters – and may succeed, but the more detailed rules there are, the more companies may argue they are only following orders.

There's also the problem that rules don't cover everything leaving continuing scope for avoidance, so that one rule may lead not to control but simply to another rule. There has already been experience of this with UITF abstracts.

UITF 3, 'Treatment of Goodwill on Disposal of a Business' (December 1991), addressed the problem of goodwill, taken to reserves on the acquisition of a subsidiary, bypassing the profit and loss account on disposal of that subsidiary. UITF 3 ruled that goodwill should be taken into account in the calculation of the gain or loss on disposal. But, just one year after issuing the Abstract, the UITF had noted that some companies were applying it in an "unsatisfactory manner" and another ruling was required (UITF Information Sheet No. 6, 17 December 1992).

Some had presented the goodwill debit in the profit and loss account separately from, rather than as part of, the profit and loss on disposal. The Abstract did not clearly indicate, as the UITF now did in its subsequent statement, that the goodwill element should be included *as part* of the profit or loss on disposal, and not distanced from it as a separate item.

Others had credited, in the profit and loss account, before the deduction of dividends, an amount equal to the goodwill element of the profit or loss on disposal, "thereby mitigating the impact on the bottom line of the profit and loss account". The UITF stated that while it is acceptable to show that dividends are paid out of accumulated reserves, this should not be done in such a way that implies that the profit for the period is calculated after crediting the goodwill release.

One rule simply led to the revelation of continuing problems and another rule to stop them. This is precisely the cat and mouse situation that the new regime was seeking to avoid by focusing on principles rather than prescriptive rules.

The DTI

The ASB looks to the DTI for backup in a number of ways. It hopes the DTI would provide funding if the war chest proves inadequate, as we saw in Chapter 3. But it counts on more substantive support too. Certainly David Tweedie hopes that if "we fought on a standard and lost, the DTI would change the law".

As a strategy this would have to be viewed with caution, however. For this would have to be second best for the new regime. The new regime was deliberately founded on ASB standards not statutes for good reason. The point of keeping standards non-statutory was that 'we can change quickly', whereas legislation is generally perceived as too slow to keep up with dynamic accounting practice. Anyway, *could* the DTI always change the law without the risk of challenge? What of Europe?

Then there's the issue of how closely in tune the ASB and DTI would actually prove to be on any specific issue. However supportive the DTI might be of the ASB's strategy in general, it may have different views over detail. It may also have different pressures and interests to satisfy. And any change of government could have an impact too. For the new regime, the preference must be to protect standards and make them win on their own terms, or at least avoid them being overruled.

A Persuasive Tactic

However, invoking the *threat* of DTI support may also impact more directly on specific cases, and encourage companies to concede to the Panel in a dispute. Directors' confident assertion that they are in the right legally, and willing to go to court, is likely to be dampened if hints are dropped that, if the Panel loses, the DTI will change the law. A court case is a daunting enough prospect without undertaking it to benefit from only one set of accounts.

External Factors and the Panel

External factors may impinge on Panel decisions too. Regulations other than those governing accounting may complicate matters. Accounting could impinge on capital adequacy ratios, for example, and companies plead concern over this. Might wider considerations of the impact on national economic matters play their part too, leading to 'self-regulation' – a cautious approach – by the Panel?

External factors may impinge on Panel enforcement in another sense. We suggested earlier (in Chapter 6) that the success of the Panel will affect the image of the new regime as a whole. But the image of the new regime as a whole will also affect the image and success of the Panel.

CONSENSUS AND CONTROL

If regulators are perceived as having general support, or as winning in disputes over the *making* of regulations, then regulators' confidence in *enforcing* those regulations is likely to be boosted, and the confidence of potential challengers reduced. If, however, there is extensive or simply loud dissent, or if regulators are forced to retreat in standard-setting disputes, then corporate confidence to challenge the ASB or the Panel is likely to be boosted.

Both the ASB and the Panel are aware of the need to nurture 'consensus', keeping the big accounting firms and business community generally on side: "As far as is possible it is the Board's aim to build a consensus on any particular accounting issues" (Tweedie, FRC 1991:15). Glasgow too observed, "we can only function with the support and respect of the City generally" (CBI Conference, 15 June 1993). Goldsmith recently met informally with large audit firms.

This support is important legally, to demonstrate that standards represent *generally accepted* accounting principles. In trying to dictate GAAP, the ASB clearly has authority on the side of its interpretation. But it is also aware that it needs the support of the commercial and professional community to keep it credible. Mary Arden QC made a point of this in her opinion on the status of accounting standards.

There is a certain irony in this since, in the past, many big names in business led the way in creative accounting while one of the reasons for replacing the ASC (a voluntary professional body) with the ASB (a statutory body comprising more than professional accountants) was that the big firms tended to dominate. Their support was necessary if there was to be any chance of getting standards accepted. If they were, according to Dearing, not unmindful' of clients' interests in specific audits, would they be any less so when it came to making the standards that would then affect financial reporting and audit? The objective in setting up the ASB was that it should be an *independent* standard-setting body.

There is a delicate balance to be found in seeking consensus from those on whom one is seeking to impose effective regulation, and the ASB is well aware of it, though Tweedie insists the new regime will opt for what it sees as the correct standards, adding to his expressed wish to build consensus:

> It should be stressed, however, that a consensus achieved at the expense of principle would not be worth having, and would quickly bring the new system into disrepute. (FRC, 1991:15)

Dissent

However, if the ASB is seen as too much at odds with the big firms and the business community generally, it may encourage legal challenge, not only on the status of standards but more generally. Despite the emphasis on consensus, there has been considerable dissent over the new regime's approach. We've seen some examples in Chapters 13 and 15.

FRS 5 was highly controversial, taking nine years to reach the standard book. That was in part under the aegis of the ASC, before the ASB took over. But there has been controversy and delay under the ASB too. The proposed Statement of Principles, though seen as an important plank of the new regime, has been in the making since it began, and has been subjected to scathing criticism, orchestrated particularly by Ron Paterson of Ernst & Young, though the ASB insists its critics have misunderstood it. The dispute over Private Finance Initiatives (PFIs) is another example.

PFIs

As we saw in Chapter 13, the ASB's proposals to bring PFIs on balance sheet via an additional application note in FRS 5 came in for scathing criticism by the Treasury and other advocates of its approach. "Fundamentally flawed" and "betraying a complete misunderstanding of how PFI works" was how the Faculty and Institute of Actuaries described them (*Accountancy*, April 1998:13).

This can only have encouraged the trend observed by "many respondents to the exposure draft". "PFI-type arrangements", they said, were being drafted by private sector organisations. Ernst & Young warned of the possibility of "a vast expansion in off-balance sheet accounting by commercial organisations" (*Accountancy*, October 1998:16).

The ASB was placed under intense pressure to compromise, but in the end stuck to its guns, although the final rules "responded to Treasury concerns". The rules focus more narrowly on the property element in contracts, and they will not apply to schemes already agreed or those where a best and final offer is being negotiated and a deal agreed by 31 December 1998. The Channel Tunnel rail link scheme, the biggest PFI project "that puts burdens on future taxpayers", will thus fall outside the new rules (*The Times*, 10 September 1998). The Treasury "welcomed the final version of the Board's proposals" (*ibid*). However, given it had just realised, "years after everyone else what a brilliant scam off balance sheet financing is", as Robert Bruce put it in *The Times* (19 December 1998), it is worth watching how it responds to the new Application Note.

Government Creative Compliance?

The Treasury has stated that it

> does not expect capitalisation judgements to change greatly and that the private sector contractor's ownership of the asset will in most instances continue to be recognised. (*Accountancy*, October 1998:16)

Public sector borrowing requirement will not be affected by the change, but "it will eventually add to measures of public spending and debt used under the Maastricht Treaty" (*The Times*, 10 September 1998). What does this mean?

Early in the controversy, the Treasury, according to Robert Bruce, adapted to the ASB attack. Bruce observed that, "having realised everything needs to be dressed up even more . . . pressure grew to pile more and more services like car parking or catering onto the deals *as window-dressing*" (*The Times*, 18 December 1997, our emphasis). 'Window-dressing', it may be recalled, was seen as the even wickeder cousin of off balance sheet financing in TR603, right back at the beginning of the attempt to regulate this form of transactions in 1985. The

Treasury had already noted that if a PFI deal has to be treated in substance as borrowing,

> the procurer will almost certainly want to look at the deal again. The public body should examine the scope for *reworking the deal* so that it is clearly for the provision of services. (*The Times*, 18 December 1997, our emphasis)

Reworking in substance or in form? Meeting the spirit of FRS 5, or creative compliance?

If the government were to circumvent the ASB's requirements this would give out a message which could only undermine the new regime, encourage creative accounting and boost challenges to attempts to control it, with, in effect, an official stamp of approval.

There is a wider political message here. If the new Labour government – or any government – wishes to clean up corporate practice, strengthen corporate governance, and control avoidance – creative compliance – in other areas such as tax, it should perhaps look with care at the example it sets in its own practice.

A WIDER REGULATORY CONTEXT

The regime's image, and therefore power – the Oz factor – might also be affected by events in the wider regulatory context. Developments in financial services or audit regulation, for example, and in international financial reporting regulation, could impact on enforcement in the new regime. Its regulatory weapons could be affected too.

Audit Regulation

Developments in the regulation of auditors could affect the routine mechanisms of enforcement. Proposals by the CCAB Working Party under Chris Swinson for a regulatory structure at arm's length from the profession have now been given the go-ahead by government (*Accountancy*, October 1998:11)

Auditor effectiveness is also being addressed in the European Union. In April 1998 the European Commission adopted a detailed programme for monitoring auditing throughout Europe. While the focus is still on professional self-regulation, the declared objective is a shift to 'monitored self-regulation'. The idea is to ensure that someone – the new Committee on Auditing, to be precise – is looking over the self-regulator's shoulders.

The principal European issue is harmonisation. But with harmonisation frequently comes regulation. Karel Van Hulle, of the European Commission, states:

> It is well known that Europe's auditing regulation is weak . . . The purpose of the Committee on Auditing is to put things right. Its objective is to contribute to raising the general standard of auditing in the EU. (*Accountancy*, July 1998:73)

Pressure is being put on the accounting profession to make audit more effective.

Impact?

What impact would this have on the new regime in the UK? Strengthened audit – or a need to appear strengthened – might at first sight seem like a boost to enforcement by the Panel. In reality it could go either way. Auditors to date, in many companies tackled by the Panel, cannot been seen as giving wholehearted, or, indeed, any support to the Panel's application of law and standards.

It would be taking too simple a line to *assume* this is evidence of weak auditors in the pockets of their clients. It could also mean that auditors reasonably disagree with the Panel's interpretation of law and standards. It may be evidence of honest differences of opinion.

A new improved audit profession could strengthen the enforcement of the new regime, providing a stronger first line of control. It could also strengthen any auditor challenge to the Panel by enhancing auditor credibility. It *could* strengthen enforcement. But is could also strengthen the challenge to enforceability. Likewise, increased concern by auditors over liability could make them more cautious in their advice, or more bullish in their defence of it.

International Accounting Regulation

In looking to the future effectiveness of the new regime in the UK, one eye should also be kept on developments in international accounting regulation. Increasing drives for harmonisation of accounting regulation worldwide could lead to pressures on UK regulators.

Odd One Out

The power to use the true and fair requirement to override literal compliance with specific rules or extend their reach, is an important weapon for the new regime. UK regulators are, however, unusual in the international context in taking this approach. Australia tried the override approach and rejected it. In the USA a true and fair view is equated with compliance with more specific rules. We have already noted the very rule-oriented approach taken in Germany.

There are changes afoot in the *administration* of accounting regulation in Germany. German accounting has traditionally been a legal matter, and the accounting profession has been underdeveloped. However, an Accounting Standards Committee has now been set up.

How this will develop and what impact it will have remains to be seen. As yet it is quite unclear what relationship the new committee's standards will have with German law. Will the Committee help define what is true and fair, as the ASB claims to in its standards? Will the existence of a professional standard-setting body soften the legal approach, and make the German approach more open to the true and fair override as allowing professional judgement? Or will the German experience provide one more example to add to the view that the UK is the odd one out?

Harmonisation

Pressures can arise from being the odd one out, especially in the context of international harmonisation programmes.

These might be *internal* pressures. Differences of this sort provide obvious pegs for UK companies to complain they are being placed at a competitive disadvantage. Indeed, this very argument was rehearsed – successfully – when FRS 5 was being drafted. According to Allan Cook, the original approach to securitisation was amended partly on the grounds that British banks, governed by European directives on risk capital, would be penalised under European rules vis-à-vis their European competitors if the ASB's proposal was adopted.

They might be *external* pressures. Will international regulation involve, as it so often does, a lowest common denominator effect? Will the ASB and UK law be seen as out of step and the weapons of the true and fair override and FRS 5 lost in the drive for harmonisation?

The IASC is looking to accomplish harmonisation in key areas by the year 2000. There are hints of a move to international standards, bypassing the ASB, *informally* before then. France, Germany, Italy and Belgium have recently passed laws allowing companies to file their consolidated accounts using internationally recognised accounting standards – IASC or US GAAP (*Accountancy*, July 1998:9). Companies in these countries say this saves money and makes their accounts more comparable. The ICAEW has been taking note of this. In considering its comments on the DTI consultative paper on the reform of UK company law, the Institute was recently reported to be considering proposing the UK follow suit.

Whether this happens or not in the UK, and the ASB would obviously resist it – Tweedie is already on record as saying it would diminish the ASB's power (*Accountancy*, July 1998:9) – this development could also put pressure on the ASB to get more in line with the IASC and US GAAP. This is a matter of real concern for the new regime, which sees its standards as tackling abuses which IASC and US GAAP don't. Bypassing them would be a major setback in the fight against creative accounting.

Lame Duck?

Harmonisation, on the other hand, could prove more threat than reality. It could simply prove politically elusive, or a lame duck in practice, with continuing scope for countries to stick to their own standards. Touche Ross's survey (1989) of accounting regulation in different Member States after the implementation of the Fourth Directive within the European Community, demonstrated just how much scope for variation remained even after a measure allegedly harmonising company accounting. Making international regulation effective is even more of a challenge than making national regulation work.

ASB Rules?

And, so far as lobbying goes, perhaps the ASB or the DTI could counter the arguments against the UK approach. Political arguments, like legal ones, are about making a case, not stating incontrovertible truths (though frequently presented as such). There is usually more than one way to present what is going on and its likely impact.

So far as lobbying within the UK is concerned, the competitive disadvantage argument could be turned on its head. It could be argued that strong regulation reassures investors and attracts them. Indeed the proposal to allow authoritative alternatives to UK standards has been countered not only by Tweedie but also by key players in business too. *Accountancy* reported:

> Many UK finance directors said they would never back such a proposal. Christopher Pearce, chairman of the 100 Group of finance directors, was perplexed. He said, ". . . we have an excellent set of standards prepared through a very rigorous process. In many cases the UK standard is much better than the comparable US or International Accounting Standard" (*Accountancy*, July 1998:9)

As for pressures from abroad to toe the line, perhaps they could be reversed. Tweedie sees the UK as the "leader of the opposition" (vis-à-vis US GAAP) in the international arena. Indeed there have been examples of the UK approach on specific issues being taken up internationally in preference to the US way. Early in the new regime, Sir Ron Dearing talked of other countries following the ASB's approach with interest. If most other countries have not set in place the same regulatory protections as the UK, it is, says Tweedie, because they didn't experience "the abuses of accounting rules that occurred in the 1980s" as the UK did.

It would be interesting to see what would happen if regulators in other key states were to acknowledge creative accounting as a fundamental problem in the way that UK regulators have, one that needs a fundamental change of approach to tackle it. Would the UK model then become the one to follow? It could be argued the UK approach to 'true and fair' would allow harmonisation in substance not form. The enforceability and practice of the new regime's weapons could become very significant beyond the UK.

CHALLENGING THE REGULATORS: FROM LITIGATION TO LOBBYING

Finally, corporate challenge needs to be seen through a wider lens too. Litigation and negotiation are not the only means available to companies to challenge regulators. Indeed, companies may side-step the perils of *individual litigation* by opting for challenge through *collective lobbying*. Law in action can take a *political* form too.

Disarming the Panel

A specific case might prompt this. So might the regular review of new standards promised by the ASB. The DTI and the Law Commission are currently reviewing company law and inviting comments from profession and industry. The issue could be very specific – European rules on equalisation reserves for insurance companies, for example, after GRE – or it might be on something more general, and fundamental. Instead of taking on the Panel in the courts, companies might seek to *disarm* it by lobbying for curtailment of or change in the statutes or standards to which the Panel looks in defining accounting practices as defective. We shall see more of this in Chapter 22.

PART VI

CONTROL?

19
Climate Control

So, can the new regime, with its new enforcement powers and new regulatory weapons, succeed in its goal? Can creative accounting be controlled?

There is no quick answer, as this book demonstrated. Even in specific cases that have reached their outcomes, the issue of who has won and who has lost is subjective and elusive. It is in the nature of bargaining that both sides may laugh all the way to the bank, or equally feel hard done by; that they may present one face publicly, another behind the scenes.

Winning and losing do not necessarily involve a zero sum. The Panel may feel it has won considerable victories in pressing big companies into compliance in the future on specific issues, or into retrospective revision in comparative figures in next year's accounts. Or it may see this as a delicately negotiated compromise which keeps it, as well as the company, out of the courts. Companies may feel they have lost, when legally they could have won, but that they could have lost much more. Or they may feel they have secured a pragmatic victory.

For the new regime the outcome of any specific case investigated is obviously important. But there has been a goal for control beyond the specific issue – the objective and hope is to improve the company's compliance in the future *in general*. There has been a goal beyond the specific *company* too. Cases investigated represent just the tip of the iceberg of accounting practice. The objective is to tackle the iceberg itself.

There has also been a goal beyond changing and enforcing

law. David Pimm, writing at the outset of the new regime, observed:

> The legislators' new tools (The Companies Act and [what became FRS 5]) adopt a general appeal to principles. It will be interesting to see whether this approach confounds the avoidance industry's search for loopholes. (Pimm, 1991:135)

There is still a search for loopholes, and there is still scope for claiming loopholes exist. Whether that claim is bound to win is another matter. It will depend very much on how broadly or narrowly the Panel, and the judges, should they come into play, interpret the reach of law and accounting standards. And it will depend on how the regime develops in the future. The ultimate objective of the new regime, however, is to stop the search for loopholes, to change the *climate* of accounting practice. Is the new regime winning on 'climate control'?

A CHANGE OF CLIMATE?

For the new regime, the ideal situation would be one where enforcement was, in practice, unnecessary, where directors either willingly embraced a new business ethic in financial reporting, or were deterred from doing otherwise by fear of enforcement.

Tweedie, at the outset of the new regime, called for:

> a change in the climate in financial reporting away from the tendency of a minority to use creative accounting and towards financial reporting that is genuinely balanced, helpful and informative. (FRC, 1991:23)

Indeed in 1991, he stated his belief that this "new climate" was already "well on the way", that the "task now is to assure good progress is maintained". Simon Tuckey QC, first chairman of the Panel, observed that there were "clear signs" that the formation of the Panel was itself "proving a potent force for good" (FRC, 1991:25). Sir Sydney Lipworth, as we saw in Chapter 1, was still asserting in 1997 that the "below the waterline effect" was "very real" (FRC, 1997:13).

There is, in short, a claim – and a fervent hope – that the Panel (and new regime behind it) has had an effect beyond its specific caseload, on the business community in general.

Changing the climate of financial reporting has always been the goal. If Lipworth is right, the precise details of this or that case before the Panel – who "really" won, who "really" lost – may be less important than the overall impact of the enforcement structure. Just as with the judges, what the Panel *does* in detail, may matter less than what it *might* do. Indeed the mere fact that a new regime was perceived as necessary could itself have an impact on the attitude of business to compliance.

A Clean-up Accounting Campaign

Any below the waterline reduction in creative accounting would not only be a product of the role of the Panel and the new regime, but a product of the increased public profile of accounting and corporate governance in the last decade, of scandals, debate, the perceived need to set up a new regime at all, the gradual definition of creative accounting as a problem.

The change in ethos would be a product of a successful campaign to label creative accounting as not just clever but too clever by half, as not smart but deviant. The ASB's use of the press for enforcement can be seen both as devaluing accounts *and* as a 'shaming' tactic, which can only be effective if the companies involved think the business community cares. A real below the waterline effect would demonstrate the successful stigmatisation of creative accounting, and a change of business attitude to law and ethics. It would mean companies and their advisers looking to the spirit of the law and approaching 'good faith' arguments in good faith.

This is clearly what the new regime has been hoping for. The ASB's approach can be seen in part as a campaign to change the attitude of business to financial reporting. The Panel can be seen as a symbol of the stigmatisation of creative accounting and a reminder to directors of their exposure to sanctions if they overstep the mark.

Back From the Abyss

The higher profile afforded to accounting in general and creative accounting in particular, over the last decade, may also have encouraged what one senior accountant described as a "collective drawing back from the abyss" by the commercial community. This, he saw as not so much the product of conversion to a Tweedie-esque vision of corporate compliance with the *spirit* of accounting standards, but more the product of a calculated assessment of the need to counter the public image of company reports as unreliable.

Whatever the motivation, any below the waterline effect of increased respect for the spirit of the law would be good news for those who have nurtured hopes that the excesses of business and finance in the 1980s – with creative accounting and its consequences not the least of them – and the adverse publicity received, would lead to a change in business ethics more generally. The rhetoric of fat cats and fantasy finances might have contributed to a backlash.

OR A PHONEY PEACE?

But is there any clear evidence of this change of climate? Tweedie's early entreaties for voluntary compliance with the spirit of the principles have given way to threats to return to a cookbook of detailed rules. The ASB's approach, according to Lipworth

> will work only if preparers and their auditors are willing to follow the spirit of a standard and not seek loopholes in it . . . the inevitable alternative – a detailed rule book – would be a major setback not only for financial reporting but also for the wider interests of UK industry and commerce. (FRC, 1996:6)

Is the perception that the "very real" below the waterline effect is nonetheless far from adequate? In any case, any apparent change of climate would need to be interpreted with care, for a number of reasons:

The Ones That Got Away

First there is a problem of distinguishing apparent from real impact. As Chapter 3 suggests, fewer cases of creative accounting coming to light might mean no more than fewer being detected. It might point out the limits of detection rather than the impact of control. Indeed the potential for more control – for the simple reason that there is an enforcement agency, however reactive – may paradoxically mean greater covering of tracks than before. We have noted suggestions of a tendency to *reduced* disclosure in accounts.

By What Measure?

Second, just how much 'unacceptable creative accounting' continues below the waterline will depend on how 'unacceptable creative accounting' is defined. The Panel now plays a key role in drawing the line between what is deemed acceptable and what is not – 'where does the *Panel* say I can't?'

Where the Panel draws the line will be affected by whether it

- takes a broad or narrow view of the reach of statute and standards;
- feels constrained by the wider regulatory context, or not;
- is checked by the threat of corporate challenge (individual or collective) or prepared to take a 'bullish' line regardless.

If it does *not* take a 'bullish' line, apparent improvement in accounting practice could be a product of where the line is being drawn by the Panel rather than any fundamental change in practice. It could be a product of *regulatory* self-restraint rather than *corporate* self-restraint.

The Hiatus Effect

Third, any apparent change of ethos might simply demonstrate no more than 'the hiatus effect' – with companies treading carefully until they get the measure of the real power of the new regime. A period of circumspection is likely to follow any revolutionary change in regulation. There was a 'hiatus effect' when the judges took a revolutionary 'new approach' to tax avoidance in the 1980s, while tax advisers assessed whether tax avoidance was really dead, and tax inspectors wielded the threat of the 'new approach' to secure compliance with *their* view of tax liabilities. The threat could be wielded to great effect because it took time for a taxpayer to be willing to put his or her head on the block to test it, or for lobbying to have its effect.

New laws and regulation can lead to a period of uncertainty until their operation in practice is tested. That period of uncertainty may be the most powerful weapon of all for regulators: the power of the hiatus effect. But if this were the basis of any new self-constraint in corporate practice, it would be no more than a phoney peace. The new regime would be living off borrowed time.

A Fickle Following?

Fourth, if any below the waterline effect is a product not of conversion to the Tweedie doctrine, not of fear of the Panel and the courts, but of strategic self-restraint – self-interest in countering the public image of company reports – then this may, as a senior accountant put it:

> contain the seeds of its own downfall . . . the risk is that sentiment can change against the ASB just as easily as it has supported the Board in the past. If this were to happen, and I believe that economic circumstances can easily arise in which it will be likely to happen, then we will be faced with all the regulatory issues all over again.

In short, the trouble with strategic self-restraint is that strategic interests can change. A change in *economic climate* could affect this. Although there are always motivations for creative accounting, economic circumstances can enhance the pressures and the opportunities. The culture of the 1980s and the creative accounting it encouraged no doubt generated as well as reflected the economic 'boom' of the time. The real test of the below the waterline effect now and in the future will be economic circumstances that stimulate new motivations for creative accounting. David Tweedie recognises concerns over whether standards "will unravel" in a change of economic climate. Can the standards take boom *and* bust?

The political climate may have an impact too as we saw in Chapter 18. If the government is to sustain any credibility in a policy that encourages good corporate governance and corporate practice more generally, it should be wary of the messages it conveys. It cannot condemn corporate creative accounting only to engage in it itself without legitimising rather than stigmatising it. This could be just another factor to undermine the ASB's hope of 'climate control', and encourage instead a climate of resistance to both the Panel and the regime as a whole. The same would be true if the profession and other regulators, national or international, were to withdraw support from the new regime.

Such changes of context could tip the balance in terms of whether companies, who have perhaps been more circumspect than in the past, opt once again for creative accounting. Any 'below the waterline effect' and associated claims of success by the new regime could prove to have shaky foundations.

The less self-interest operates to motivate corporate self-restraint, the more important it becomes that the threat of the Panel proves a real deterrent. The idea that its mere existence is what counts may prove wrong. The precise detail of what it actually does, and how, may take on real significance. The Panel will have to be seen to be exercising effective control. To project that image, its message may have to be more than 'medium'. It may have to do more – routinely – than require compliance in the future. What's more, the *basis* of its control may become an issue.

20
Cost-Benefit Control

In all the reported cases where the Panel has required corrective action the company has complied. Whether this is viewed as success or not depends on the measure used. If the measure is effective imposition of the corrective action required by the Panel in the cases it has found and chosen to pursue, then it has a 100% success rate. If the measure is revision of defective accounts, the success rate is very low. Is it the long-term effect that matters or the short-term outcome? Is it rigid application of the law now, or securing compliance in the future? What of the ones that got away?

Taking the Panel's enforcement record on its own terms, however, how has it been accomplished? On what basis? Can it last?

The Bases of Control

To date the Panel has enforced the law without challenge in the courts – or more precisely, it has enforced its view of how the law applies, without the legal enforceability of that view being tested. All companies investigated have conceded.

There seem to be three factors that lead to companies conceding to the Panel.

- **The Oz factor** – For some directors the Oz factor has clearly been enough: the 'you won't stand a dog's chance against them' approach. If challenged by the Panel they concede. They assume the Panel has law on its side.

- **The uncertainty factor** – For others, uncertainty of the reach of regulations like FRS 5 or 'true and fair' can act as a constraint. The law is too much of an unknown quantity.
- **The cost-benefit factor** – Others, however, have insisted they are right in law. Companies such as Trafalgar House or Guardian Royal Exchange have not publicly conceded defeat on legal grounds. They have presented themselves as forced to concede because of enormous practical and commercial pressures.

This underlines the fact that the Panel could be very effective as an enforcement agency quite simply because of the impact of these practical factors. The Panel is under practical pressures too, as we have seen, but whatever the pressures on the Panel, and whatever leverage that gives companies in bargaining, at the end of the day the Panel may be able to hold out longest. And, if the Panel is sufficiently benign in its demands, for companies, on a cost-benefit analysis, it is usually just not worth challenging the regulators in court.

The commercial decision for the company, and the wise one for directors, may be to concede. The Panel's view of 'proper' accounting prevails. The Panel wins without ever having to go to court.

While the Oz and uncertainty factors could change with a successful challenge in the courts, the practical and commercial costs of going to court may be just too great for directors to risk staging that challenge.

Cost-Benefit Control

The result is successful enforcement of the Panel's view, with enforceability issues tempering the outcomes, but never put to the test in court. Very effective. But the effect is based, *not* on proven Panel control on legal grounds, but on corporate concession on practical grounds.

Can this last? Yes. Cost-benefit control could continue indefinitely.

Whatever the *legal* basis of the accounting treatment, whatever the *motivation* of directors in choosing it, and despite *auditor* approval and 'independent' support, the bottom line in enforcement may be that challenging the Panel in court is simply not on as far as the company is concerned. The *practical* power of the Panel may matter more than its formal *legal* powers. The Panel may always be able to secure the compliance it requires, unless, that is, the balance of costs and benefits changes. And it might.

When the Benefits of Contesting Outweigh the Costs

- **Changing contexts** – We noted above that changes in the economic climate could lead to changes in the accounting climate. If the potential gains were high enough, there might be a greater temptation to use creative accounting techniques. Economic change could also tip the balance in an investigation in favour of a greater willingness to challenge the Panel. It would affect the stakes. The greater the benefits to be gained from successful resistance, the more it is likely to be tried. Likewise a change in political climate, challenges to the regime or the wider regulatory context, hints of dissent rather than consensus might encourage a test case.
- **Not benign enough** – How far can the Panel go down the softly softly road, we asked earlier, without being seen as merely soft? In 'climate control' we suggested the Panel may *have* to project a tougher image. On the other hand, the tougher the Panel becomes, the less the benefits for companies in co-operating, and the less there is to lose by contesting.

  If the demands proffered – or the compromise secured by bargaining – is merely to amend comparative figures in the next year's accounts, or adopt a different treatment in the future, there may be little incentive to contest. The costs of conceding are not high enough, and the potential costs of contesting are too high. But if the Panel were to require, let's say, revision of accounts *now* as a matter of routine – if the benign big gun was to become less benign and more big gun – would this tip the balance the other way?
- **The Panel goes too far** – With so few cases on such different issues it is difficult to make sensible comparisons regarding the Panel's approach over time. Nonetheless there are hints that the Panel is beginning to flex its muscles rather more

> than it did to begin with. As Sydney Treadgold, the Panel's secretary, noted to us, the Panel began with a clean sheet. It had no history. It has in large measure had to map out its own way forward. What is more, some of its key weapons have only recently become available.
>
> FRS 5 came into play for accounting periods ending after September 1994, with the first Panel case appearing in 1997. The Panel has also begun to show signs of using the true and fair requirement more assertively. Compare the Pentos case in 1994 with RMC in 1998. In Pentos the Panel treated an area in which there was a lack of clear rules as a grey area. It did not take action against Pentos but referred the issues to the ASB to fill the gap by ruling for the future on appropriate treatment. In RMC the Panel has been seen, for the first time, as clearly extending the reach of the true and fair requirement to reach the parts true and fair has never reached before.

How will companies respond if the RMC approach becomes the pattern? Will they begin to feel the Panel is going too far? They may want to know whether the courts will in fact permit the Panel to extend the reach of the true and fair requirement in this way. What if the Panel adopts a broader view of the reach of law and takes a more bullish line on loopholes? Companies may want to test what limits there are on Panel power. Large companies may resist Panel demands to revise their accounts. Muscle flexing by the Panel may seem to demonstrate considerable potential for effective control. But the very threat of more effective control may be enough to stimulate greater resistance.

The more the Panel uses its legal powers to break into new territory, the more likely it is that companies will want to test – and they will hope – limit those powers by challenging in the courts. We'll consider the consequences of that in Chapter 21 – or challenging the powers of the Panel itself – as we'll see in Chapter 22.

21
Battles, Wars and the Spirit of the Law

What if companies challenge in the courts? Would the Panel's view be upheld? And what would be the consequences for the control of creative accounting more generally? The success of the Panel in combat with a specific company and the success of the regime in its campaign against creative accounting will not necessarily be in harmony.

We saw in Chapter 6 how a Panel defeat could encourage creative accounting, but also how the Panel could win but the regime lose. This could happen, for example, where a principle like reporting 'substance' was 'clarified' into rules for creative accountants to use or circumvent in the future, pointing to authoritative court decisions in support. This could be damaging to a regime bent on regulating through principles, not detailed rules, precisely to avoid providing such opportunities.

A Good Case to Lose

It might also be that the Panel could lose but the regime win. The regime may focus attention on the importance of applying principles, but much of the Panel's record of corrective action could be read as focusing on securing compliance with rules, or with *its* interpretation of rules.

This could result in the Panel shooting the regime in the foot. The GRE case, for example, from the point of view of a regime aimed at the application of principles and the spirit of the law, might have been a good case to lose in court. The lesson drawn from a Panel win might well have been: rigid adherence to current rules is all that counts.

Driven to Rules?

Judges could drive the ASB to rules. Principles are there in part to fill the 'gap' in specific rules. But what if judges duck this challenge and intervene only where clear rules are available? What if judges say: where does it say you can't do that? The ASB might find itself in the position of having to supply rules to win judicial control.

Combats and Campaigns

Victory or defeat for the Panel in any specific case, success for the new regime in terms of *its* chosen strategy for controlling creative accounting, could, then, be two very different matters. The mechanism for *enforcing* the new regime's regulations could, ironically, end up undermining them.

All on Side?

Alternatively, ASB, Panel and judges might find themselves of one mind. Indeed, even the occasional company victory in a dispute over what is substance, what is true and fair, might not impact too heavily if the judges upheld the *principles* at stake:

- commercial substance counts, not legal form;
- true and fair can override specific rules;
- the spirit of the law is what has to be applied.

Defeat for the Panel would mean the judges thought the *Panel* had got it wrong this time, but the *regime* had got it right. The principles would be safe to be applied again next time.

Even concern over case law 'rules' being used for new forms of creative compliance *could* be negated. Judges might apply these principles afresh each time according to the specific circumstances of the next specific case. If every case can be seen as unique in some way, even past precedents can be treated as irrelevant to the particular circumstances of this particular case. Judges have certainly done that often enough in other contexts. Perhaps they will simply ask afresh each time: is *this* true and fair? Is *this* substance?

There is scope for flexibility in law, as we saw in Chapter 16. Judges might distinguish cases on their substance, or apply doctrines like collateral advantage to set them aside. Rigid adherence to precedent could work against the new regime, but this scope for flexibility in law, if judges are so minded, would work for it.

The new regime's attack on creative accounting could prove effective not just at the level of practical enforcement, but at the level of legal enforceability.

Spirit of the Age, Spirit of the Law?

Far from bluff, the Panel's hand could prove to contain all the trump cards – not just the practical pressures inherent in the threat of court proceedings, but courts apparently intent on applying the spirit of the law, in the spirit of the ASB, and looking through artificial enhancement of accounts.

Tweedie's approach would be endorsed. An emphasis on broad principles like reporting substance and giving a true and fair view might be seen as the only way to lead to effective control. The spirit of the age might favour the spirit of the law.

If this were to prove a feasible scenario for the future, would it mean the end of creative accounting? Or would there still be tensions to confront?

22
Creative Control?

There are strong vested interests in creative accounting. Perhaps strong vested interests in taking the moral high ground will grow too, and 'climate control' is all about encouraging that. But interests in successful creative accounting – and marketing it – are all too clear. There may also be divergent standpoints to be taken on where the moral high ground lies.

SPIRIT OF LAW V. RULE OF LAW?

Some might see matters for concern – moral or political – in a regime which focuses on the *spirit* of the law. What, they might ask, about the *rule* of law?

Indeed they might point to both the enforcement process, and the regulations to be enforced, to question the *legitimacy* of the new regime.

Whose Granny?

Questions might be raised over the subjective nature of some of the key regulations in the new regime. 'Substance' and 'true and fair' could be pointed to as giving too much leeway for different interpretations – which one will the Panel choose? Which one will the judges choose? Tweedie might say "your granny would know what's right", but whose granny? An 'uncertainty' lobby could be mounted on this basis.

CHALLENGING UNCERTAINTY

The uncertainty card is a strong one to play in the context of business regulation. The Financial Reporting Review Panel is a product of the experiences of the 1980s, but so was the Legal Risk Review Committee, founded in 1991 on the grounds that:

> markets cannot function efficiently without a sound legal foundation. Promoting legal certainty, even though it is not the only relevant concern, is therefore of fundamental medium- to long-term importance. (Final Report of the Legal Risk Review Committee, Bank of England, October 1992:1)

That commercial transactions, investment decisions need legal certainty is persuasive rhetoric. How, it is argued, are businesses to engage in commercial deals if they cannot depend on their legal status? As far back as 1985, the date of the first stage of what was to become FRS 5, the Law Society emphasised the need to be able to "assess the probable consequences of any proposed transaction" (1986:33).

Uncertainty Won't Do

Though, as we observed in Chapter 16, law is always prone to some degree of uncertainty, the demand for certainty is a classic lobbying tool – the more so when there are real costs and sanctions involved.

Too much uncertainty won't do, it could be argued.

- It won't do when directors may be held personally liable.
- It won't do when auditors might end up vulnerable to negligence suits or disciplinary action.
- It won't do when companies suffer for decisions that could be interpreted as 'perfectly legal'.

Companies could criticise the Panel, or the new regime more generally, precisely *as* a cross-eyed javelin thrower. No one, they might claim, knows where the javelin will land and that won't do.

Clearances

In other areas, 'uncertainty' has led to demands for a system of clearances so that companies can *know* before committing themselves to a particular structure or transaction, how it would be treated by the regulatory agency involved. The Panel has to date expressly ruled this out. But pressure could arise on the back of an uncertainty lobby.

The introduction of a system of clearances would not be a popular move for regulators. Not only would it have a major impact on resources but also there would be concern over clearances being abused. Unless the whole transaction is scrutinised, regulators can find themselves giving the go-ahead on one part only to find it takes on a completely different function when seen as part of a whole. Clearances, unless very carefully dealt with, can end up endorsing creative compliance.

But the issue might go beyond solving the practical inconvenience of uncertainty in law. The *leverage* this gives to regulators might also become a bone of contention, particularly when set in the context of the consequences for a company of going to court. Indeed the new 'big gun' of civil court proceedings might come under fire.

ENFORCED OR FORCED?

Dearing said criminal proceedings were an inappropriate means of enforcement in an area like this where so much subjective judgement was involved. It is not a big step from there to arguing that civil proceedings in public courts are problematic too. Going to court is enough to damage a company beyond repair, be it found right or wrong in law. So companies concede. The Panel therefore wins by default without ever having its view tested in court.

Justice without trial is, in fact, the norm – overwhelmingly – for criminal and civil cases in the UK and elsewhere. Those who plead guilty or settle out of court often do so believing themselves to be innocent or in the right, but excluded from justice by practical pressures. The corporate position vis-à-vis the Panel is far from unusual. If it causes concern on behalf of large companies it should cause concern more generally. The corporate sector, however, is a more powerful lobby than suspects of crime.

There might be pressure for some more neutral and confidential procedure for resolving disputes without the collateral damage inherent in public court cases – some *ex parte* procedure – "referring a matter to the court for ruling in conditions of confidentiality" perhaps. There may be advantages here for the Panel too, but it would lose the sanction of publicity.

FROM CREATIVE ACCOUNTING TO CREATIVE CONTROL

Or, the weapons of 'true and fair' and 'substance over form' might themselves come under attack. It could be argued not only that they leave companies uncertain on how to comply with the law, but that, combined with the collateral damage associated with going to court to contest the Panel, they give the Panel too much power.

This may make for very effective control – with companies unwilling to risk adopting a certain treatment or defending it in court. A senior auditor reported to us that he tells his clients: "You could argue this way or that way, but we can't be sure which way the Panel would argue. If you go for either you could be open to attack."

The question could arise: is this legitimate discretion or too much power? In the 1980s companies were accused of using the requirement to give a true and fair view to justify defining any practice they liked as lawful. Might not the Panel – and indeed the judges – be open to the accusation that they are using true and fair to define any practice *they* don't like as unlawful? Do regulations framed as principles leave too much scope for *creative control*? Creative accounting may be unacceptable, but is countering it with creative control any less so?

Panel Power

The power of the Panel on, to date, practical, and, potentially, legal grounds, could become an issue for the future. In our research we have been struck by the real concern of companies to be assured of the confidentiality of our interviews. The reasons given were invariably concern *not* to be seen to be critical of the Panel.

What's more, regulators themselves acknowledge they have immense powers at their disposal, whether they were to be found legally right or not, in terms of the practical consequences of taking a company to court. The Panel

> can do immense damage. The service of a writ itself will do such irreparable damage that if it's wrong it will have created real injustice. The power of the Panel is almost unanswerable.

Of course, it is answerable in the courts. But, the implication is, by that time irreparable damage may already have been done. No wonder the Panel has been described as having "draconian powers" at its disposal – though this regulator insisted, they have *not* been abused. Indeed, as we observed in Chapters 12 and 17, the Panel can be seen, on the whole, as treading quite gingerly in terms of its use of the 'big powers' of true and fair and FRS 5.

'Self Regulation'

Such issues may never – publicly – be aired. The Panel may take great care to self-regulate in our sense of exercising self-restraint, great care not to risk the charge of abuse. Perhaps we can see here another reason for the *benign* big gun approach – the recognition that the big guns of the new regime are *too* big to use in this context without great caution. They are too susceptible to the charge of abuse of power, too vulnerable to resistance – resistance on the basis that there is too much power and too much discretion.

Ultimately, the success of the new regime may depend on whether it can sustain an image of just application of the law – letter and spirit – and escape the charge of unacceptable creative control. And whether it can do so without compromising its goal of curbing creative accounting.

23
The Cross-Eyed Javelin Thrower

So, is the new regime winning the battle to control creative accounting, and will it win in the long run? Can the cross-eyed javelin thrower reach its target?

Double-edged Sword

The new regime was set up with a new enforcement agency, new enforcement procedures, new – and revitalised – regulations geared to controlling creative accounting, and a new boost in legal status. But the practice of enforcement is a complex business, and law is a double-edged sword – an instrument of control but also a basis for arguing escape routes from it.

An image of successful *enforcement* has been maintained. It is one that must be treated warily – there can be no doubt creative accounting, much in the old style, is still going on, and the corrective action accomplished has been of a limited nature, a product, we would judge, of both astute policy and unavoidable tensions. But images count too and have an impact – the Oz factor can be a very effective deterrent. And the ASB is still developing new weapons.

Testing Times

However, the regime has yet to be tested on the *enforceability* – legal and political – of its weapons to control creative accounting. Indeed, there may be tensions within the new regime on the real reach of these weapons. Standard-setters may see themselves as producing regulations that can root out creative accounting. Those who have to enforce them may be less assured. The whole process is taking place in a wider political and regulatory context and developments there will have a knock-on effect. The cast will change. David Tweedie is a man with a mission, but he is in place for only two more years. Will his successor share his views?

Wider Relevance

One thing is sure. The success or failure of the new regime has relevance for contexts far wider than the UK and far wider than accounting. The campaign to control creative accounting has put the spotlight on an issue that goes to the heart of business and legal ethics – the tendency to see minimalist compliance with advantageously interpreted regulation, literal compliance with the letter of the law, as good enough.

The ASB has raised critical questions about the acceptability of this approach, and called for much more emphasis on the spirit of the law. The same tack has subsequently been taken for corporate governance more generally, with the Hampel Report calling for an end to mere "box-ticking" compliance (1997).

How feasible it will be to accomplish a new business ethic of compliance with the spirit of the law – and the ability to enforce it – raises a whole range of questions. Fundamental legal issues are involved too. But the bid to control creative accounting is certainly as good a testing ground for this regulatory goal as there could be.

Watch This Space

No one can know yet whether the cross-eyed javelin thrower will reach his target. But the crowd *has* been kept on the edge of its seats. And there it should certainly stay. All those interested not only in the practice of creative accounting or its control, but also in corporate governance, in business ethics, and in the feasibility of effective regulation more generally, should keep their eyes firmly on the arena of financial reporting.

Appendix 1

ACCOUNTING STANDARDS BOARD

Foreword to Accounting Standards
June 1993

(Footnotes omitted)

Introduction

1. This foreword explains the authority, scope and application of accounting standards issued or adopted by the Accounting Standards Board (the Board). The foreword also considers the procedure by which the Board issues accounting standards and their relationship to International Accounting Standards, issued by the International Accounting Standards Committee.

2. The Board at its meeting on 24 August 1990 agreed to adopt the 22 extant Statements of Standard Accounting Practice (SSAPs) issued by the Councils of the six major accountancy bodies following proposals developed by the Accounting Standards Committee (ASC). Adoption by the Board gave these SSAPs the status of accounting standards within Part VII of the Companies Act 1985 (the Act) and within Part VIII of the Companies (Northern Ireland) Order 1986 (the Order). This status will apply until each SSAP is amended, rescinded or replaced by new accounting standards.

3. Accounting standards developed by the Board are designated Financial Reporting Standards (FRSs). Accounting standards developed by the ASC and adopted by the Board continue to be known as SSAPs.

4. FRSs are based on the Statement of Principles for Financial Reporting currently in issue, which addresses the concepts underlying the information presented in financial statements. The objective of this Statement of Principles is to provide a framework for the consistent and logical formulation of individual accounting standards. The framework also provides a basis on which others can exercise judgement in resolving accounting issues.

5. The Board may issue pronouncements other than FRSs, including the Urgent Issues Task Force 'Abstracts'. The Board will indicate the authority, scope and application of pronouncements other than FRSs as they are issued. UITF Abstracts are the subject of a separate foreword.

Aims of the Accounting Standards Board

6. The aims of the Board are set out in the document 'The Accounting Standards Board – Statement of Aims'.

Authority of accounting standards

7. FRSs issued and SSAPs adopted by the Board are 'accounting standards' for the purposes of the Act, which requires accounts, other than those prepared by small or medium-sized companies (as defined by the Act), to state whether they have been prepared in accordance with applicable accounting standards and to give particulars of any material departure from those standards and the reasons for it. References to accounting standards in the Act are contained in paragraph 36A of Schedule 4, paragraph 49 of Part I of Schedule 9 and paragraph 18B of Part I of Schedule 9A. The equivalent references in the Order are in paragraph 36A of Schedule 4, paragraph 49 of Part I of Schedule 9 and paragraph 18B of Part I of Schedule 9A.
8. Directors of companies incorporated under the Companies Acts are required by the Act to prepare accounts that give a true and fair view of the state of affairs of the company, and where applicable the group, at the end of the financial year and of the profit or loss of the company or the group for the financial year.
9. The Consultative Committee of Accountancy Bodies (CCAB) is committed to promoting and supporting compliance with accounting standards by its member bodies and by their members, whether as preparers or auditors of financial information.
10. The Councils of the CCAB bodies therefore expect their members who assume responsibilities in respect of financial statements to observe accounting standards. The Councils have agreed that:

a) where this responsibility is evidenced by the association of members' names with such financial statements in the capacity of directors or other officers, other than auditors, the onus will be on them to ensure that the existence and purpose of accounting standards are fully understood by fellow directors and other officers. Members should also use their best endeavours to ensure that accounting standards are observed and that significant departures found to be necessary are adequately disclosed and explained in the financial statements.
b) where members act as auditors or reporting accountants, they should be in a position to justify significant departures to the extent that their concurrence with the departures is stated or implied. They are not, however, required to refer in their report to departures with which they concur, provided that adequate disclosure has been made in the notes to the financial statements.

11. The CCAB bodies, through appropriate committees, may enquire into apparent failures by their members to observe accounting standards or to ensure adequate disclosure of significant departures.
12. The Board notes the continuing application of previously adopted SSAPs in the Republic of Ireland through their on-going promulgation by the Institute of Chartered Accountants in Ireland (ICAI). It further notes ICAI's intention of maintaining close liaison with the Board on promulgating, with appropriate modifications for legal differences, FRSs for application in the Republic of Ireland. The objective of the Board and ICAI is a regime of accounting standards common to both the United Kingdom and the Republic of Ireland.

Scope and application of accounting standards

13. Accounting standards are applicable to financial statements of a reporting entity that are intended to give a true and fair view of its state of affairs at the balance sheet date and of its profit or loss (or income and expenditure) for the financial period ending on that date. Accounting standards need not be applied to immaterial items.

14. Accounting standards should be applied to United Kingdom and Republic of Ireland group financial statements (including any amounts relating to overseas entities that are included in those financial statements). Accounting standards are not intended to apply to financial statements of overseas entities prepared for local purposes.

15. Where accounting standards prescribe information to be contained in financial statements, such requirements do not override exemptions from disclosure given by law to, and utilised by, certain types of entity.

Compliance with accounting standards

16. Accounting standards are authoritative statements of how particular types of transaction and other events should be reflected in financial statements and accordingly compliance with accounting standards will normally be necessary for financial statements to give a true and fair view.

17. In applying accounting standards it is important to be guided by the spirit and reasoning behind them. The spirit and reasoning are set out in the individual FRSs and are based on the Board's Statement of Principles for Financial Reporting.

18. The requirement to give a true and fair view may in special circumstances require a departure from accounting standards. However, because accounting standards are formulated with the objective of ensuring that the information resulting from their application faithfully represents the underlying commercial activity, the Board envisages that only in exceptional circumstances will departure from the requirements of an accounting standard be necessary in order for financial statements to give a true and fair view.

19. If in exceptional circumstances compliance with the requirements of an accounting standard is inconsistent with the requirement to give a true and fair view, the requirements of the accounting standard should be departed from to the extent necessary to give a true and fair view. In such cases informed and unbiased judgement should be used to devise an appropriate alternative treatment, which should be consistent with the economic and commercial characteristics of the circumstances concerned. Particulars of any material departure from an accounting standard, the reasons for it and its financial effects should be disclosed in the financial statements. The disclosure made should be equivalent to that given in respect of departures from specific accounting provisions of companies legislation.

20. The Financial Reporting Review Panel (the Review Panel) and the Department of Trade and Industry have procedures for receiving and investigating complaints regarding the annual accounts of companies in respect of apparent departures from the accounting requirements of the Act, including the requirement to give a true and fair view. The Review Panel will be concerned with material departures from accounting standards, where as a result the accounts in question do not give a true and fair view, but it will also cover other departures from the accounting provisions of the Act. The Review Panel is empowered by regulations made under the Act to apply to

the court for a declaration or declarator that the annual accounts of a company do not comply with the requirements of the Act and an order requiring the directors of the company to prepare revised accounts. The Department of Trade and Industry has similar powers.

The public sector

21. The prescription of accounting requirements for the public sector in the United Kingdom is a matter for the Government. Where public sector bodies prepare annual reports and accounts on commercial lines, the Government's requirements may or may not refer specifically either to accounting standards or to the need for the financial statements concerned to give a true and fair view. However, it can be expected that the Government's requirements in such cases will normally accord with the principles underlying the Board's pronouncements, except where in the particular circumstances of the public sector bodies concerned the Government considers these principles to be inappropriate or considers others to be more appropriate.
22. In the Republic of Ireland accounting standards will normally be applicable to reporting entities in the public sector as such entities are either established under companies legislation or are established under special legislation which requires them to produce financial statements which give a true and fair view.

The issue of a Financial Reporting Standard

23. Topics that become the subject of FRSs are identified by the Board either from its own research or from external sources, including submissions from interested parties.
24. When a topic is identified by the Board as requiring the issue of an FRS the Board commissions its staff to undertake a programme of research and consultation. This programme involves consideration of and consultation on the relevant conceptual issues, existing pronouncements and practice in the United Kingdom, the Republic of Ireland and overseas and the economic, legal and practical implications of the introduction of particular accounting requirements.
25. When the issues have been identified and debated by the Board a discussion draft is normally produced and circulated to parties who have registered their interest with the Board. When the issues require a more discursive treatment a discussion paper may be published instead. The purpose of either of these documents is to form a basis for discussion with parties particularly affected by, or having knowledge of, the issues raised in the proposals. An exposure draft of an accounting standard (a Financial Reporting Exposure Draft or FRED) is then published to allow an opportunity for all interested parties to comment on the proposals and for the Board to gauge the appropriateness and level of acceptance of those proposals.
26. The exposure draft is refined in the light of feedback resulting from the period of public exposure. There may follow another period of public or selective exposure prior to the issue of an FRS. Although the Board weighs carefully the views of interested parties, the ultimate content of an FRS must be determined by the Board's own judgement based on research, public consultation and careful deliberation about the benefits and costs of providing the resulting information.

Applicability of an accounting standard to transactions entered into before the standard was issued

27. When a new accounting standard is issued the question arises whether its provisions should be applied to transactions which took place prior to promulgation of the standard. The general policy of the Board is that the provisions of accounting standards should be applied to all material transactions irrespective of the date at which they are entered into. This is because exemption of certain transactions leads to similar transactions being accounted for differently in the same set of accounts, and can also hinder the comparison of the accounts of one entity with another.

28. In a few instances, application of the provisions of accounting standards to past transactions will entail a considerable amount of work and may result in information which is difficult for the user of accounts to interpret. In such a case, in drafting the standard, the Board will consider incorporating an exclusion for transactions which took place prior to the promulgation of the standard.

29. In some instances, a new standard may have unforeseen consequences where financial statements are used to monitor compliance with contracts and agreements. The most widespread example is the covenants contained in banking and loan agreements, which may impose limits on measures such as net worth or gearing as shown in the borrower's financial statements.

30. The Board considers that the developing nature of accounting requirements is a long-established fact that would be known to the parties when they entered into the agreement. It is up to the parties to determine whether the agreement should be insulated from the effects of a future accounting standard or, if not, the manner in which it might be renegotiated to reflect changes in reporting rather than changes in the underlying financial position. The Board, therefore, has no general policy of exempting transactions occurring before a specific date from the requirements of new accounting standards.

Early adoption of Financial Reporting Exposure Drafts

31. An exposure draft is issued for comment and is subject to revision. Until it is converted into an accounting standard the requirements of any existing accounting standards that would be affected by proposals in the exposure draft remain in force.

32. Some companies or other reporting entities may wish to provide additional information reflecting proposals in an exposure draft. In the Board's view there are two ways that this can be achieved:

a) insofar as the information does not conflict with existing accounting standards, it could be incorporated in the financial statements. It should be remembered, however, that the proposals may change before forming part of an accounting standard and the consequences of a change to the proposals should be considered.
b) the information could be provided in supplementary form.

Reviews of accounting standards

33. Accounting standards are issued against the background of a business environment that evolves over time. The Board is, therefore, receptive to comments on accounting standards, recognising that, for some, a substantial period may be needed before their effectiveness can be judged, while in other cases there may be special reasons why an earlier review is necessary.

However, the Board believes that it will normally be appropriate to allow new accounting standards a period in which to become established before commencing a process of formal post-issue review.

Accounting standards and the legal framework

34. In its debates on any accounting topic the Board initially develops its views by considering how its principles of accounting apply to the possible accounting options available for that topic. However, in deciding what is the most appropriate treatment the Board must also consider the environment in which its standards are to be applied. The legislation with which reporting entities must comply forms an important part of the environment. Accordingly, FRSs are drafted in the context of current United Kingdom and Republic of Ireland legislation and European Community Directives with the aim of ensuring consistency between accounting standards and the law.

35. The status of accounting standards under United Kingdom legislation is addressed in the Opinion by Miss Mary Arden QC 'The true and fair requirement', which is published as an appendix to this Foreword.

International Accounting Standards

36. FRSs are formulated with due regard to international developments. The Board supports the International Accounting Standards Committee in its aim to harmonise international financial reporting. As part of this support an FRS contains a section explaining how it relates to the International Accounting Standard (IAS) dealing with the same topic. In most cases, compliance with an FRS automatically ensures compliance with the relevant IAS. Where the requirements of an accounting standard and an IAS differ, the accounting standard should be followed by entities reporting within the area of application of the Board's accounting standards.

Withdrawal of Explanatory Foreword to Statements of Standard Accounting Practice

37. The 'Explanatory Foreword' to SSAPs, issued by the ASC in May 1975 and revised in May 1986, is superseded by this Foreword and is accordingly withdrawn.

APPENDIX

Accounting Standards Board The true and fair requirement

Opinion

1. This Opinion is concerned with the effect of recent changes in the law on the relationship between accounting standards and the requirement in Sections 226 and 227 of the Companies Act 1985 (as amended) that accounts drawn up in accordance with the Companies Act 1985 give a true and fair view of the state of affairs of the company, and where applicable the group, at the end of the financial year in question and of the profit or loss of the Company or group for that financial year. (I shall call this requirement the 'true and fair requirement'). As is well known, the true and fair requirement is overriding. Thus both sections provide that where in special circumstances with the requirements of the Act as to the matters to be included in the accounts would be inconsistent with the true and fair requirement there must be a departure from those requirements to the extent necessary to give a true

and fair view (sections 226(5) and 227(6)). The meaning of the true and fair requirement, as it appeared in earlier legislation, was discussed in detail in the joint Opinions which I wrote in 1983 and 1984 with Leonard Hoffmann QC (now the Right Hon Lord Justice Hoffmann).

2. As stated in those Opinions, the question whether accounts satisfy the true and fair requirement is a question of law for the Court. However, while the true and fair view which the law requires to be given is not qualified in any way, the task of interpreting the true and fair requirement cannot be performed by the Court without evidence as to the practices and views of accountants. The more authoritative those practices and views, the more ready the Court will be to follow them. Those practices and views do not of course stand still. They respond to such matters as advances in accounting and changes in the economic climate and business practice. The law will not prevent the proper development of the practices and views of accountants but rather, through the process of interpretation, will reflect such development.

3. Up to August 1990 the responsibility for developing accounting standards was discharged by the Accounting Standards Committee ('the ASC'). Since August 1990 that responsibility has been discharged by the Accounting Standards Board ('the Board'). The Foreword to Accounting Standards approved by the Board describes in particular the circumstances in which accounts are expected to comply with accounting standards. For this purpose the key paragraph is paragraph 16, which provides

> 'Accounting standards are authoritative statements of how particular types of transaction and other events should be reflected in financial statements and accordingly compliance with accounting standards will normally be necessary for financial statements to give a true and fair view'.

The Foreword also describes the extensive process of investigation and consultation which precedes the issue of a standard and explains that the major accountancy bodies expect their members to observe accounting standards and may enquire into apparent failures by their members to observe standards or ensure adequate disclosure of departures from them.

4. What is the role of an accounting standard? The initial purpose is to identify proper accounting practice for the benefit of preparers and auditors of accounts. However, because accounts commonly comply with accounting standards, the effect of the issue of standards has also been to create a common understanding between users and preparers of accounts as to how particular items should be treated in accounts and accordingly an expectation that save where good reason exists accounts will comply with applicable accounting standards.

5. The Companies Act 1989 now gives statutory recognition to the existence of accounting standards and by implication to their beneficial role in financial reporting. This recognition is achieved principally through the insertion of a new section (Section 256) into the Companies Act 1985 and of a new disclosure requirement into Schedule 4 to that Act. Section 256 provides:

> '256 (1) In this Part 'accounting standards' means statements of standard accounting practice issued by such body or bodies as may be prescribed by regulations.
>
> 2) References in this Part to accounting standards applicable to a company's annual accounts are to such standards as are, in accordance

with their terms, relevant to the company's circumstances and to the accounts.

3) The Secretary of State may make grants to or for the purposes of bodies concerned with:

a) issuing accounting standards,
b) overseeing and directing the issuing of such standards, or
c) investigating departures from such standards or from the accounting requirements of this Act and taking steps to secure compliance with them.

4) Regulations under this section may contain such transitional and other supplementary and incidental provisions as appear to the Secretary of State to be appropriate.'

In addition the notes to financial statements prepared under Schedule 4 must now comply with the following new requirement:**

'36A. It shall be stated whether the accounts have been prepared in accordance with applicable accounting standards and particulars of any material departure from those standards and the reasons for it shall be given.'

6. Another significant change brought about by the 1989 Act is the introduction of a procedure whereby the Secretary of State or a person authorised by him may ask the Court to determine whether annual accounts comply with inter alia the true and fair requirement (Section 245B of the Companies Act 1985). The Financial Reporting Review Panel ('the Review Panel') has been authorised by the Secretary of State for this purpose. By agreement with the Department of Trade and Industry the ambit of the Review Panel is normally public and large private companies, with the Department exercising its powers in other cases.

7. The changes brought about by the Companies Act 1989 will in my view affect the way in which the Court approaches the question whether compliance with an accounting standard is necessary to satisfy the true and fair view requirement. The Court will infer from Section 256 that statutory policy favours both the issue of accounting standards (by a body prescribed by regulation) and compliance with them: indeed Section 256(3)(c) additionally contemplates the investigation of departures from them and confers power to provide public funding for such purpose. The Court will also in my view infer from paragraph 36A of Schedule 4 that (since the requirement is to disclose particulars of non-compliance rather than of compliance) accounts which meet the true and fair requirement will in general follow rather than depart from standards and that departure is sufficiently abnormal to require to be justified. These factors increase the likelihood, to which the earlier joint Opinions referred, that the Courts will hold that in general compliance with accounting standards is necessary to meet the true and fair requirement.

8. The status of accounting standards in legal proceedings has also in my view been enhanced by the changes in the standard setting process since 1989. Prior to the Companies Act 1989 accounting standards were developed by the ASC, which was a committee established by the six professional accountancy

(** This requirement also applies to group accounts drawn up under Schedule 4A. In addition the accounts of banking and insurance companies and groups drawn up under Schedules 9 and 9A must make the same disclosures. There is an exemption for small and medium-sized companies and for certain small and medium-sized groups.)

bodies who form the Consultative Committee of Accountancy Bodies ('the CCAB') and funded by them. The standard-setting process was reviewed by a committee established by the CCAB under the chairmanship of Sir Ron Dearing CB. The report of that Committee (the Dearing Report), which was published in 1988 and is entitled The Making of Accounting Standards, contained a number of recommendations, including recommendations leading to what are now paragraph 36A and Section 245B and the further recommendation that the standard-setting body should be funded on a wider basis. As a result of the implementation of these recommendations the standard-setting body no longer represents simply the views of the accountancy profession. Its members are appointed by a committee drawn from the Council of the Financial Reporting Council Limited ('the FRC'). The Council includes representatives of the Government, representatives of the business and financial community and members of the accountancy profession. Moreover the Board is now funded, via the FRC, jointly by the Government, the financial community and the accountancy profession.

9. The statements referred to in Section 256 are of standard accounting practice. Parliament has thus recognised the desirability of standardisation in the accountancy field. The discretion to determine the measure of standardisation is one of the matters left to the Board. By definition, standardisation may restrict the availability of particular accounting treatments. Moreover the Act does not require that the practices required by a standard should necessarily be those prevailing or generally accepted at the time.

10. As explained in the earlier Joint Opinions in relation to statements of standard accounting practice, the immediate effect of the issue of an accounting standard is to create a likelihood that the court will hold that compliance with that standard is necessary to meet the true and fair requirement. That likelihood is strengthened by the degree to which a standard is subsequently accepted in practice. Thus, if a particular standard is generally followed, the court is very likely to find that accounts must comply with it in order to show a true and fair view. The converse of that proposition, that non-acceptance of a standard in practice would almost inevitably lead a court to the conclusion that compliance with it was not necessary to meet the true and fair requirement, is not however the case. Whenever a standard is issued by the Board, then, irrespective of the lack in some quarters of support for it, the court would be bound to give special weight to the opinion of the Board in view of its status as the standard-setting body, the process of investigation, discussion and consultation that it will have undertaken before adopting the standard and the evolving nature of accounting standards.

11. The fact that paragraph 36A envisages the possibility of a departure from an 'applicable accounting standard' (in essence, any relevant standard: see section 256(2), above) does not mean that the Companies Act permits a departure in any case where the disclosure is given. The departure must have been appropriate in the particular case. If the Court is satisfied that compliance with a standard is necessary to show a true and fair view in that case, a departure will result in a breach of the true and fair requirement even if the paragraph 36A disclosure is given.

12. Experience shows that from time to time and for varying reasons deficiencies in accounting standards appear. Following a recommendation in the Dearing Report, the Board has established a sub-committee called the Urgent Issues Task Force ('the UITF') to resolve such issues on an urgent basis in appropriate cases. The members of the UITF include leading members of the accountancy profession and of the business community. The agenda of the UITF is published in advance to allow for public debate. The UITF's consensus pronouncements (contained in abstracts) represent the considered views of a large majority of its members. When the UITF reaches its view, it is considered by the Board for compliance with the law and accounting standards and with the Board's future plans. If an abstract meets these criteria the Board expects to adopt it without further consideration. It will then be published by the Board. The expectation of the CCAB, the Board and the profession is that abstracts of the UITF will be observed. This expectation has been borne out in practice. Accordingly in my view, the Court is likely to treat UITF abstracts as of considerable standing even though they are not envisaged by the Companies Acts. This will lead to a readiness on the part of the Court to accept that compliance with abstracts of the UITF is also necessary to meet the true and fair requirement.

13. The joint Opinions were particularly concerned with the effect of standards on the concept of true and fair. The approach to standards taken in the joint Opinions is consistent with the approach of the Court in *Lloyd Cheyham* v. *Littlejohn* [1987] BCLC 303 at 313. In that case Woolf J. (as he was then) held that standards of the ASC were 'very strong evidence as to what is the proper standard which should be adopted'.

14. As regards the concept of true and fair, I would emphasise the point made in the joint Opinions that the true and fair view is a dynamic concept. Thus what is required to show a true and fair view is subject to continuous rebirth and in determining whether the true and fair requirement is satisfied the Court will not in my view seek to find synonyms for the words 'true' and 'fair' but will seek to apply the concepts which those words imply.

15. It is nearly a decade since the joint Opinions were written. Experience and legislative history since then have both illustrated the subtlety and evolving nature of the relationship between law and accounting practice. Accounting standards are now assured as an authoritative source of the latter. In consequence it is now the norm for accounts to comply with accounting standards. I would add this. Just as a custom which is upheld by the courts may properly be regarded as a source of law, so too, in my view, does an accounting standard which the court holds must be complied with to meet the true and fair requirement become, in cases where it is applicable, a source of law in itself in the widest sense of that term.

Mary Arden
Erskine Chambers
Lincoln's Inn
21 April 1993

Appendix 2

THE COMPANIES (REVISION OF DEFECTIVE ACCOUNTS AND REPORT) REGULATIONS 1990

(SI 1990/2570)

CITATION AND COMMENCEMENT

1. These Regulations may be cited as the Companies (Revision of Defective Accounts and Report) Regulations 1990 and shall come into force on 7th January 1991.

INTERPRETATION

2. In these Regulations:

"the Act" means the Companies Act 1985;

"date of the original annual accounts" means the date on which the original annual accounts were approved by the board of directors under section 233 of the Act;

"date of the original directors' report" means the date on which the original directors' report was approved by the board of directors under section 234A of the Act;

"date of revision" means the date on which revised accounts are approved by the board of directors under Regulation 4 below or (as the case may be) a revised report is approved by them under Regulation 5 below;

"original", in relation to annual accounts or a directors' report, means the annual accounts or (as the case may be) directors' report which are the subject of revision by, respectively, revised accounts or a revised report and, in relation to abbreviated accounts (within the meaning of Regulation 13(1) below) or a summary financial statement, means abbreviated accounts or a summary financial statement based on the original annual accounts or directors' report;

"revised accounts" mean revised annual accounts of a company prepared by the directors under section 245 of the Act, either through revision by replacement or revision by supplementary note; in the latter case the revised accounts comprise the original annual accounts together with the supplementary note;

"revised report" means a revised directors' report prepared by the directors under section 245 of the Act, either through revision by replacement or revision by supplementary note; in the latter case the revised report comprises the original directors' report together with the supplementary note;

"revision by replacement" means revision by the preparation of a replacement set of accounts or directors' report in substitution for the original annual accounts or directors' report; and

"revision by supplementary note" means revision by the preparation of a note indicating corrections to be made to the original annual accounts or directors' report.

CONTENT OF REVISED ACCOUNTS OR A REVISED REPORT

3(1) Subject to Regulation 16(1), the provisions of the Act as to the matters to be included in the annual accounts of a company shall apply to revised accounts as if the revised accounts were prepared and approved by the directors as at the date of the original annual accounts.

3(2) In particular, sections 226(2) and 227(3) of the Act shall apply so as to require a true and fair view to be shown in the revised accounts of the matters therein referred to viewed as at the date of the original annual accounts.

3(3) Paragraph 12(b) of Schedule 4 to the Act shall apply to revised accounts as if the reference therein to the date on which the accounts were signed was to the date of the original annual accounts.

3(4) The provisions of the Act as to the matters to be included in a directors' report apply to a revised report as if the revised report was prepared and approved by the directors of the company as at the date of the original directors' report.

APPROVAL AND SIGNATURE OF REVISED ACCOUNTS OR A REVISED REPORT

4(1) Section 233 of the Act (approval and signing of accounts) shall apply to revised accounts, save that in the case of revision by supplementary note, it shall apply as if it required a signature on the supplementary note instead of on the company's balance sheet.

4(2) Where copies of the original annual accounts have been sent out to members under section 238(1) of the Act, laid before the company in general meeting under section 241(1) of the Act or delivered to the registrar under section 242(1) of the Act, the directors shall, before approving the revised accounts under section 233 of the Act, cause statements as to the following matters to be made in a prominent position in the revised accounts (in the case of a revision by supplementary note, in that note):

- (a) in the case of revision by replacement:
  - (i) that the revised accounts replace the original annual accounts for the financial year (specifying it);
  - (ii) that they are now the statutory accounts of the company for that financial year;
  - (iii) that they have been prepared as at the date of the original annual accounts and not as at the date of revision and accordingly do not deal with events between those dates;
  - (iv) the respects in which the original annual accounts did not comply with the requirements of the Act; and

(v) any significant amendments made consequential upon the remedying of those defects;

(b) in the case of revision by a supplementary note:

(i) that the note revises in certain respects the original annual accounts of the company and is to be treated as forming part of those accounts; and

(ii) that the annual accounts have been revised as at the date of the original annual accounts and not as at the date of revision and accordingly do not deal with events between those dates,

and shall, when approving the revised accounts, cause the date on which the approval is given to be stated in them (in the case of revision by supplementary note, in that note); section 233(5) of the Act shall apply with respect to a failure to comply with this paragraph as if the requirements of this paragraph were requirements of the Act.

5(1) Section 234A of the Act (approval and signing of directors' report) shall apply to a revised report, save that in the case of revision by supplementary note, it shall apply as if it required the signature to be on the supplementary note.

5(2) Where the original directors' report has been sent out to members under section 238(1) of the Act, laid before the company in general meeting under section 241(1) of the Act or delivered to the registrar under section 242(1) of the Act, the directors shall before approving the revised report under section 234A of the Act, cause statements as to the following matters to be made in a prominent position in the revised report (in the case of a revision by supplementary note, in that note):

(a) in the case of a revision by replacement:

(i) that the revised report replaces the original report for the financial year (specifying it);

(ii) that it has been prepared as at the date of the original directors' report and not as at the date of revision and accordingly does not deal with any events between those dates;

(iii) the respects in which the original directors' report did not comply with the requirements of the Act; and

(iv) any significant amendments made consequential upon the remedying of those defects;

(b) in the case of revision by a supplementary note:

(i) that the note revises in certain respects the original directors' report of the company and is to be treated as forming part of that report; and

(ii) that the directors' report has been revised as at the date of the original directors' report and not as at the date of the revision and accordingly does not deal with events between those dates, and shall, when approving the revised report, cause the date on which the approval is given to be stated in them (in the case of a revision by supplementary note, in that note); section 234(5) of the Act shall apply with respect to a failure to comply with this paragraph as if the requirements of this paragraph were requirements of Part VII of the Act.

AUDITORS' REPORT ON REVISED ACCOUNTS AND REVISED REPORT

6(1) Subject to the next paragraph, a company's current auditors shall make a report or (as the case may be) further report under section 235 of the Act to the company's members under this Regulation on any revised accounts prepared under section 245 of the Act and:

(a) section 237 (duties of auditors) shall apply *mutatis mutandis*; and

(b) section 235(1) shall not apply with respect to the revised accounts.

6(2) Where the auditors' report on the original annual accounts was not made by the company's current auditors, the directors of the company may resolve that the report required by paragraph (1) is to be made by the person or persons who made that report, provided that that person or those persons agree to do so and he or they would be qualified for appointment as auditor of the company.

6(3) Subject to Regulations 16(1), an auditors' report under this Regulation shall state whether in the auditors' opinion the revised accounts have been properly prepared in accordance with the provisions of the Act as they have effect under these Regulations, and in particular whether a true and fair view, seen as at the date the original annual accounts were approved, is given by the revised accounts with respect to the matters set out in section 235(2)(a) to (c) of the Act.

The report shall also state whether in the auditors' opinion the original annual accounts failed to comply with the requirements of the Act in the respects identified by the directors (in the case of revision by replacement) in the statement required by Regulation 4(2)(a)(iv) or (in the case of revision by supplementary note) in the supplementary note.

6(4) The auditors shall also consider whether the information contained in the directors' report for the financial year for which the annual accounts are prepared (which is, if the report has been revised under these Regulations, that revised report) is consistent with those accounts; and if they are of the opinion that it is not they shall state that fact in their report under this Regulation.

6(5) Section 236 of the Act (signature of auditors' report) shall apply to an auditors' report under this Regulation as it applies to an auditors' report under section 235(1) *mutatis mutandis*.

6(6) An auditors' report under this regulation shall, upon being signed under section 236 as so applied, be, as from the date of signature, the auditors' report on the annual accounts of the company in place of the report on the original annual accounts.

6A(1) Subject to the next paragraph, where a company's reporting accountant has, prior to the preparation of the revised accounts, made a report for the purposes of section 249A(2) of the Act on the original annual accounts, he shall make a further report to the company's members under this regulation on any revised accounts prepared under section 245 of the Act and section 249C of the Act shall apply *mutatis mutandis*.

6A(2) The directors of the company may resolve that the further report is to be made by a person who was not the original reporting accountant, but is qualified to act as the reporting accountant of the company.

6A(3) Subsections(2) to (4) of section 236 of the Act shall apply to a report under this Regulation as they apply, by virtue of section 249E(2)(A) of the Act, to a report made for the purposes of section 249A(2) of the Act.

6A(4) A report under this Regulation shall, upon being signed by the reporting accountant, be, as from the date of the signature, the report on the annual accounts of the company for the purposes of section 249A(2) of the Act in place of the report on the original annual accounts.

6B(1) Where as a result of the revisions to the accounts a company which, in respect of the original accounts, was exempt from audit by virtue of subsection (1) of section 249A of the Act, becomes a company which is eligible for exemption from audit only by virtue of subsection (2) of that section, it shall cause a report to be prepared in accordance with section 249C of the Act in respect of the revised accounts.

6B(2) Where as a result of the revisions to the accounts, the company is no longer entitled to exemption from audit under section 249(1) or (2) of the Act, the company shall cause an auditors' report on the revised accounts to be prepared.

6B(3) The report made in accordance with section 249C of the Act or auditors' report shall be delivered to the registrar within 28 days after the date of revision of the revised accounts.

6B(4) Subsections (2) to (5) of section 242 of the Act shall apply with respect to a failure to comply with the requirements of this Regulation as they apply with respect to a failure to comply with the requirements of subsection (1) of that section but as if -

(a) the references in subsections (2) and (4) of that section to "the period allowed for laying and delivering accounts and reports" were references to the period of 28 days referred to in paragraph (3); and

(b) the references in subsection (5) to "the documents in question" and "this Part" were, respectively, a reference to the documents referred to in paragraph (3) and to the provisions of Part VII of the Act as applied by these Regulations.

AUDITORS' REPORT ON REVISED REPORT ALONE

7(1) Subject to the next paragraph, a company's current auditors shall make a report or (as the case may be) further report under section 235 of the Act to the company's members under this Regulation on any revised report prepared under section 245 of the Act if the relevant annual accounts have not been revised at the same time.

7(2) Where the auditors' report on the annual accounts for the financial year covered by the revised report was not made by the company's current auditors, the directors of the company may resolve that the report required by paragraph (1) is to be made by the person or persons who made that report, provided that that person or those persons agree to do so and he or they would be qualified for appointment as auditor of the company.

7(3) The report shall state that the auditors have considered whether the information given in the revised report is consistent with the annual accounts for the relevant year (specifying it) and:

(a) if they are of the opinion that it is; or

(b) if they are of the opinion that it is not,

they shall state that fact in their report.

7(4) Section 236 of the Act (signature of auditors' report) shall apply to an auditors' report under this Regulation as it applies to an auditors' report under section 235(1) *mutatis mutandis.*

EFFECT OF REVISION

8(1) Upon the directors approving revised accounts under Regulation 4, the provisions of the Act shall have effect as if the revised accounts were, as from the date of their approval, the annual accounts of the company in place of the original annual accounts.

8(2) In particular, the revised accounts shall thereupon be the company's annual accounts for the relevant financial year for the purposes of:

(a) sections 239 (right to demand copies of accounts and reports) and 240(5) (requirements in connection with publication of accounts) of the Act; and

(b) sections 238 (persons entitled to receive copies of accounts and reports), 241 (accounts and reports to be laid before company in general meeting) and 242 (accounts and reports to be delivered to the registrar) if the requirements of those sections have not been complied with prior to the date of revision.

9(1) Subject to the following provisions of these Regulations, upon the directors approving a revised report under Regulation 5 the provisions of the Act shall have effect as if the revised report was, as from the date of its approval, the directors' report in place of the original directors' report.

9(2) In particular, the revised report shall thereupon the directors' report for the relevant financial year for the purposes of:

(a) sections 239 (right to demand copies of accounts and reports); and

(b) sections 238 (persons entitled to receive copies of accounts and reports), 241 (accounts and reports to be laid before company in general meeting) and 242 (accounts and reports to be delivered to the registrar) if the requirements of those sections have not been complied with prior to the date of revision.

PUBLICATION OF REVISED ACCOUNTS AND REPORTS

10(1) This Regulation has effect where the directors have prepared revised accounts or a revised report under section 245 of the Act and copies of the original annual accounts or report have been sent to any person under section 238 of the Act.

10(2) The directors shall send to any such person:

(a) in the case of a revision by replacement, a copy of the revised accounts, or (as the case may be) the revised report, together with a copy of the auditors' report on those accounts, or (as the case may be) on that report; or

(b) in the case of revision by supplementary note, a copy of that note together with a copy of the auditors' report on the revised accounts, or (as the case may be) on the revised report,

not more than 28 days after the date of revision.

10(3) The directors shall also, not more than 28 days after the revision, send a copy of the revised accounts or (as the case may be) the revised report, together with a copy of the auditors' report on those accounts or (as the case may be) on that report, to any person who is not a person entitled to receive a copy under the last paragraph but who is, as at the date of revision:

(a) a member of the company;

(b) a holder of the company's debentures; or

(c) a person who is entitled to receive notice of general meetings,

unless the company would be entitled at that date to send to that person a summary financial statement under section 251 of the Act. Section 238(2) and (3) of the Act shall apply to this paragraph as they have effect with respect to section 238(1)

10(4) Section 238(5) shall apply to a default in complying with this Regulation as if the provisions of this Regulation were provisions of section 238 and as if the reference therein to "the company and every officer of it who is in default" was a reference to each of the directors who approved the revised accounts under Regulation 4 above or revised report under Regulation 5 above.

10(5) Where, prior to the date of revision of the original annual accounts, the company had completed sending out copies of those accounts under section 238, references in the Act to the day on which accounts are sent out under section 238 shall be construed as referring to the day on which the original accounts were sent out (applying section 238(6) as necessary) notwithstanding that those accounts have been revised; where the company had not completed, prior to the date of revision, the sending out of copies of those accounts under that section, such references shall be to the day, or the last day, on which the revised accounts are sent out.

LAYING OF REVISED ACCOUNTS OR A REVISED REPORT

11(1) This Regulation has effect where the directors have prepared revised accounts or a revised report under section 245 of the Act and copies of the original annual accounts of report have been laid before a general meeting under section 241 of the Act.

11(2) A copy of the revised accounts or (as the case may be) the revised report, together with a copy of the auditors' report on those accounts, or (as the case may be) on that report, shall be laid before the next general meeting of the company held after the date of revision at which any annual accounts for a financial year are laid, unless the revised accounts, or (as the case may be) the revised report, have already been laid before an earlier general meeting.

11(3) Section 241(2) to (4) shall apply with respect to a failure to comply with the requirements of this Regulation as they have effect with respect to a failure to comply with the requirements of section 241(1) but as if:

(a) the reference in section 241(2) to "the period allowed for laying and delivering accounts and reports" was a reference to the period between the date of revision of the revised accounts or (as the case may be) the revised report and the date of the next general meeting of the company held after the date of revision at which any annual accounts for a financial year are laid; references in section 241(2) and (3) to "that period" shall be construed accordingly; and

(b) the references in section 241(4) to "the documents in question" and "this Part" were, respectively, a reference to the documents referred to in the last paragraph and the provisions of Part VII of the 1985 Act as applied by these Regulations.

DELIVERY OF REVISED ACCOUNTS OR A REVISED REPORT

12(1) This Regulation has effect where the directors have prepared revised accounts or a revised report under section 245 of the Act and a copy of the original annual accounts or report has been delivered to the registrar under section 242 of the Act.

12(2) The directors of the company shall, within 28 days of the date of revision, deliver to the registrar:

(a) in the case of a revision by replacement, a copy of the revised accounts or (as the case may be) the revised report, together with a copy of the auditors' report on those accounts or (as the case may be) on that report; or

(b) in the case of a revision by supplementary note, a copy of that note, together with a copy of the auditors' report on the revised accounts or (as the case may be) on the revised report.

12(3) Section 242(2) to (5) shall apply with respect to a failure to comply with the requirements of this Regulation as they apply with respect to a failure to comply with the requirements of section 242(1) but as if:

(a) the references in section 242(2) and (4) to "the period allowed for laying and delivering accounts and reports" was a reference to the period of 28 days referred to in the last paragraph; the reference in section 242(2) to "that period" shall be construed accordingly; and

(b) the references in section 242(5) to "the documents in question" and "this Part" were, respectively, a reference to the documents referred to in the last paragraph and the provisions of Part VII of the 1985 Act as applied by these Regulations.

SMALL AND MEDIUM-SIZED COMPANIES

13(1) This Regulation has effect (subject to Regulation 16(2)) where the directors have prepared revised accounts under section 245 of the Act and the company has, prior to the date of revision, delivered to the registrar accounts which take advantage of the exemptions for a small or medium-sized company conferred by section 246 of the Act (referred to in these Regulations as "abbreviated accounts").

13(2) Where the abbreviated accounts so delivered to the registrar would, if they had been prepared by reference to the revised accounts, not comply with the provisions of the Act (whether because the company would not have qualified as a small or (as the case may be) medium-sized company in the light of the revised accounts or because the accounts have been revised in a manner which affects the content of the abbreviated accounts), the directors of the company shall cause the company either:

(a) to deliver to the registrar a copy of the revised accounts, together with a copy of the directors' report and the auditors' report on the revised accounts; or

(b) (if on the basis of the revised accounts they would be entitled under the Act to do so) to prepare further accounts under section 246 in accordance with the provisions of that section and Schedule 8 to the Act and deliver them to the registrar together with a statement as to the effect of the revisions made.

13(3) Where the abbreviated accounts would, if they had been prepared by reference to the revised accounts, comply with the requirements of the Act, the directors of the company shall cause the company to deliver to the registrar:

(a) a note stating that the annual accounts of the company for the relevant financial year (specifying it) have been revised in a respect which has no bearing on the abbreviated accounts delivered for that year; together with

(b) a copy of the auditors' report on the revised accounts.

13(4) Revised abbreviated accounts or a note under this Regulation shall be delivered to the Registrar within 28 days after the date of revision of the revised accounts.

13(5) Section 242(2) to (5) shall apply with respect to a failure to comply with the requirements of this Regulation as they apply with respect to a failure to comply with the requirements of section 242(1) but as if:

(a) the references in section 242(2) and (4) to "the period allowed for laying and delivering accounts and reports" was a reference to the period of 28 days referred to in the last paragraph; the reference in section 242(2) to "that period" shall be construed accordingly; and

(b) the references in section 242(5) to "the documents in question" and "this Part" were, respectively, a reference to the documents referred to in paragraphs (2)(a) or (b) or (as the case may be) (3)(a) and (b) and to the provisions of Part VII of the 1985 Act as applied by these Regulations.

13A(1) This Regulation has effect (subject to Regulation 16(2)) where the directors have delivered to the registrar abbreviated accounts which do not comply with the provisions of the Act for reasons other than those specified in Regulation 13(2) above.

13A(2) The directors of the company shall cause the company -

(a) to prepare further abbreviated accounts under section 246 in accordance with the provisions of that section and Schedule 8 to the Act, and

(b) to deliver those accounts to the registrar within 28 days after the date of revision together with a statement as to the effect of the revisions made.

13A(3) Section 242(2) to (5) shall apply with respect to a failure to comply with the requirements of this Regulation as they apply with respect to a failure to comply with the requirements of section 242(1) but as if-

(a) the references in section 242(2) and (4) to "the period allowed for laying and delivering accounts and reports" was a reference to the period of 28 days referred to in the last paragraph; the reference in section 242(2) to "that period" shall be construed accordingly, and

(b) the references in section 242(5) to "the documents in question" were a reference to the documents referred to in paragraph (2)(a) and to the provisions of Part VII of the 1985 Act as applied by these Regulations.

SUMMARY FINANCIAL STATEMENTS

14(1) This Regulation has effect (subject to Regulation 16(3)) where the directors have prepared revised accounts or a revised report under section 245 of the Act and a summary financial statement based upon the original annual accounts or report has been sent to any person under section 251 of the Act.

14(2) Where the summary financial statement would, if it had been prepared by reference to the revised accounts or revised report, not comply with the requirements of section 251 or the Companies (Summary Financial

Statement) Regulations 1992 made thereunder, the directors of the company shall cause the company to prepare a further summary financial statement under section 251 and to send that statement to:

(a) any person who received a copy of the original summary financial statement; and

(b) any person to whom the company would be entitled, as at the date the revised summary financial statement is prepared, to send a summary financial statement for the current financial year;

and section 251(1) to (4) and (7) shall apply *mutatis mutandis* to a summary financial statement hereunder.

14(3) A summary financial statement prepared under the last paragraph shall contain a short statement of the revisions made and their effect.

14(4) Where the summary financial statement would, if it had been prepared by reference to the revised accounts or revised report, comply with the requirements of section 251 and the Companies (Summary Financial Statement) Regulations 1992, the directors of the company shall cause the company to send to the persons referred to in paragraph (2) above a note stating that the annual accounts of the company for the relevant financial year (specifying it) or (as the case may be) the directors' report for that year have or has been revised in a respect which has no bearing on the summary financial statement for that year.

If the auditors' report under Regulation 6 or 7 above on the revised accounts or revised report is qualified, a copy of that report shall be attached to the note sent out under this paragraph.

14(5) A summary financial statement revised, or a note prepared, under this Regulation shall be sent to the persons referred to in paragraph (2) above within 28 days after the date of revision of the revised accounts or revised report.

14(6) Section 251(6) of the Act shall apply with respect to a failure to comply with the requirements of this Regulation as if the provisions of this Regulation were provisions of section 251 and as if the reference therein to "the company and every officer of it who is in default" was a reference to each of the directors of the company who approved the revised accounts under Regulation 4 above or the revised report under Regulation 5 above.

COMPANIES EXEMPT FROM AUDIT BY VIRTUE OF SECTION 249A OF COMPANIES ACT 1985

14A(1) Where a company is exempt by virtue of section 249A(1) of the Act from the provisions of Part VII of the Act relating to the audit of accounts, these Regulations shall have effect as if any reference to an auditors' report, or to the making of such a report, were omitted.

14A(2) Where a company is exempt by virtue of section 249A(2) of the Act from the provisions of Part VII of the Act relating to the audit of accounts, regulations 10 to 13 shall have effect as if-

(a) references to the auditors' report on any accounts were references to the report made for the purposes of section 249A(2) in respect of those accounts, and

(b) references to the auditors' report on a revised directors' report were omitted.

DORMANT COMPANIES

15 Where a company has passed a resolution under section 250 of the Act exempting itself from the requirements of Part VII of the Act relating to the audit of accounts, these Regulations shall apply as if they omitted any reference to an auditors' report, or to the making of such a report.

MODIFICATIONS OF ACT

16(1) Where the provisions of the Act as to the matters to be included in the annual accounts of a company or (as the case may be) in a directors' report have been amended after the date of the original annual accounts or (as the case may be) directors' report but prior to the date of revision, references in Regulations 3 and 6(3) above to the provisions of the Act shall be construed as references to the provisions of the Act as in force at the date of the original annual accounts or (as the case may be) directors' report.
16(2) Where the provisions of section 246 of, and Schedule 8 to, the Act as to the matters to be included in abbreviated accounts (within the meaning of Regulation 13(1) above) have been amended after the date of delivery of the original abbreviated accounts but prior to the date of revision of the revised accounts or report, references in Regulation 13 or 13A to the provisions of the Act or to any particular provision thereof shall be construed as references to the provisions of the Act, or to the particular provision, as in force at the date of delivery of the original abbreviated accounts.
16(3) Where the provisions of section 251 of the Act, or of the Companies (Summary Financial Statement) Regulations 1992, as to the matters to be included in a summary financial statement have been amended after the date of the sending out of the original summary financial statement but prior to the date of revision of the revised accounts or report, references in Regulation 14 to section 251 or to those Regulations shall be construed as references to that section or those Regulations as in force at the date of the sending out of the original summary financial statements.

Appendix 3

FINANCIAL REPORTING REVIEW PANEL PROCEDURES FOR HANDLING INDIVIDUAL CASES

PN23, September 1993

Introduction

1. This note sets out the revised version of the procedures originally adopted for the Review Panel ('the Panel') and considered by the Secretary of State for Trade and Industry prior to the making of an Order on 9 January 1991 authorising The Financial Reporting Review Panel Limited for the purposes of section 245B of the Companies Act 1985 (The Companies (Defective Accounts) (Authorised Person) Order 1991 – Statutory Instrument 1991 No. 13). Under this Order the Panel is empowered to apply to the court under section 245B of the Companies Act 1985 for a declaration or declarator that the annual accounts of a company do not comply with the requirements of that Act and for an order requiring the directors of the company to prepare revised accounts. A parallel Order – Statutory Rules of Northern Ireland 1991 No. 269 – was made on 24 June 1991 in respect of the Companies (Northern Ireland) Order 1986. This current version of the procedures is in substitution of the June 1991 version and will apply to all Panel enquiries that start after 27 September 1993.

2. The Department of Trade and Industry (DTI) has agreed with the Financial Reporting Review Panel that normally the Panel will deal with the accounts of public and large private companies. The companies concerned are public limited companies (PLCs) (except PLCs that are subsidiaries in a small or medium-sized group), companies within a group headed by a PLC, and any company not qualifying as small or medium-sized as defined by section 247 of the Companies Act 1985 or any company within a group which does not qualify as small or medium-sized as defined by section 249 of the Act. DTI will handle all other cases. The Review Panel will examine departures from the accounting provisions of the Companies Act 1985 whether or not they also involve departures from accounting standards. DTI remains responsible for all complaints relating to the directors' report and summary financial statements.

3. These procedures, which have been adopted pursuant to Article 36(b), should be read in conjunction with the relevant provisions of the company's

Articles of Association. An extract from the Articles is annexed. A full copy of the company's Memorandum and Articles of Association is available on application.

General principles

4. The Panel's aim is that its procedures shall be effective and proper. Since the concern of the Panel is the possible need for revision of the published annual accounts of companies the matters it deals with will normally call for speedy action, and the Panel's procedures must therefore be quick; but speed will not be achieved at the expense of fairness to all concerned.

5. The Panel will seek to operate by discussion and persuasion as far as possible, and will seek recourse to the court only when the possibility of voluntary agreement has been properly explored.

6. The Panel will not itself monitor or actively initiate scrutinies of company accounts for possible defects. It will examine matters drawn to its attention, either directly (e.g. by complaint or qualified audit report in respect of companies listed on the London Stock Exchange) or indirectly (e.g. by Press comment).

7. The Panel will concentrate on the particular matter drawn to its attention. While its enquiries may extend beyond this issue they will not necessarily involve an examination of all aspects of the company accounts in question.

8. Where it holds hearings or other meetings with a company or others the Panel will operate in an informal way and not seek to follow a court-like procedure. Nevertheless, if they wish, companies may be represented by Counsel or other professional advisers. While the Panel's procedures will be informal the requirements of natural justice will be fully observed.

9. The Panel will encourage the company under enquiry to be accompanied by its auditors at meetings or hearings with the Panel. Where this does not prove practicable the Panel may seek separate contact with the auditors.

10. The Panel will be prepared to receive representations from, or to give consideration to a hearing with, third parties where it appears to the Panel that they may have relevant information to contribute. The company under enquiry will be informed of the substance of such representations.

11. Complainants to the Panel will always be informed of the outcome of their complaint, in as much detail as is legally and commercially practicable.

12. Subject to its responsibility to the court when it has made an application to it, the Panel will take great pains to safeguard all commercial confidential information provided to it. The Panel will strive to avoid any public comment on individual cases (potential or actual) until they are in the public domain (see paragraphs 39 to 43 below).

13. As is indicated in paragraphs 22 to 31 below the Panel will normally deal with individual cases of substance through specially constituted Groups of members, whose appointment, functions, composition and powers are set out in paragraphs 36, 37, 39 and 40 of the Articles of Association annexed. As paragraph 24 indicates, the involvement of a Group may be preceded by one or more informal meetings with the company.

14. No member will be appointed to a Group or otherwise become involved in any case (eg as in paragraphs 18 and 24 below) where there is reason to believe that there may be any conflict of interest. This issue will be drawn specifically to members' attention on each occasion they are invited to join a Group or otherwise become involved in a case.

15. As far as possible each Group will be chaired by the Review Panel Chairman. Where he is unable to chair a particular Group he will endeavour to ensure that the membership of the Group in question includes a lawyer. (See also paragraph 26).
16. The Panel will not modify its procedures or timetable to assist one or other party in a takeover bid. It will not unreasonably delay any enquiry that it may believe appropriate but it will not feel in any way bound to operate within the bid timetable. The Panel will liaise closely with the Executive of the Take-over Panel during the course of any enquiry that affects that Panel.

NOTE: References to a 'company' in this note of procedures should be read as references to the directors of that company where the context requires it – see for example sections 245A(1) & (2) and 245B(1) of the Companies Act 1985. References to the Chairman and Deputy Chairman should be read in conjunction with Article 36(h).

Detailed approach

17. When a case comes to notice the Secretary
    (i) will acknowledge receipt of any notice or reference which comes by letter from an individual or corporate complainant.
    (ii) will inform the Chairman and Deputy Chairman of it, and
    (iii) will provide them with preliminary advice from the accountants on the common staff of The Financial Reporting Council Limited (FRC). The Accounting Standards Board Limited (ASB) and The Financial Reporting Review Panel Limited (FRRP).

18. The Chairman, assisted by the Deputy Chairman, and consulting if he so chooses two or more Panel members, will decide on the next steps. If the Chairman feels it would materially assist him to form a view as to whether there is a case of substance he may also seek outside specialist advice, taking care to ensure that there is no apparent conflict of interest and that due confidentiality is observed.
19. If it appears that there is, or may be, a case of substance, the Chairman will proceed as outlined in paragraphs 20 to 33 below. If it appears that the case does not fall into this category but that there are minor matters which should be explored further he will proceed as outlined in paragraphs 34 to 37 below. If he concludes that the case is not one that should be pursued further the Secretary will inform the complainant (if any) accordingly.

Cases of apparent substance

20. After considering the preliminary advice referred to in paragraphs 17 and 18 above, the Chairman, or Deputy Chairman if appropriate, will write to the Chairman of the company concerned. The letter will be couched in the terms of section 245A(1) of the Companies Act 1985 (i.e. it will indicate that there is, or may be, a question whether the accounts under enquiry comply with the requirements of the Act, and will indicate the respects in which it appears that such a question arises, or may arise); will draw attention to the powers of the Panel, including its right to make an application to the court; will enclose a copy of the Panel's procedures; and will invite the directors to comment.
21. The period allowed for a reply will be one month, so as to relate to the Secretary of State's powers specified in the Act, but the directors will be

invited to reply earlier if they are able and willing to do so. During this period the Panel Secretary will, if the company requests, meet directors or officials of the company to assist the company's understanding of the Panel's procedures and the content of the letter referred to in paragraph 20.

22. After any letter in accordance with paragraph 20 has been sent the Secretary will, if appropriate, make contact with the company to arrange a contingent date or dates for a meeting with the Group formed for the purpose of the enquiry or with the Chairman, as the case may be. The company will be invited to arrange for its auditors to attend the meeting.

23. At the time the paragraph 20 letter is despatched the Chairman will decide whether to form a Group immediately or whether to await the company's reply to the letter and any informal meeting or meetings that may follow it.

24. As soon as possible after the directors' reply to the paragraph 20 letter has been received the Chairman will decide whether to proceed immediately to a Group meeting or whether first to seek further information from, or any informal discussion with, the company. In reaching this decision the Chairman will consult the Deputy Chairman and may consult those Panel members involved in the preliminary review of the case (paragraph 18 above) or members of the Group formed for the purpose of the enquiry, if it is in existence at that time. A similar procedure, if appropriate, will apply in respect of information supplied to the Panel at an informal meeting or meetings with the directors or officials of the company or in subsequent letters from the company.

25. If and when the Chairman concludes that the matter warrants the formal involvement of a Group he will instruct the Secretary to make arrangements for its formation. The company will be informed by the Secretary of the membership of the Group as soon as possible after its formation.

26. It will be the practice of a Group to engage an accountant and if appropriate other advisers for any enquiries that it appears may result in an application to the court. For such enquiries a Group will always have legal advice available to it, provided either internally or externally. The time at which external advisers are engaged will depend on the circumstances of the case. The Secretary will inform the company of such proposed appointments in order that the company may advise the Panel of any conflict of interest that might arise were a particular adviser to be engaged.

27. If and when the Chairman concludes that the point has been reached where the Panel's enquiries should be pursued formally by a Group he, or the Secretary on his behalf, will arrange (or confirm) with the company the date and time of the meeting ('hearing') between the Group and the directors and other officials of, or advisers to, the company.

28. The hearing will be in private. All those present will be identified to the hearing by name, function and connection with the parties concerned.

29. At its discretion the Group may on occasion give a separate hearing to third parties who appear to have useful and relevant information to contribute. As stated in paragraph 9 above, where the auditors to a company do not attend with the company a separate meeting may be sought with them.

30. After the hearing and any subsequent hearings or meetings that may take place the Group will deliberate as to the next steps. If it remains unsatisfied with the company's explanations or the corrective action proposed by the company the Chairman will write to the directors setting out the grounds on

which the Group is unsatisfied. Where the Group has received third party submissions pursuant to paragraph 29 and not made available to the company a summary of these will be included in the letter. The letter will inform the directors that on the basis of the explanations so far given to it the Panel is minded to make an application to the court under section 245B(1)(b) of the Companies Act 1985. The directors will be given 14 days to make any further comments before such action is set in hand.

31. The Group will convene to consider the company's reply to the letter at paragraph 30. If the further explanations or the company's voluntary action do not satisfy the Group it will formally resolve, subject to the majority specified in the Articles, to make an application to the court.

32. The application to the court will thereupon be made in the name of the company – The Financial Reporting Review Panel Limited – through solicitors and Counsel instructed on its behalf.

33. On application to the court the Secretary will inform the Registrar of Companies in accordance with section 245B(2) of the Companies Act 1985. At this point, and in a manner which takes account of market sensitivities, a public announcement of the application will be made. (See paragraphs 39 to 43 below for more details of the Panel's policy and procedures on publicity).

Minor cases

34. Where the Chairman's preliminary view, reached in accordance with paragraphs 17 and 18 above, is that the issues raised, although apparently minor, nevertheless warrant further exploration, the Secretary will write to the company inviting its comments and seeking a reply within 14 days.

35. The Secretary will report the reply to the Chairman and Deputy Chairman with any further advice he has sought from the common staff accountants or others. In the light of this information, and any amplification of it, the Chairman will then decide whether the matter should:

- (i) not be pursued further; or
- (ii) be pursued as a case of apparent substance, or
- (iii) continue to be pursued as a minor matter.

36. If it is decided not to pursue the case further, the Secretary will inform the company and the complainant (if any) accordingly. If it is decided to pursue the matter as one of apparent substance the Chairman will write to the company a suitably adapted version of the letter in paragraph 20 above and will thereafter follow the procedures set out in paragraphs 20 to 33 above.

37. If the defect appears not to be one warranting treatment as a matter of apparent substance but to be one that is desirable to remedy in some way the Chairman, assisted by such members of the Panel as he may choose, will hold informal discussions with the company accordingly.

Other matters

Supervision of voluntary or compulsory revision

38. Appropriate arrangements will be put in place by the Group (or Chairman as appropriate) for the supervision of the voluntary revision of accounts. A failure to carry out the voluntary revision agreed will re-start the procedures outlined above. It will be for the court to decide how to secure

compliance with any order it makes, and how, if appropriate, the Panel should be involved.

Public statements by the Panel or Group

39. The Panel will not normally make any announcement about an enquiry before it makes an application to the court. Nor will it either confirm or deny that a particular company is under enquiry. Once contacted by the Panel it will be for the company in question to decide, in consultation if appropriate with the London Stock Exchange, whether it should make any announcement at that stage but in the event that the company wishes to publish any statement concerning its contact with the Panel, the Panel will consider whether it is appropriate to associate itself in any way with that statement and will act accordingly.
40. As indicated in paragraph 33 above the Panel will make an announcement at the time it makes any application to the court.
41. The Panel will normally make an announcement when a company has agreed voluntarily to revise its accounts or take other corrective action, e.g. in its subsequent accounts. The timing of this announcement will be discussed with the company and when appropriate the London Stock Exchange.
42. The Panel may on occasion issue a statement in other circumstances e.g. when a company's accounts have been examined by it but where the departure has not been adjudged sufficiently serious to justify an application to the court or to call for voluntary revision or other corrective action. Any such case will be considered on its merits in consultation with the company and when appropriate the London Stock Exchange.
43. Where a company has itself decided to make an announcement about contact with the Panel (see paragraph 39 above) and the outcome of that contact has not been announced by the Panel it will be for the company to decide whether to make an announcement about the conclusion of that contact. At its discretion the Panel may issue a statement commenting on any such announcement.

Advice

44. In no circumstances will the Panel provide advice to a company or its auditors as to whether a particular accounting treatment would or would not meet the requirements of the Act.

The position of auditors and directors

45. In order to assist those responsible for the regulation of auditors the Panel will draw to the attention of an auditor's professional body any case where, at the instance of the Panel, the company has voluntarily accepted, or the court has declared, that its accounts were defective and where the auditor had not qualified his report in that respect. As part of this process, and subject to considerations of confidentiality, the Panel will provide the relevant professional body with such detailed information as appears appropriate.
46. The Panel may, on request, and subject to considerations of confidentiality, provide similar information to professional bodies in order to assist them to fulfil their responsibilities for the supervision of the professional conduct of individual members.

EXTRACT FROM THE ARTICLES OF ASSOCIATION OF THE FINANCIAL REPORTING REVIEW PANEL LTD

The Review Panel

34. a) The company shall have a Review Panel whose membership shall consist of:

(i) a Chairman;

(ii) a Deputy Chairman; and

(iii) other members of the Review Panel appointed in accordance with this Article and the members of the Review Panel shall be officers of the Company.

b) The Appointments Committee may, having regard to the appointee's ability to contribute towards the Company's objects, at any time:

(i) appoint or re-appoint any person or persons as members of the Review Panel (whether or not for a specified period); and

(ii) appoint or re-appoint any member of the Review Panel to the office of Chairman or Deputy Chairman (whether or not for a specified period).

c) The Appointments Committee may at any time remove from office any person so appointed or re-appointed.

d) Any appointment, re-appointment or removal made under clause (b) or (c) above, shall be notified in writing to the Company at its registered office and shall be signed by the duly authorised representative of the Appointments Committee. Each such notice shall specify the date from which it is to take effect and, in the case of an appointment or re-appointment, shall be accompanied by the appointee's written consent to act.

e) A member of the Review Panel shall retire from office upon the expiry of the period specified in the most recent notice of his appointment or re-appointment received by the Company pursuant to clause (d) above or, if no particular period is specified therein, upon the third anniversary of such appointment or re-appointment.

35. The office of member of the Review Panel shall be vacated if the member of the Review Panel:

a) is removed from office pursuant to the provisions of Article 34; or

b) resigns his office by notice in writing received at the registered office of the Company; or

c) is absent from meetings of a Group to which he has been appointed pursuant to Article 36, for more than three consecutive meetings of that Group without the consent of the Chairman.

Function and proceedings of the Review Panel

36. a) It shall be the function of the Review Panel, subject to and in a manner that is consistent with the nature and scale of the Company's financial resources, as may be notified by the directors to the Chairman from time to time, to perform and discharge any of the Company's functions and powers that enable or assist it to identify, to address and generally to act in respect of any question that there is or may be as to whether the annual accounts of any particular company comply with the requirements prescribed by legislation or regulation for the time

being in force in the United Kingdom or the Republic of Ireland to which such accounts are subject.

b) The Chairman may, after such consultation with such other members of the Review Panel as he considers appropriate, adopt procedures and practices in accordance with which the operation and workings of the Review Panel or any Group are to be regulated and the Chairman may also revise or withdraw any procedures or practices that are so adopted.

c) The Chairman shall appoint to a Group not less than 4 members of the Review Panel under the chairmanship of a further member of the Review Panel (who may, but need not, be the Chairman or Deputy Chairman) as he may specify, to comprise the Review Panel for the purposes of determining any matter that is referred to it and of taking any further action (if any) in respect thereof.

d) Each Group shall be invested with all of the functions, powers and duties of the Review Panel in respect of the matters to which its appointments relates.

e) Where during the proceedings of a Group:
   (i) a member of the Group ceases to be a member of the Review Panel; or
   (ii) the Chairman is satisfied that a member of the Group will be unable for a substantial period to perform his duties as a member of the Group, the Chairman may appoint any member of the Review Panel to be a member of the Group in his place.

f) The Chairman may also appoint any member of the Review Panel to be an additional member of a Group, whether the person so appointed was or was not a member of the Review Panel at the time when the Group was originally selected.

g) A group shall be authorised to obtain such independent professional advice in relation to any aspect of the Group's activities as the Group considers necessary or desirable for pursuing any matter that is referred to it and to consult any member of the Review Panel with respect to any matter or question with which the Group is concerned.

h) The Deputy Chairman may perform those functions of the Chairman that are referred to in clauses (c) and (e) of this Article during any period of temporary absence or incapacity of the Chairman or in respect of any matter in relation to which the Chairman considers himself to have a conflict of interest. The Chairman may also appoint one or more other members to act as aforesaid in the place of the Deputy Chairman if the Deputy Chairman himself is or may be unable or unwilling to act during such period or in respect of any such matter. In the event that the Chairman is unable or unwilling to make such an appointment then the appointment may be made by the Appointments Committee.

Meetings of the Review Panel

37. Subject to these Articles, the Review Panel or a Group, as the case may be, may meet for the despatch of business, adjourn and otherwise regulate its meeting as it thinks fit. The quorum necessary for a meeting of the Review Panel or a Group, as the case may be, shall be not less than one half of the members of the Review Panel or of the Group. Questions arising at any

meeting of the Review Panel shall be decided by a majority of votes. In the case of an equality of votes the Chairman shall have a second or casting vote. Questions arising at any meeting of a Group shall be decided negatively unless a two-thirds majority comprising not less than four affirmative votes is in favour of an affirmative decision.

38. A member of the Review Panel may hold any other office under the Company other than the office of director or the office of auditor.

Appointments and minutes

39. All acts done bona fide by a meeting of the directors or by a person acting as a director, and all acts done by the Review Panel or by a Group or by a person acting as a member of the Review Panel and all acts done by a committee or working group of the Review Panel or of a Group shall, notwithstanding that it be afterwards discovered that there was a defect in the appointment of any director, member of the Review Panel, a Group or any member of a committee or working group thereof, or that any of them were disqualified from holding office, or had vacated office, be as valid as if every such person had been duly appointed and was qualified and had continued to be a director, member of the Review Panel, member of the Group or member of the committee or working group.

40. The directors or, as the case may be, the Review Panel or a Group, shall, where applicable, cause minutes to be made in books provided for the purpose:

a) of all appointments and termination of appointments of officers of the Company included members of the Review Panel;
b) of the names of the persons present at each meeting of the directors, of the Review Panel or a Group, and of any committee or working group thereof;
c) of all resolutions and proceedings at all meetings of the Company, and of the directors, and of the Review Panel or a Group, and of any committee or working group thereof; and
d) of all appointments made pursuant to Article 36(h) and of their duration.

Appendix 4

FRRP Record 1991–98

	1991–92[1]	1992–93[2]	1993–94[3]	1995	1996	1997	1998	Totals 1991–98
No. of cases drawn to Panel's attention[4]	78	45	46	43	49	24	32	317
Cases still under consideration from prior period	N/A	19	11	10[5]	15	13	5	
Total no. of cases under consideration during period	78	64	57	53	64	37	37	
Cases still under consideration at end of period	19	11	14[9]	15	13	5	7	
Cases disposed of during period	59	53	43	38	51	32	30	306[5]
(i) Not pursued beyond initial examination [6]	28(47%)	11(20%)	14(33%)	19(50%)	24(47%)	11(34%)	15(50%)	122
(ii) Action concluded [7]	31(53%)	42(80%)	29(67%)	19(50%)	27(53%)	21(66%)	15(50%)	184
[of which Public Statements issued]	[10(32%)[8]	[9(21%)]	[6(21%)]	[4(21%)]	[8(29%)]	[5(24%)]	[7(47%)][9]	[49]

Sources: FRC, 1991, 1992, 1993, 1995, 1996, 1997

1. Mid-1991–Oct 1992.
2. Nov 1992–Oct 1993.
3. Nov 1993–end of 1994:
4. Source of referral 1991–94:

	1991–92	1992–93	1993–94	Totals	1995	1996
QAR or recorded non-compliance	25(32%)	5(11%)	6(13%)	36(21%)		
(a) Individuals, corporate bodies	30(38%)	22(49%)	21(46%)	73(43%)	*	**
(b) Press	23(27%)	18(40%)	19(41%)	60(36%)		

* Sources not indicated but a "significant reduction in the number of cases referred to the Panel by individuals or corporate bodies (FRC, 1996:31)

** Sources non indicated but the "majority came from individual or corporate complainants." (FRC, 1997:55)

5. According to FRC, 1995, 14 cases were outstanding at the end of the 1993–94 period. According to FRC 1996, only 10 cases were 'carried forward'. We reported to this the Panel in 1996 and, after internal inquiry, the Panel confirmed that the cases were "lost" but had probably been concluded.
6. "Because they either did not fall within the jurisdiction of the Panel, or were referred to another regulator, or no point of substance arose."
7. "After consideration by the Panel and, where appropriate, discussion with the companies concerned."
8. Percentage of enquiries and action concluded.
9. According to FRC, 1999, enquiries were concluded after discussion in 7 cases and remedial action required in 8. However, only 7 PN's were issued. After internal enquiry, the Panel confirmed that its figures were incorrect. 8 cases were concluded; 7 required remedial action.

Appendix 5

PANEL PRESS NOTICES – REPORT

(with occasional supplementary information)

PN 2/8 July 1991/Jun 1992 240 Companies and Auditors

Concern

Non-compliance with the Companies Act requirement to state whether accounts have been prepared in accordance with applicable accounting standards and to give particulars of any material departures from those standards and the reasons for such departures. "A scrutiny of company accounts has shown that many are failing to comply with this requirement."

Outcome

All companies confirm that applicable accounting standards have been complied with, or have explained reasons for any departure, and give the Panel an assurance that their companies' accounts will in future contain the statement required by the Act.

PN 4 Jan 1992 Ultramar (oil and gas group)

Concern

Treatment of unrelieved portion of Advanced Corporation Tax in the December 1990 consolidated profit and loss account: it was treated as part of the cost of dividends contrary to SSAP 8, which requires that irrecoverable ACT be included as part of the tax charge for the year. As a consequence, the consolidated profit and loss account failed to show the aggregate amount of dividends paid and proposed, contrary to Companies Act Sched 4 para 3(7). The effect was to increase EPS to 32.2p instead of 28.9p (*FT*, 29 January 1992). The approach taken was highlighted in the notes.

Outcome

Ultramar is no longer an independent entity [it was taken over by LASMO].

So there will be no future accounts (though directors gave an assurance of compliance with SSAP 8 in future accounts). The Panel did not seek revision but made the information public "for the information and guidance of others."

PN 5 Jan 1992 Williams Holdings (industrial conglomerate)

Concern

A note in the accounts indicated that exceptional items on asset disposals and reorganisation – one-off costs incurred as part of its continuing operations – had been reported net of tax and EPS was shown before exceptional items. So, the December 1990 consolidated profit and loss account was contrary to the Companies Act and the statement of EPS contrary to SSAP 3 (now FRS 3). There was also non-disclosure of the names of undertakings acquired and sold. (The accounts were not qualified but the treatment was highlighted in a note to the accounts.) The effect was to boost EPS from 21.2p to 22.3p.

Outcome

The directors reiterated the opinions expressed in the note but accepted that SSAP and Companies Act requirements had not been met. They gave written assurances regarding compliance in future accounts.

PN 6 Jan 1992 Shield Group (property development and estate agency)

Concern

Prior year adjustments made in the March 1991 accounts to restate the March 1990 financial statements to reflect reduced carrying value of certain properties, investments and loans. This retrospective treatment was contrary to SSAP 6.

Outcome

The directors accepted that the requirements of SSAP 6 had been met. They remained of the view that the basis adopted in the 1991 accounts provided the best estimate of the actual losses and the timing of the losses suffered by the group in view of market uncertainties prevailing when the 1990 accounts were prepared. But, at the Panel's request, they re-stated, in the Interim Report, the profit and loss account in accordance with SSAP 6. In the re-stated accounts, Shield made provisions of £3.58 million for the year to March 1991 against £784,000 when the accounts were first published. It also increased stated losses before exceptional items by £876,000 to £3.75 million (*FT*, 1 February 1992). The effect was to nearly double the company's losses per share. [Interim Report published same day as PN.]

PN 7 Feb 1992 Forte (hotels)

Concern

Accounting policies in the January 1991 accounts regarding (i) capitalisation of interest; (ii) treatment of expenses on major IT projects; (iii) absence of depreciation of freehold and long-leasehold properties; and (iv) variance between balance sheet signing and auditors' report dates.

Outcome

No cause of action found (satisfactory explanations, though some additional information on depreciation policy will be given in future accounts).

PN 10 Aug 1992 Williamson Tea Holdings (tea holding company)

Concern

The disclosure and the explanation of the treatment of certain items relating to overseas assets, including the non-depreciation of leasehold and lease rental properties, and why and how asset revaluations were depreciated and transferred to reserves (March 1991 accounts).

Outcome

Fuller information on accounting policies will be given in future accounts [to be issued later this month].

PN 11 Aug 1992 Associated Nursing Services (1st time) (nursing homes)

Concern

1. The treatment of start-up costs. The company stated that it would capitalise the costs of building nursing homes until either three months after they were registered or until they had achieved break-even occupancy, rather than treat them as items of current expenditure;
2. The adequacy of the explanation of an accounting policy change (March 1991 accounts).

Outcome

No cause of action found (satisfactory explanation, though directors decided to include a clear and finite time limit to the capitalisation of start-up costs and intend to ensure that future changes in accounting policy includes the former policy as well as a description of the new policy).

PN 12 Oct 1992 GPG (investments)

Concern

The September 1991 accounts were prepared in accordance with FRED 1 (The Structure of Financial Statements – Reporting of Financial Performance, issued in December 1991) and thus failed to comply with SSAPs 6, on extraordinary items and prior year adjustments, and 3, on earnings per share (a £5.8 million profit mainly generated by disposal of a subsidiary was treated as an exceptional item. The gain was classified as a 'discontinued operation' which would make it an extraordinary item under existing accounting guidelines. The result was to increase pre-tax profits from £5 million to £10.8 million and increase EPS from 1.58p to 3.38p).

Outcome

The Panel told the company that this was unacceptable even though the accounts clearly identified the departures: companies must "comply with current accounting standards." The Panel said that in normal circumstances it would be likely to seek revision of the accounts. But, in this case, because it understood that the accounting standard incorporating the most significant proposals of FRED 1 was close to issue, the Panel concluded that no further action should be taken on this occasion. (FRS 3, "with few changes in substance" (Ernst & Young, 1997:1259) was issued in October 1992. This effectively converts all extraordinary items into exceptional ones. GPG's shares had been suspended since December 1990. See ASB, Foreword to Accounting Standards, para 31, on 'Early adoption of FREDs'.)

PN 13 Oct 1992 Trafalgar House (property, construction and engineering, shipping, hotels)

Concern

The Panel's main concerns were:

- the reclassification of certain properties from current to fixed assets (write-down of properties to reserves. This resulted in a deficit of £102.7 million, which was charged directly to the revaluation reserve of only £84 million rather than to the profit and loss account);
- the amount of Advanced Corporation Tax carried forward in balance sheet.

Also, the Panel questioned the accounting treatment of a number of other matters including:

- the disclosure of the company's investment in BREL; and
- compliance with Companies Act format required for the profit and loss account (September 1991 accounts).

Outcome

On the basis of independent legal and accounting advice, TH directors did not accept the Panel view on the two principal matters (reclassification and ACT). The Panel was therefore "minded" to apply to the court for an order requiring the directors to prepare revised accounts. But the directors undertook to make appropriate changes and adjustments in future accounts. A £122.4 million profit was cut by £102.7 million to £19.7 million as a result of the reclassification; shareholders' funds were reduced by £20 million, as a result of the ACT change, to £684.6 million (*FT*, 16 October 1992). (The Panel indicated that TH was also issuing a separate Press Notice.)

PN 14 October 1992 British Gas (utility)

Concern

The presentation of the change of financial year from 31 March to 31 December 1991. The company included in the December profit and loss account the results of a three-month period already included in the previous March 1991 profit and loss account (i.e. three months 'double-counted'). The nine-month profit and loss account was presented in the notes, contrary to Companies Act ss. 223(3), 227. The effect was to boost pre-tax profits by £1 billion (from £496 million to £1.47 billion) (*FT*, 27 October 1992). The directors wanted to show 12-month figures "to reflect the fact that two-thirds of profits were generated in the first quarter of the year, reflecting the highly seasonal demand for gas."

Outcome

The Panel accepted the directors' assurance that there was no intention to mislead and that the company acted in good faith. The Panel said the note failed to meet Companies Act requirements either as to the location or content of the profit and loss account, nor did it contain the relevant EPS figure. The directors undertook to ensure that the 1991 comparative figures in 1992 accounts covered a nine-month period in compliance with the Companies Act.

PN 15 Oct 1992 S.E.P. Industrial Holdings (hardware, plumbing and heating)

Concern

1. The treatment of an amount in respect of stock provisions as a prior year item; and
2. The non-deprecation of freehold properties contrary to SSAP 12 (September 1991 accounts).

Outcome

1. The Panel was satisfied with the directors' explanation in respect of the prior year item. (No cause of action.)
2. The directors accepted that departure from SSAP 12 was not justified and gave an assurance of compliance in future accounts.

PN 16 Feb 1993 Eurotherm (control equipment)

Concern

The correctness and consistency of the treatment of a provision for the costs of closure of a manufacturing activity. In the October 1990 accounts, the original provision (of £2.8 million) for the costs of closing a manufacturing activity was treated as an extraordinary item; in the October 1991 accounts, the write-back element of the over-provision (£513,000) was treated as an exceptional item netted against the year's reorganisation costs. The effect was to increase pre-tax profits by 8% to £7.2 million (*FT*, 23 February 1993).

Outcome

In its 1992 accounts, the company adopted FRS 3 and restated the prior years in accordance with it (in a detailed Note). The restatement did not affect shareholders' equity, but it did have the effect of reducing 1990 EPS from 19.6p to 12.3p. It made no difference to the 1991 and 1992 results (*FT*, 23 February 1993). [PN same day as 1992 accounts with restated information.]

PN 17 March 1993 Foreign & Colonial Investment Trust (1st time) (investment trust)

Concern

1. The adequacy of information regarding directors' emoluments: non-disclosure of certain remuneration receivable by the five executive directors from the company's investment manager, an associate of one of its subsidiaries, relating to services to that company;
2. Whether or not subsidiary undertakings should have been consolidated (December 1991 accounts).

Outcome

The directors agreed to provide additional information with appropriate comparative figures in the 1992 accounts concerning the proportion of remuneration receivable by the directors from the company's investment manager which relates to services to FCIT and its subsidiary undertaking. The directors remained of the view that the treatment adopted was in accordance with requirements because the inclusion of subsidiary undertakings was not material. In the light of subsequent developments [unspecified], directors decided in the company's 1992 accounts to present consolidated accounts with appropriate comparative figures. [PN same day as 1992 accounts.]

PN 18 Apr 1993 Warnford Investments (property investment)

Concern

Non-compliance with SSAP 19 (Investment Properties): a property was not shown at open market value. The company argued that commercial confidentiality justified departure – the company had only one freehold property which was under negotiation to be sold, and to reveal the price would have compromised the company. This reason was stated clearly in a note to the December 1991 accounts and in the qualified audit report. According to the *FT*, Frank Martyn, finance director, stressed that it was shown at market value in the consolidated group accounts, so non-compliance had no effect on the group's value or earnings. He stated: "It made no difference whatsoever to the market's perception of the company" (*FT*, 3 April 1993).

Outcome

(The Panel rejected the commercial confidentiality justification for the departure.) The directors gave an assurance of future compliance with SSAP 19.

PN 19 Apr 1993 Penrith Farmers' & Kidd's (farmers and auctioneers)

Concern

Certain of the 1991 comparative figures had properly been restated in the March 1992 accounts. But the accounts did not give the particulars and reasons for these adjustments.

Outcome

Because of the extent of the additional information needing to be provided, it was concluded "by both the company and the Review Panel" that it could best be provided in a Supplementary Note. The Panel was satisfied that the adjustments did not affect the company's reported profits or the balance sheet totals and that the sums themselves were not significant. [Supplemenatary Note issued same day as PN. First case of revision of accounts.]

PN 20 Jul 1993 Breverleigh Investments (real estate)

Concern

Three departures from requirements in the June 1992 accounts:

1. The assets and liabilities and results of Breverleigh's (77.5% owned) subsidiary company were not included (contrary to the CA s 229, SSAP

14, as amended by ASB's Interim Statement 'Consolidated Accounts'). (The subsidiary had net liabilities of £339,000 and showed a loss for the year of £279,000. Breverleigh showed a pre-tax profit of £887 before an extraordinary loss of £198,000 (*FT*, 11 August 1993)).

2. A cash flow statement was not provided (contrary to FRS 1).
3. A failure to include a statement that the accounts had been prepared in accordance with applicable accounting standards and with particulars and reasons for any reported departures from those standards (contrary to the CA Sched 4, para 36A).

Outcome

The directors accepted that the departures were not justified and the chairman assured the Panel of full compliance in the 1993 accounts, including appropriate adjustment of the 1992 comparative figures to correct the non-consolidation of the subsidiary company.

PN 21 Aug 1993 Royal Bank of Scotland Group (bank)

Concern

The change in accounting policy for the deferment of acquisition expenses for insurance policies in the company's Direct Line Insurance subsidiary (in line with market practice and a SORP issued by the Association of British Insurers). The change led to a credit of £9.1 million relating to 1991 and earlier years, but this amount was treated in the September 1992 group accounts as an exceptional item and credited to profit in 1992. (The effect was to nearly double profits to £20.9 million.)

Outcome

The company regarded the amount as not material but the Panel rejected this. The Panel accepted the change in accounting policy but rejected treatment of credit as an exceptional item: the amount should have been shown as a prior year adjustment in accordance with SSAP 6. The company undertook to amend the comparative figures in the 1993 accounts and to include appropriate explanatory notes. (The effect was to reduce 1992 profits by £9.1 million.)

PN 22 Sep 1993 Control Techniques (electronic drives)

Concern

The Panel's enquiry "brought to light" a classification error in the group cash flow statement required by FRS 1. The accounts had wrongly shown the cash impact of the disposal of two subsidiaries. The reconciliation from operating profit to net cash flow from operating activities excluded the elements of working capital of the businesses sold. The effect was to incorrectly show the company with a net inflow before financing of £100,000, while the amended version shows it with a net outflow of £1.14 million for the year (*FT*, 27 September 1993). (September 1992 accounts.)

Outcome

Company issued an announcement (same day as PN) together with a revised group cash flow statement. It circulated amended numbers on 'Topic', the Stock Exchange news service (*FT*, 27 September 1993).

PN 24 Oct 1993 BM Group (construction equipment)

Concern

1. The cash equivalent element of the cash flow statement included significant items (including bank loans not repayable in more than five years), not permitted by the definition of cash equivalents in FRS 1 (cash is defined as "liquid assets realisable within three months").
2. The incorrect description of exceptional profit and the related goodwill written back: amounts arose not from the sale of companies by the parent company to one of its subsidiaries as described, but from the placing on the market of some of the parents' shares in the subsidiary after a temporary increase in the parents' shareholding. (June 1992 accounts.)

Outcome

Directors' assurance of full compliance in future accounts with appropriate amendment to the comparative figures.

PN 25 Oct 1993 Ptarmigan Holdings [now Graystone] (engineering components)

Concern

The change in the company's policy for goodwill arising on consolidation. It used to write-off goodwill immediately to reserves in respect of all acquisitions. In the June 1992 accounts, goodwill was capitalised on acquisition and amortised over its estimated useful economic life.

Outcome

The company satisfied the Panel that, in accordance with Companies Act Sched. 4, para. 15, the directors had special reasons for departing from the requirement that accounting policies should be applied consistently. But they agreed to the Panel's view that disclosure of the reasons for change was inadequate. The company decided to provide a fuller explanation in future accounts and in the listing particulars. [Listing particulars issued on same day as PN.]

PN 26 Nov 1993 Chrysalis Group (music and media)

Concern

The accounting treatment, in the August 1992 accounts, of the company's 18.7% investment in an associated company, Metro Radio. The company wrote off £3.94 million in goodwill against reserves after buying 3.18 million shares for £4.99 million. The investment was then revalued to its original cost by an amount equal to goodwill previously written off, contrary to SSAP 1. The treatment was highlighted in the accounts, which stated it was "not in accordance with accounting standards". There was no such statement in the 1991 accounts after the shares were first acquired. Neither Stoy Hayward in 1991 nor KPMG Peat Marwick in 1992 qualified the accounts to draw attention to the treatment (*FT*, 30 November 1993).

Outcome

The directors accepted that the accounting treatment adopted was not in accordance with SSAP 1. The directors remained of the view that the aggregate value of the investment shown was justified, but recognised that the total should have been attained by attributing fair values to the intangible assets of the associated company when Chrysalis acquired its interest. The directors undertook to make appropriate adjustments, including reclassification of the revaluation reserve, and to provide a full explanation in future accounts. The adjustment will have no effect on the reported total net assets of the group.

PN 27 Jan 1994 Intercare Group (health care products)

Concern

Two departures from FRS 1 in the October 1992 group cash flow statement:

1. Amounts shown as cash flows – as the cash outflow on the acquisition of subsidiaries and as cash inflow from financing – included sums that were not cash flows as they related to shares issued as consideration for an acquisition.
2. The cash consideration given for acquisitions of subsidiaries did not include the negative balances of cash and cash equivalents acquired in the subsidiary undertakings. The Panel did not regard the FRS requirement satisfied via information in a footnote and a further note from which the correct figure could be derived. The Panel also noted that the figures shown for interest receivable and interest payable were not on a cash basis, contrary to FRS 1, although the difference was not a material amount.

Outcome

The directors accepted they have not complied with FRS 1 and assured full compliance in future accounts. They did so in the company's Annual Report and Accounts published on the same day as the PN: the relevant comparative amounts in the group cash flow statement were restated.

PN 28 Feb 1994 Pentos (retailer)

Concern

The adequacy of information about the company's treatment of reverse premiums (payments made by landlords to attract tenants) received in respect of property leases. The amount taken to the profit and loss account in the year was included in 'other operating expenses (Net)' and was not separately disclosed. (The pre-tax profits of £4 million had included reverse premiums of £6.3 million.) (December 1992 accounts.)

Outcome

The directors stated their intention to explain their accounting policy more fully in the forthcoming accounts. As part of this explanation, the directors intend to disclose the amounts of reverse premiums received in 1993 and the comparative amounts for 1992. The directors "shared the Panel's view that it would be helpful to bring forward the company's clarification of its accounting policy and information" in respect of the amounts included in the 1992 accounts and did so in a statement [issued on the same day as the PN; The Panel referred accounting treatment of reverse premiums to the ASB; UITF12 (1994) was the result].

PN 29 May 1994 BET (business services conglomerate)

Concern

The Panel welcomed the company's decision to adopt FRS 3 ahead of its mandatory commencement date but was concerned about its treatment of exceptional items: the company included £76 million under the heading 'operating exceptional items'. The exact nature of the items – £42 million of accounting adjustments and £34 million relating to reorganisation costs – had been disclosed in a note, but while acknowledging this, the Panel "felt that this did not fulfil the requirement of the standard that these items should be shown on the profit and loss account under the statutory format headings to which they relate." The Panel was believed to have been concerned about the presentation of the exceptional items in boxes, and comments in the chairman's statement which drew attention away from the pre-tax profit line stressed in FRS 3 (*FT*, 25 May 1994). The company believed its original treatment was "more helpful in showing its underlying performance" (*FT*, 25 May 1994). (March 1993 accounts.)

Outcome

The company decided to restate within its 1994 accounts the comparative exceptional items with accompanying explanations. According to BET, "This was a technical detail probably of most interest to those in the accounting profession. The analysts did not ask one question about it" (*FT*, 25 May 1994).

PN 30 Nov 1994 Butte Mining (1st time) (excavation group)

Concern

1. A bank overdraft of £750,000 incorrectly shown in the balance sheet as falling due after more than one year.
2. A receipt of £560,000 from the sale of an equity investment not shown in the cash flow statement because the investment was incorrectly treated as a cash equivalent.
3. The repayment of a £500,000 loan was not shown in the cash flow statement because the loan was incorrectly treated as a cash equivalent.

The Panel rejected the directors' contention that the treatments adopted were justified through use of the true and fair override (June 1993 accounts). The directors argued that the overdraft could not be shown as falling due within a year and still give a true and fair view of the company's affairs. They claimed the overdraft was "entangled with a Montana law suit and could not fall due within a year. The company, however, did not want to 'become party to a test case'" (*FT*, 3 November 1994).

Outcome

"As a consequence" of the Panel's action, a Supplementary Note was issued as part of the 1994 accounts in order to revise the 1993 accounts. The revision includes corresponding adjustments to the 1992 accounts. The Panel reminded the directors of the requirement to send copies not only to those entitled to receive the 1994 accounts but also to those entitled to receive the 1993 accounts when they were originally issued. [Supplementary Note issued *before* PN.]

PN 31 Nov 1994 Clyde Bowers

Concern

The treatment adopted, and the adequacy of disclosures, in respect of the company's disposal in 1993 of half of its 100% interest in its subsidiary company (Clydeview Precision Engineering and Supplies Limited) to some of the company directors. The treatment (of both the sale and the option) was contrary to FRS 3 and the Companies Act Sched. 4; and the information did not comply with the Companies Act Sched. 5 and FRS 1. The company included two items relating to the sale under 'gain on sale of investment' in its August 1993 accounts, which included a loss on disposal of the remaining 50% holding and a provision of £90,907 against the potential loss on disposal of the option.

Outcome

At the Panel's request, the directors issued a statement outlining the transaction and the accounting for it in more detail; and have included fuller information in the August 1994 accounts just published. Appropriate adjustments have also been made in these accounts to the prior year figures. [Statement and following year's accounts produced few days before PN.]

PN 32 Mar 1995 Alliance Trust (investment trusts)

Concern

The Panel became involved following the company's approach for guidance to the Stock Exchange on the question of consolidation (1994 accounts). Alliance had not consolidated a subsidiary because the directors considered the amounts involved were not material. The value attributable to it was £23,028 million out of total investments of £1,042,252 million.

Outcome

The company decided to produce consolidated accounts incorporating the results of its subsidiary in accordance with FRS 2. [PN coincides with company's summarised results announcement.]

PN 33 Jun 1995 Courts (home furnishings retailer)

Concern

Under the company's accounting policy for instalment and hire purchase transactions, the total amount due under long-term credit agreements was included in turnover and operating profit and transfers were made to a deferred profit reserve. Turnover included the full invoiced amount of each transaction, including the unearned service charges. Only a portion of the profit went into pre-tax profits, with the balance and the service charge income going to the deferred profit reserve (*FT*, 22 June 1995). The matter at issue was the conformity of this policy with the Companies Act Sched. 4, paras 12, 13 and SSAP 21 (March 1994 accounts).

Outcome

The company changed its accounting policy in future accounts: transfers to a deferred profit reserve will no longer arise. Only the part of the service charge income earned in the accounting period can be included in turnover and operating profits. [Preliminary results announcement noting Panel consideration of accounts made same day as PN.]

PN 34 Nov 1995 Caradon (building materials manufacturer and supplier)

Concern

The conformity of the accounts with FRS 4. The analysis of shareholders' funds between equity and non-equity did not meet FRS 4, paras 40 to 44: non-equity interests (7.25% Convertible Cumulative Redeemable Preference Shares of 15p) were shown as £24.3 million (being their nominal value), whereas the amount attributable to non-equity interests calculated in accordance with FRS 4 was £163.1 million. Also, the brief summary of the rights of each class of shares required by FRS 4 para. 56 was incomplete (December 1994 accounts).

Outcome

The directors included in the company's September 1995 interim results statement an analysis of shareholders' funds between equity and non-equity interests both at 30 June 1995 and 31 December 1994 calculated in accordance with FRS 4. The directors agree to include corresponding information on the face of the balance sheet in future accounts and to ensure that the analysis of shareholders rights contains the full information required by FRS 4. (Interim results statement issued three weeks prior to PN.]

PN 35 Dec 1995 Ferguson International Holdings (conglomerate)

Concern

The February 1995 consolidated accounts show the fair value of the acquisition consideration of another company of £38.2 million, but did not show gross goodwill of £30.7 million calculated by reference to that fair value; only the net amount of goodwill of £6.9 million, remaining after advantage had been taken of the merger relief provisions of the Companies Act s. 131 was disclosed. The matter of concern was the conformity of the accounts with the Companies Act Sched. 4A, paras 9, 14 and SSAP 22.

Outcome

The directors agreed to take corrective action in future accounts: shareholders' funds will be restated to show separately gross goodwill and share premium relief and to disclose cumulative amounts of goodwill written off.

PN 36 Feb 1996 Securicor Group (distribution, security and communications)

Concern

The conformity of the analysis of the shareholders' funds between equity and non-equity interests with FRS 4, especially paras 40, 41, in the special circumstances of the company's participating preference shares (September 1994 accounts).

Outcome

The future accounts included, in a Note, an analysis in conformity with FRS 4, with earlier figures restated accordingly, together with an explanation of the effect on the analysis of further distributions to shareholders. [1995 accounts published same day as PN.]

PN 37 Mar 1996 Newarthill (building construction and engineering)

Concern

FRS 4 had not been followed in respect of the recognition of the financial cost of redeemable convertible preference shares issued by a company subsidiary. Also, there had been non-compliance with the requirement to give details of any material departure from applicable accounting standards (CA Sched. 4, para. 36A). (October 1994 accounts.)

Outcome

Revised (and audited) accounts issued, incorporating the application of FRS 4, under the provisions of the Companies Act s. 245 and S.I. 1990 No. 2570, published and not qualified. [Revised accounts issued same day as PN.]

PN 38 Mar 1996 Brammer (industrial services)

Concern

Assets held for rental had been classified in the December 1994 accounts as stock within current assets contrary to SSAP 21. The Panel believed SSAP 21 was applicable and the assets should have been classified as fixed assets in accordance with SSAP 21, para. 42 and the Companies Act s. 262.

Outcome

The directors agreed with the Panel and in the company's 1995 Preliminary Results Statement announced their acceptance that SSAP 21 should be followed. In future accounts the rental inventory is to be reclassified as fixed assets and prior year figures adjusted accordingly. The changes did not affect the profit for the year or shareholders' equity. [Preliminary results Statements issued same day as PN.]

PN 39 Apr 1996 Foreign & Colonial Investment Trust [2nd time] (investment trust)

Concern

The adequacy of the explanation given for the departure from SSAP 1 in the December 1994 consolidated balance sheet treatment of an associated undertaking. In accounting for the associated undertaking in its 1994 accounts, FCIT had shown it in the revenue accounts using the equity method, as recommended in SSAP 1. The carrying value in the consolidated balance sheet was at directors' or market valuation. The difference between the two methods was revealed in the subsequent 1995 accounts: at £5.5 million under the equity method compared to £49.7 million at valuation. The Panel said FCIT had not explained this treatment adequately.

Outcome

The directors provided fuller explanation in future accounts. [Future accounts just published.] They explained that "as the investment ... forms part of the group's investment portfolio the directors believe adoption of the equity method in the balance sheet would not show a true and fair view."

PN40 May 1996 Alexon Group (women's wear retailer)

Concern

The conformity of the analysis of shareholders' funds between equity and non-equity interests with FRS 4, especially para. 41. Alexon included accrued dividends on its preference shares (which were in arrears) within shareholders' funds rather than showing them as a liability, even though they also showed them as an appropriation in the profit and loss account as required by FRS 4 (January 1995 accounts).

Outcome

The analysis of shareholders' funds has been restated in future accounts to accord with the method specified by FRS 4. The effect is to reduce equity shareholders' funds and increase non-equity shareholders' funds by £17,970,000, and to include the accrued preference dividends within the non-equity shareholders' funds. This has resulted in an increase in total shareholders' funds by the amount of the accrued preference dividends, previously included within creditors. The directors also included a fuller explanation of the rights of the company's cumulative preference shares and of its deferred shares. [Future accounts same day as PN.]

PN 41 May 1996 Ransomes (agricultural equipment maker)

Concern

The conformity of the analysis of shareholders' funds between equity and non-equity interests with FRS 4. Conformity would result in a £47.9 million decrease in equity interests and a £47.9 million increase in non-equity interests. The change relates to the inclusion of the premium arising on the issue of the 8.25p preference shares in 1989. This amount had previously been regarded as having been set-off by the write off of goodwill of £47.9 million. Total shareholders' funds remain unchanged. (September 1995 accounts.)

Outcome

The company included in its 1996 Interim Results Statement a restatement of the analysis at 30 September 1995 which conforms with FRS 4 and the directors have confirmed that the analysis to be included in the 1996 accounts will similarly conform with FRS 4. The 1996 accounts will also include some additional information about the rights of the non-equity shares. [Interim Statement same day as PN.]

PN 42 Jul 1996 Sutton Harbour Holdings (water transport)

Concern

The treatment of government grants and the adequacy of information given about the use of the true and fair override. (March 1995 accounts.)

Outcome

The Panel accepted the directors' justification for their departure from SSAP 4 (Government Grants) in the particular circumstances of the company, but disclosures about use of override did not fully meet the Companies Act; they were also inadequate in respect of the non-depreciation of investment properties. The directors have included in the 1996 accounts disclosures conforming to the Companies Act requirements as to the use of the true and fair override. The directors have also taken the opportunity to amplify some disclosures in other areas of the accounts. [Future accounts published same day as PN.]

PN 43 Oct 1996 Butte Mining (2nd time) (excavation group)

Concern

The accounting treatment of shares in Gem River Corporation received by the company in consideration of services rendered by the company to GRC. The issue was the extent to which a profit on the transaction should have been included in the profit and loss account at the balance sheet date, given that the tradability of the shares was subject to restrictions. The accounts published a profit in the profit and loss account on the whole transaction. In the Panel's view, having regard to the Companies Act Sched. 4 para. 12 and SSAP 2 para. 14(d), profit should only have been included on the shareholding that had been realised at the time the accounts were completed. At that date, the remaining shares were subject to an Escrow agreement prohibiting their trading on the Alberta Stock Exchange, on which they were listed, until certain conditions relating to the success of a GRC mining operation were fulfilled and certain periods of time had elapsed (GRC had to find and sell sapphires). Consequently, in the Panel's view, the ultimate cash realisation of these shares could not be assessed with reasonable certainty and profit should not have been recognised on this element. A consequential downward adjustment was also needed to the turnover figure at present published. The published profit on ordinary activities before and after taxation was stated in the accounts at present at £339,000. Directors calculated the effect of revision would be to translate this into a loss of £628,000, i.e. a reduction of £967,000. (June 1995 accounts.)

Outcome

The directors gave an undertaking to prepare and issue as soon as possible a revision of the 1995 accounts under the Companies Act s. 245. The directors' "last-minute undertaking to produce this revision enabled the Panel to refrain from issuing the proceedings under s. 245B of the Companies Act 1985 that were at an advanced stage of preparation" (FRC, 1997:59). The revised accounts will also provide some clarification of the position of the non-equity shareholders in respect of the dividend attaching to the company's Convertible Cumulative Redeemable Preference Shares. [First ever PN prior to revision, supplementary note, interim statement etc. apart from PN 10 – adjustment 'later this month'. Four directors of Butte Mining were prosecuted in a fraud case in 1997–98 (the Old Bailey trial lasted 11 months), relating to Butte's £60 million stock market flotation (in October 1987) and subsequent events, including an alleged failure to disclose beneficial interests and concealing the identity of beneficiaries of the issue. In May 1998, John Clarke, the founder director, was found guilty, as was Clive Smith and Malcolm Clews. All received prison sentences. Roy Bichan was acquitted. Shares in Butte were suspended in 1996 because the company failed to publish annual results within the six months of the year-end. The company subsequently requested to be delisted from the Stock Exchange. According to the directors, this was because "the costs of complying with listing requirements were too onerous to be worthwhile" (*The Times*, 21 January 1997). The Exchange apparently insisted the company convene a meeting to approve the sale of mining land in Montana. It was the rights issue to buy a Montana-based operation that led to the Serious Fraud Office inquiry and legal action.]

PN 44 Feb 1997 Associated Nursing Services (2nd time) (nursing homes)

Concern

1. The accounting treatment of two joint venture companies as associated undertakings rather than as quasi-subsidiaries. One case involved a deadlocked joint venture company with a bank. In the Panel's view, the financial and operating policies of the company were substantially predetermined by underlying agreements; and through its interest in the JV ANS gained benefits arising from the net assets of the company such that it had control. In the other case a venture capital arrangement with five venture capital funds had been set up through an intermediary. In the Panel's view the financial and operating policies were again substantially predetermined by underlying agreements. In this case ANS only held a minority of the ordinary share capital but the investor's interests were effectively limited and the Panel took the view that ANS gained benefits arising from the net assets of the company such that it had control. In the Panel's view therefore the substance of the arrangements was such that the companies were quasi-subsidiaries as defined by FRS 5. So they should not have been accounted for by the equity method but treated, as FRS 5 requires, as though they were subsidiaries. Under the accounting treatment adopted by the company only the company's share of the net assets of the companies in question was reflected in the consolidated balance sheet.
2. The accounting treatment of certain sale and leaseback transactions involving a 25-year lease, renewable for a further 25 years, and a call option held by ANS.

For both concerns, the issue was the same: whether the treatment reflected the substance of the transaction under FRS 5. (March 1995 and March 1996 accounts.)

Outcome

1. The directors accepted the Panel view that the accounts did not comply with FRS 5; they accepted that the substance of the transactions was such as to require that, in accordance with FRS 5, the full amount of the JV companies' assets and liabilities should be included in the consolidated balance sheet with appropriate changes to the consolidated profit and loss account.

2. The directors accepted the Panel's view that the nature of the transaction was such that not all the significant rights or other access to benefits relating to the asset in question and not all the significant exposure to the risk inherent in those benefits had been transferred to the purchaser. So, in accordance with FRS 5, an asset should have remained on the consolidated balance sheet and the sale proceeds should have been included in borrowings, with consequential profit and loss account adjustments.

Following "extended discussions" between the Panel and the directors, the directors undertook to prepare and issue as soon as possible a revision of accounts for two years' set of accounts under the provisions of the Companies Act s. 245.

PN 45 Apr 1997 Reckitt & Colman (household goods)

Concern

The adequacy of information and explanations given in respect of fair value adjustments made in connection with an acquisition and specifically whether the requirements of FRS 6 and the Companies Act sched. 4A, para. 13(5) had been met. The company purchased the acquisition for c. £1 billion late in 1994 and it was only possible to make a provisional fair value adjustment when the acquisition was recorded in the company's financial statements to 31 December 1994. The provisional adjustment resulted in an increase of £750.46 million to the net assets acquired. In the company's 1995 accounts, a further and final fair value adjustment of £81.2 million was included in respect of the acquisition, with a corresponding adjustment to goodwill (in accordance with FRS 7, paras 23–25). However, no further information was provided in respect of the adjustments as required by FRS 7 para. 27. In the Panel's view, this second stage required a similar level of disclosure and explanation so as to comply with the requirements of FRS 6 para. 25 and the Companies Act sched. 4A, para. 13(5) and should include an analysis of the adjustments and an explanation of the reasons for them. (December 1995 accounts.)

Outcome

The directors included in the 1996 accounts a note in respect of the 1995 fair value adjustments giving the relevant additional information required by FRS 6 and the Companies Act. [1996 accounts published same day as PN.]

PN 46 Aug 1997 M & W Mack (retail chain)

Concern

Non-compliance with UITF Abstract 13: the April 1996 accounts did not include the income, expenses and assets of W & M Mack Limited ESOP. (April 1996 accounts.)

Outcome

The directors included the income, expenses and assets of the ESOP in the 1997 accounts and restated the 1996 comparative figures to give the requisite information.

PN 47 Oct 1997 Burn Stewart Distillers (Scotch whisky producers)

Concern

The company made a material sale in December 1995 of whiskies to Hurlingham International, a marketing consultancy which planned to develop new spirit brands. Hurlingham paid £3 million immediately with the balance payable by 31 December 1996. The company, following the advice of its auditor Price Waterhouse, rightly, according to the Panel, did not reflect the sale in the results for the period (June 1996) because not all the significant benefits and risks relating to the stock had been transferred to the purchaser. The transaction was for £5.1 million and, if completed according to its terms, would have resulted in a profit of £2.3 million. However, the actual outcome – and profit – depended on a variety of factors outside the directors' control.

At the time, the company said it expected to recover the full profit, but Ian Bankier, the managing director, stated that publicity surrounding the transaction meant the company had booked a £1.4 million profit from it. This helped the pre-tax profits for the year ending 30 June 1996 to reach £3.56 million and took turnover to £70.1 million. The reported profit for the group in 1996 (after excluding the transaction in question) was cut by 75% to £1.01 million. In the view of the Panel, although the transaction was rightly not recorded as a sale, FRS 5 para. 30 still required disclosure of the transaction so that users were able to understand its commercial effects and the consequences of its exclusion from the accounts. The company had refused to give details of the transaction on grounds of commercial confidentiality (supplementary information from *FT*, 3 October 1997).

Outcome

The directors accepted the Panel's view that the information given in the accounts did not fulfil the disclosure requirements of FRS 5. They included the information in their preliminary announcement and will circulate to shareholders an amendment to their 1996 accounts. [PN same day as announcement.]

PN 48 Nov 1997 Stratagem Group (1st time) (diversified industrials)

Concern

The adequacy of the information and explanations given in respect of fair value adjustments made in connection with the £4.3 million acquisition of NRC Refrigeration Ltd in January 1996 and specifically whether the requirements of FRS 6 and CA Sched. 4A para. 13(5) had been met (August 1996 accounts). The accounts included a table showing, for each class of assets and liabilities of NRC Refrigeration Ltd, the book values as recorded in that company's accounts immediately before the acquisition (totalling net liabilities of £1.2 million) and the fair values at the date of acquisition (totalling net liabilities of £6.1 million). While this table met part of the requirements of FRS 6 it did not show the fair value adjustments of £4.9 million analysed into revaluations, adjustments to achieve consistency of accounting policies, and other significant adjustments, as required by FRS 6, para. 25(b), and the table did not include an explanation for the adjustments as required by the Companies Act, Sched. 4A, para. 13(5). The Panel "felt it important to maintain the principle that such information in connection with an acquisition should be fully disclosed" (*FT*, 11 November 1997).

Outcome

The directors included in the 1997 accounts (now published) a note in respect of the 1996 fair value adjustments giving the relevant additional information required by FRS 6 and the Companies Act 1985.

PN 49 Feb 1998 Guardian Royal Exchange (insurance)

Concern

In accordance with the Companies Act as amended to implement EU Directives, Guardian Royal Exchange's insurance subsidiaries set aside in their accounts 'equalisation reserves' (equivalent to provisions: to smooth fluctuations in loss ratios in future years or to cater for special risks). The law requires them to be treated as charges against profits and as liabilities.

In the December 1996 consolidated accounts, the directors excluded these amounts. They considered that these reserves should not be treated as a charge against profits and as a liability so as to achieve consistency of treatment with Guardian Royal Exchange's subsidiaries where the creation of equalisation reserves was not required. As disclosed by the company in its 1996 accounts, had the liabilities in question not been excluded from the consolidation, pre-tax profit of £651 million would have been reduced by £33 million and earnings per share of 48.7p by 2.76p. The exclusion also resulted in liabilities being understated and shareholders' funds of £2,306 million being overstated by £75 million.

In the Panel's view, specific requirements of the Companies Act as it applies to insurance companies, which requires inclusion of subsidiaries' reserves, and certain equalisation reserves in subsidiaries in other EU Member States, as a charge and a liability, were not complied with. Nor could this requirement be overridden by reference to GAAP or the use of the true and fair override. The legal requirement for the inclusion as a charge and a liability in the consolidation of the subsidiaries' equalisation reserves makes the requirement *ipso facto* an element of UK GAAP both for the purposes of individual UK companies and for the consolidated accounts of a UK parent company.

Outcome

The directors agreed in future, after extended discussions, to include as a charge and a liability in the consolidation all relevant UK subsidiaries' equalisation reserves and also their EU subsidiaries' equalisation reserves where such is required by local legislation. The 1996 comparative figures will reflect these changes. The "necessary steps" for a court application had, in this case, been "at an advanced stage". [The 1997 accounts were published around the same time as the PN.]

PN 50 April 1998 Stratagem Group (2nd time) (diversified industrials)

Concern

There were two matters at issue, both of which related to compliance with FRS 3 as regards the treatment of exceptional items in the August 1997 consolidated accounts. FRS 3 para. 20 specifies that certain exceptional items should be shown separately on the face of the profit and loss account after operating profit and before interest. All other exceptional items are required to be credited or charged in arriving at the profit or loss on ordinary activities by inclusion under the statutory format headings to which they relate.

1. In the profit and loss account an item described as "Settlement of law suit" was shown as an exceptional item positioned after profit on ordinary activities. The Panel took this matter up since the costs of settlement of a law suit would not normally fall to be treated as a paragraph 20 item under FRS 3.
2. The positioning of the paragraph 20 items in the company's consolidated profit and loss account. Paragraph 20 requires that the items it covers to be shown after operating profit and before interest. However in the company's accounts the paragraph 20 items were shown after operating profit but after, rather than before, interest.

Outcome

1. In "the light of the explanations provided by the directors the Panel is satisfied that these costs were in fact an integral part of a fundamental restructuring, which is one of the items specified by paragraph 20 of FRS 3." The directors accepted the Panel's view that this should have been made clear in the description of the item.
2. "In the light of their discussions with the Panel" the directors included in the company's 1998 Interim Statement (issued the same day as the PN) and will be including in the company's 1998 accounts, a "clarificatory" note explaining the circumstances of the law suit. The 1997 comparative figures shown in the Interim Statement and to be shown in the company's 1998 accounts will locate the paragraph 20 exceptional items in their correct position.

PN 51 May 1998 RMC Group (building materials)

Concern

The non-disclosure, in the Group's 1995 consolidated accounts, of fines levied on certain of the Group's subsidiaries in 1995. The fines arose from the breach of Orders (prior to 1988) made by the Restrictive Trade Practices Court and which, together with legal costs, totalled £4.97 million. The Panel accepted that the background to the matter had been disclosed in the Group Report and Accounts each year from 1988 to 1994 and was noted in the 1994 Group accounts as a contingent liability. The Panel also acknowledged that the fines, when levied, had been publicly announced and were disclosed in the 1995 accounts of the subsidiaries in question. They were not, however, disclosed in the Group's 1995 accounts and the users of those accounts would thus not have been made aware of them. The fines were deemed not material in the context of the company's group accounts: pre-tax profits were over £350 million in 1995.

Outcome

The directors provided further information about the fines in the Directors' Report accompanying the Group's 1997 accounts just published. They took note of the concern put to them by the Panel that the payment of the fines was an important matter that ought to be brought specifically to the attention of the users of the accounts because of the nature and circumstances of the fines. While this was a matter of judgement, in the Panel's view this was a material matter, the special nature and circumstances of which were such that its materiality needed to be determined primarily by reference to its qualitative aspects. The Panel also took the view that disclosure in previous Reports and Accounts of the possibility or likelihood of the fines in question – e.g. in the contingent liabilities note – did not affect the need for disclosure in the Group accounts when the fine was imposed.

PN 52 July 1998 Reuters Holdings (news agency)

Concern

The directors adopted FRS 10 ahead of its mandatory implementation date. In the December 1997 consolidated profit and loss account, the goodwill amortisation charge was not included in operating costs but was shown separately below the sub-total 'Operating Profit'. In the Panel's view the amortisation charge should have been classified as an operating charge and thus deducted before operating profit was arrived at.

Outcome

The directors stated in the company's 1998 Interim Statement (published the same day as the PN) that in the company's 1998 accounts goodwill amortisation will be charged as a cost in arriving at operating profit and the 1997 comparative figures will be amended accordingly.

PN 53 Aug 1998 H & C Furnishings (formerly Cantors; now Harveys Furnishings; home furnishings)

Concern

1. "A point of principle": the fair value attributed to the consideration paid by Cantors for the acquisition of a larger listed company, Harveys Holdings, in the April 1997 accounts. The consideration was the issue of shares in Cantors to Harveys' shareholders. FRS 7 para. 78 indicates that the market price on the date of acquisition would normally provide the most reliable measure of fair value in these circumstances, though para. 79 gives guidance where the market price is unreliable and allows an alternative method of valuation. At the date of acquisition (July 1996), the market price of Cantors' shares was £1.65, but the directors took the view that the market price was unreliable as a means of determining the fair value. Instead they adopted the share valuation (£1) ruling at the date four months earlier when the transaction had been negotiated. The Panel rejected the directors' interpretation. It considered information about the movements in Cantors' share price, noting that there had been a substantial and continuing rise between March and July 1996 which continued after the acquisition. In the circumstances there seemed to the Panel no grounds for adopting the earlier share price.

2. Non-compliance with a number of disclosure requirements (FRS 1 (Revised); FRS 3; FRS 8; SSAP 15; and Companies Act Schedules 4 and 6)

Outcome

1. The directors agreed to revise the accounts by way of a Supplementary Note to base the valuation of the consideration paid for the acquisition on a share price of £1.65.
2. The directors agreed to make the following revisions to remedy the non-compliance: to amend the order of items on the face of the profit and loss account, provide a reconciliation of the earnings per share excluding property profits and reorganisation costs, disclose more details of the effect of acquisitions and present a Statement of Total Recognised Gains and Losses to comply with FRS 3; adopt the format of the cash flow statement required by FRS 1 (Revised); enhance the explanation of the change in accounting policies to comply with Schedule 4 of the Companies Act 1985; incorporate related party disclosures originally made in the directors' report to comply with FRS 8; disclose aggregate gains on share options exercised by the directors as required by Schedule 6 of the Companies Act 1985; and reclassify a deferred tax asset to prepayments and accrued income to comply with SSAP 15. [Supplementary Note contained in Harvey Furnishing's 1998 Report and Accounts published same day as PN.]

PN 54 Sept 1998 Photo-Me International (photo booths, copiers and print services)

Concern

Certain sales to group undertakings (comprising equipment subsequently capitalised in the individual companies' accounts) had been included in total turnover in the April 1997 Group Profit and Loss Account. In the view of the Panel this was contrary to the Companies Act Sched. 4A which provides that Group Accounts should as far as practicable be prepared as if the undertakings included in the consolidation were a single company (para. 1(1)) and that debts and claims between undertakings included in the consolidation, and income and expenditure relating to transactions between such undertakings, should be eliminated (para. 6(1)).

The directors invoked the true and fair override to justify departing from the provisions regarding intra-group sales. As the notes to the accounts stated, the directors had taken the view that excluding such sales from turnover would understate the group's activities and as such would fail to give a true and fair view.

The Panel considered but did not accept this justification.

Outcome

As indicated in the company's 1998 Preliminary Announcement [published same day as PN], the directors accepted the Panel's view. This is reflected in the 1997 comparative figures and in the basis on which the 1998 results are presented in the Preliminary Announcement. The amendment to the 1997 comparative figures will be reflected in the company's 1998 report and accounts to be published shortly.

PN 55 Oct 1998 Concentric

Concern

The extent of the company's disclosure in its September 1997 accounts relating to its acquisition of Weed Instrument Inc in July 1997 for £4.4 million. The acquisition was referred to in the chairman's statement and the Group Profile but the cost was not disclosed in the financial statements. The profit and loss account recorded the contribution made to turnover and profit before tax and a note referred to the goodwill write-off arising on the transaction of £2.3 million.

In the Panel's view, the disclosures did not satisfy the requirements of FRS 6 'Mergers and Acquisitions', particularly in that no fair value table was produced as required by paragraph 25 or paragraph 13(5) of the Companies Act Schedule 4 in support of the calculation for goodwill. The table should include reference to the book values of the net assets required, and any adjustments made in accordance with FRS 7 'Fair Value Accounting' and the fair values taken into account in arriving at the goodwill figure. The fair value of the consideration is also required to be disclosed after paragraph 47 of SSAP 22 'Goodwill'.

Similarly in the Panel's view, the disclosures did not satisfy the requirements of FRS 1 (revised) 'Cash Flow Statements'. There was no reference to the acquisition in the consolidated cash flow statement which requires cash flows related to an acquisition to be included in the heading 'Acquisitions and Disposals', where the cash paid for the entry should be shown separately from any balances acquired on acquisition. Relevant amounts acquired on acquisition of a subsidiary but excluding cash balances and overdrafts are also required to be separately disclosed in the analysis of net debt. In addition, a note summarising the effects of acquisitions of subsidiary undertakings should be included indicating how much of the consideration comprised cash.

Outcome

The company accepted the Panel's conclusions and sought to rectify the matter at the first available opportunity. It made certain disclosures voluntarily in its interim report with the intention of providing the relevant disclosure requirements in full in its next set of financial statements, when the 1997 comparative figures will be amended accordingly.

Appendix 6

PANEL PRESS NOTICES – ANALYSIS
(Number refers to Press Notice number – up to PN55)

Adjustment in future		Accounts Revised	Other	No Action
		Full		
4	31	37	32[1]	7
5	33	43		11
6	34	44[3]		12[6]
10	35			15[2]
13	36			50[2]
14	38			
15[2]	39			
16	40			
17	41			
18	42	*Partial*		
20	45	19		
21	46	30[4]		
22	48	47[5]		
24	49	53		
25	50[2]			
26	51			
27	52			
28	54			
29	55			
	38	7	1	5

NOTES

1. Company accepted guidance to produce consolidated accounts.
2. Two matters raised by Panel. On first, no cause of action found; on second, directors gave assurance that future accounts would comply.
3. Two years' sets of accounts.
4. Accounts revised via Supplementary Note issued as part of following year's accounts (to be sent also to those entitled to receive faulty accounts).
5. Revision via amendment circulated to shareholders.
6. Panel would "in normal circumstances" have sought revision.

Bibliography

Accounting Standards Board (1992) *FRS 2 Accounting for Subsidiary Undertakings.*

Accounting Standards Board (1993) Financial Reporting Exposure Draft (FRED)4, 'Reporting the Substance of Transactions'.

Accounting Standards Board (1993) *Foreword to Accounting Standards.*

Accounting Standards Board (1993) *FRS 4 Capital Instruments.*

Accounting Standards Board (1994) *FRS 5 Reporting the Substance of Transactions.*

Accounting Standards Board (1994) *FRS 7 Fair Values in Acquisitions Accounting.*

Accounting Standards Board (1997) FRED 17 *Measurement of Tangible Fixed Assets.*

Accounting Standards Board (1998) *FRS 10 Goodwill and Intangible Assets.*

Accounting Standards Board (1998) *FRS 13 Derivatives and other financial instruments: disclosures.*

Accounting Standards Board (1998) *Amendment to FRS 5 Reporting the Substance of Transactions: Private Finance Initiative and Other Contracts.*

Accounting Standards Committee (1981) SSAP *Accounting for Investment Properties.*

Accounting Standards Committee (1984) *SSAP 21 Accounting for Leases and Hire Purchase Contracts.*

Accounting Standards Committee (1988) *ED 42 Accounting for Special Purpose Transactions.*

Accounting Standards Committee (1990) *ED 49 Reflecting the Substance of Transactions in Assets and Liabilities.*

Accounting Standards Committee (1990) *ED 50 Consolidated Accounts.*

Aldwinckle, R. (1987) 'Off-balance sheet finance – the legal view, *Accountancy*, June, 644.

Alexander, D. (1993) 'A European True and Fair View?', 1 *European Accounting Review* 59–80.

Arden, M. (1997) 'True and fair view: a European perspective', 6:4 *European Accounting Review* 675–679.

Ashton, R.K. (1986) 'The Argyll Foods Case. A legal analysis', *Accounting and Business Research* 3.

Atchley, K. (1986) 'Argyll case adopted as a rogues' charter?', 194 *The Accountant* 12–13.

Ayres, I. and Braithwaite, J. (1992) *Responsive Regulation* (Clarendon, Oxford).

Beattie, V., Brandt, R. and Fearnley, S. (1997) 'Look to your laurels: How do key audit players view auditor independence?', *Accountancy*, July, 140–141.

Biener, H. (1979) 'Auswirkungen der Vierten Richtlinie der EG auf den informationsgehait der Rechnunslegung Deutscher Unternehmen', *Betriebswirtschaftliche Forschung und Praxis*, 1–16.

Brandt, R., Fearnley, S., Hines, T. and Beattie, V. (1997) 'The Financial Reporting Review Panel: An analysis of its activities' in ICAEW, *Financial Reporting Today: Current and Emerging Issues The 1998 Edition* (Accountancy Books, London).

Collins, S., Marwood, P., and Maxwell, D. (1997) *Tax and Financial Aspects of Leasing* (Butterworths, London).

Commission of the European Communities (1976) 'Group Accounts: Proposal for a Seventh Directive', *Bulletin of the European Communities* supplement September

Crichton, J. (1990) 'A new approach to consolidated accounts', *Accountancy* 32.

Cross, Lord (1973) 'The Lawyer and justice', Presidential address to the Holdsworth Club, University of Birmingham.

Cross, R. (1976) *Statutory Interpretation* (Butterworths, London).

Darlow, C., Morley, S., Bruce-Radcliffe, G., Boff, J. (1994) *Property Development Partnerships* (Longman, London)

Dearing Committee (1988) *The Making of Accounting Standards* (ICAEW, London).

Department of Trade and Industry (1982) *The True and Fair View and Group Accounts*. London, 15 January 1982 (reprinted in Tolley, 1988:1380).

Department of Trade and Industry (1988) *Implementation of the Seventh Directive*, 30 August.

Ernst & Young (1990, 1997) *UK GAAP* (Longman, London; Macmillan, Basingstoke).

Ernst & Young (1998) *Associates and Joint Ventures: A Guide to FRS 9* (Ernst & Young).

Ernst & Young (1998) *Goodwill and Intangible Assets: A Guide to FRS 10* (Ernst & Young).
Ernst & Young (1998) *Derivatives and Other Financial Instruments: Disclosures: A Guide to FRS 13* (Ernst & Young).
FASB (1983) SFAS No. 76 (FASB, Norwalk, Connecticut).
FASB (1984) *In-Substance Defeasance of Debt*. Technical Bulletin No. 84 (Norwalk, Connecticut).
FASB (1987) SFAS 94 (Norwalk, Connecticut).
FASB (1996) SFAS 125 'Accounting for Transfers and Servicing of Financial Assets and Extinguishment of Liabilities' (Norwalk, Connecticut)
Financial Reporting Council (1991) *The State of Financial Reporting: A Review* (FRC, London).
Financial Reporting Council (1992) *The State of Financial Reporting* (FRC, London).
Financial Reporting Council (1995) *The State of Financial Reporting* (FRC, London).
Financial Reporting Council (1996) *Progress Report 95* (FRC, London).
Financial Reporting Council (1997) *Progress Report 96* (FRC, London).
Financial Reporting Council (1998) *Progress Report 97* (FRC, London).
Financial Reporting Council (1999) *Annual Review 1998* (FRC, London).
Fisse, W.B. and Braithwaite, J. (1983) *The Impact of Publicity on Corporate Offenses* (Albany, NY, State University of New York).
Griffiths, I. (1986) *Creative Accounting* (Sidgwick & Jackson, London).
Griffiths, I. (1995) *New Creative Accounting* (Macmillan, London).
Hampel, R. (1997) *Preliminary Report of the Committee on Corporate Governance*.
Hawkins, K. (1984) *Environment and Enforcement* (Clarendon, Oxford).
ICAEW (1985) *TR603 Off-balance sheet finance and window dressing*.
Kirk, R. (1995) 'Accounting Standards: Moving into Second Gear', 73 *Management Accounting* 51–54.
Law Commission Consultation Paper No. 153, Scottish Law Commission Discussion Paper No. 105 (1998) *Company Directors: Regulating Conflicts of Interests and Formulating a Statement of Duties: A joint consultation paper* (London, HMSO).
Law Society (1986) *Off-balance sheet finance and window dressing: memorandum by the Society's Standing Committee on Company Law* (Law Society, London).
Law Society Company Law Committee (1990) *Comments on ED49 – Reflecting the Substance of Transactions in Assets and Liabilities* (No. 232, Law Society, London).
Law Society (1990) *Comments on ED50 – Consolidated Accounts* (No. 236, Law Society, London).

Law Society (1990) ED50 *Accounting for Investments* (Law Society, London).

Legal Risk Review Committee, Bank of England (1992) *Final Report.*

Maw, N., Lord Lane of Horsell, Craig-Cooper, M. (1994) *Maw on Corporate Governance* (Dartmouth, Aldershot).

Nailor, H. (1990) *Reflecting the Substance of Transactions in Assets and Liabilities* (Coopers & Lybrand Deloitte, London).

Niessen, H. (1990) 'Image fidele: Reflexions sur une notion de droit communautaire en matiere comptable' in Tresarrieu, J. Ph. (ed) *Reflexions sur la comptabilite: Hommage a Bertrand d'Illiers* (Economica, Paris).

Ordelheide, D. (1990) 'Soft Transformations of Accounting Rules of the 4th Directive in Germany', 3 *Les cahiers internationaux de la comptabilite* 1–15.

Ordelheide, D. (1993) 'True and fair view: a European and German perspective', 1 *European Accounting Review* 81–90.

Ordelheide, D. (1996) 'True and fair view: a European and a German perspective II' 5:3 *European Accounting Review* 495–506.

Ottolenghi, S. (1990) 'From Peeping Behind the Corporate Veil to Ignoring it Completely', 53 *Modern Law Review* 338.

Paterson, R (1993) *Off Balance Sheet Finance* (Macmillan, London).

Pijper, T. (1993) *Creative Accounting: The Effectiveness of Financial Reporting in the UK* (Macmillan, London).

Pimm, D.A. (1991) 'Off Balance Sheet Finance' in ICAEW *Financial Reporting 1990–91: A Survey of UK Reporting Practice* (ICAEW, London) p.137.

Rosenblatt, M. (1984) 'In-substance defeasance removes long-term debt from balance sheet', *Corporate Finance* (Euromoney).

Smith, T. and Hannah, R. (1991) *Accounting for Growth* (UBS Phillips & Drew).

Smith, T. (1992, 1996) *Accounting for Growth: Stripping the Camouflage from Company Accounts* (Century Business, London).

Tolley (1988) *Tolley's Company Law* (Tolley Publishing Company, Croydon).

Touche Ross (1989) *Accounting for Europe* (Touche Ross, London).

Tweedie, D. (1988) 'Off-balance Sheet Finance', paper presented at the 17th British-German seminar, Munich, October.

Tweedie, D. and Kellas, J. (1987) 'Off-balance sheet financing', *Accountancy*, April.

Van Hulle, K. (1993) 'Truth and Untruth about True and Fair: A Commentary on "European True and Fair Comment"', 1 *European Accounting Review*.

Van Hulle, K. (1997) 'The true and fair override in the European Accounting Directives' 6:4 *European Accounting Review* 711–720.
Van Hulle, K. (1998) 'Ironing out differences in European auditing standards', *Accountancy*, July, 73.
Whewell, R. (1998) 'The unsatisfactory affair of insurance accounting', *Accountancy*, February, 82.

Cases Index

Company Index

General Index

Statutory Materials Index

Statutory Instruments

Subject Index